THE ALPS

Landscapes of the Imagination

Landscapes

THE ALPS
A *Cultural History*

ANDREW BEATTIE

Signal Books
Oxford

First published in 2006 by
Signal Books Limited
36 Minster Road
Oxford OX4 1LY
www.signalbooks.co.uk

A catalogue record for this book is available from the British Library

ISBN 1-904955-24-X Paper

Cover Design: Baseline Arts
Design & Production: Devdan Sen
Cover images: André Jenny/alamy; Mike Morley/istockphoto.com; Devereaux Library
Photos:
Andrew Beattie: pp.35, 44, 47, 60, 65, 84, 89, 132, 149, 205
Alpine Club, London pp.181, 211, 214
Devdan Sen: pp i, 102, 197
p x Arjan Schreven/istockphoto.com; p.2 Jessie Glass/istockphoto.com; p.10 Michael J. Hambrey; p.17 Tomislav Stajduhar/istockphoto.com; p.51 Kim Pin Tan/istockphoto.com; p.69 Catherine Reymond/istockphoto.com; p.104 Thomas Brueckl/istockphoto.com; p.113 Bojan Tezak/istockphoto.com; p.137 Rocky Chang/istockphoto.com; p.162 photomorgana/istockphoto.com; p.203 Bart Sadowski/istockphoto.com; p.216 Mads Frederiksen/istockphoto.com; p.224 Chris Sanzey/istockphoto.com; p.236 Arjan Schreven/istockphoto.com

Printed in India

CONTENTS

Preface and Acknowledgements

In 1922 the mountaineer Francis Sydney Smythe travelled through France to the Alps and was overwhelmed by his first glimpse of the mountains, from the windows of a railway carriage rattling over the Jura: "As the train... began its downward rush towards the Swiss lowlands I saw the Alps... there swept over me a thrill of pure excitement and amazement such as comes to a human being only once or twice in a lifetime," he later wrote. "Fortunate indeed are those who gain the vision of the mountains at an early age, and splendid their adventure."

The Alps do indeed offer the prospect of a splendid adventure, and this book aims to help travellers in the mountains—whether they come here as walkers, skiers, mountaineers or even city sightseers—to place what they see in some sort of historical and cultural context. But a book that attempts to cover the geography, history and culture of such a region, not to mention the impressions of those writers and artists who have been inspired by its landscapes, is an ambitious one: stretching in a broad arc across Europe, from Nice to Vienna, the range encompasses not only thousands of peaks and valleys and lakes, but also numerous cities of historical importance such as Grenoble, Lucerne and Innsbruck. For centuries the mountains have been fought over by empires, eulogized by writers, investigated by scientists, and visited by tourists—which gives the author of a book such as this an ample supply of material to consider and raises problems over selection; but whatever is eventually included in such a cultural study, always rising above the history and the science and the memoirs, is the scenery itself, whose beauty has never been dimmed, despite the popularity of the mountains: "Makalu is indescribably impressive," wrote the mountaineer George Mallory, "but on the whole the Himalayas are disappointing and infinitely less beautiful than the Alps."

So, what follows is not intended to be a conventional guide book to the mountains; rather, the aim is to trace the cultural history of this landscape, and to see it as geologists, botanists, poets, novelists, composers, military strategists and members of its own communities have seen it, through the ages. And to start on this formidable task—to achieve an overview, if you like—it is probably best to begin somewhere *high*.

■

Thanks to Elaine Galloway for dragging me to the "Singalonga Sound of Music" at Catford Town Hall; to Ben Pollard and Peter Cheshire for their company in Munich and Neuschwanstein; to Tim Pepper and Lyn Stone for theirs in Ticino; and my family for theirs in Verbier. Thanks also to Keith Miles and his wife Slava of the British-Slovene Society for sharing their enthusiasm for the Kekec stories and the Julian Alps.

Introduction

The View from The Jungfraujoch

It takes forty minutes of travelling through a tunnel to get there: a slow, jolting journey in the darkness, along a railway line that burrows through one of the most famous mountains in the world. The cogwheels under the carriages whine and grind continuously as they slowly drag the train up the steep gradient. At the top, passengers emerge from the station buildings slightly dazed, breathing in the crystal-clear air and blinking in the dazzling Alpine light; some even start suffering from the first signs of altitude sickness. Once the train's passengers come to their senses, they realize that the scene into which they have been disgorged is a sort of Alpine Disneyland. There are dripping ice sculptures, ski runs across thick snowfields, people riding on sledges behind teams of slavering husky dogs, a high-speed elevator that rises through a cliff to a lookout tower called the Sphinx, an Indian restaurant, and even a post office; notices in multiple languages exhort people not to move around too quickly lest they become short of breath, while discreet teams of medics keep a watchful eye out for anyone suffering the effects of being 3,500 metres above sea level. The place they have come to is the Jungfraujoch, a precipitous ridge that runs between two formidable mountains, and is home to the highest railway station in the world: the "Top of Europe", the posters call it.

Not surprisingly, the panoramic view from the Top of Europe is spectacular. In the far distance, beyond the glittering Alpine wasteland whose whiteness is blinding in the sun, the views from the terrace outside the station buildings stretch as far as the Vosges and the Jura, low and purple and hazy on the horizon. Right up close are the dramatic peaks of the Eiger (3,970m), the Mönsch (4,099m) and the Jungfrau (4,158m), all of them grey and forbidding and usually obscured in continuously-circling clumps of cloud and mist. The tunnels of the Jungfraujoch railway run up inside the Eiger, behind its famously treacherous north face, the ascent of which has long been counted as one

of the world's great mountaineering challenges; the mountain's name translates as "ogre", which hints at the role that beasts, devils and goblins have long played in Alpine folklore. Below the viewing terraces of the Jungfraujoch the mighty Aletsch glacier, the longest in Europe, peels away towards the Rhône valley, along the wide rocky chasm it has carved for itself; in the Ice Age hundreds of glaciers like the Aletsch covered the whole of the Alps, gouging out deep valleys and creating finger-like and often stunningly beautiful lakes. Thousands of metres below the viewing terraces in the other direction is the green meadowland of the Lauterbrunnen valley, from where the train ride up to the Jungfraujoch begins. The fields are speckled with houses that seem the size of pinpricks; once these would have been part of remote farming communities, but now the villages below the Jungfrau such as Wengen and Grindelwald live solely off tourists, who have been coming here in their droves for more than a hundred years.

Each year, the fabulous view from the Jungfraujoch terrace, of villages and farms, peaks and glaciers, deep valleys and distant mountains, is enjoyed by two million people, who travel up from the balmy lakeside resort of Interlaken to experience this perpetually icy wilderness. Even if the weather is cloudy, few return disappointed; the sheer elation of being somewhere so obviously high, so precariously perched, so remote, so cold, so snowy, so windy and so famous is in itself enough.

But the significance of the Jungfraujoch goes beyond the magnificence of its location. Many of the human and natural forces that over time have shaped the landscape and culture of the Alps can be observed from the terraces outside the station: the glaciers that carved out the lakes and valleys, and cut away at the mountainsides to create needle-sharp peaks such as the Eiger; the formidable climbing challenges presented by the steep faces and the harsh weather; the remote communities that for centuries lived in fear of the beasts and dragons which lived in the peaks, only to turn the mountains to their advantage when the first tourists began coming to the region; the steep terrain that encouraged such ingenious engineering solutions when the first railways were built; the "Alpine wonderland" circus of dog sledges and ice caverns that confirms the Alps as one of the great tourist playgrounds of the world; and the sheer magnificence of the scenery that has attracted legions of writers, artists, film-makers and composers, following the leads of the poets Shelley and Byron whose 1816 visit to Lake Geneva and Chamonix started the snowball of Alpine tourism rolling. "The immensity [of the mountains] staggers the imagination," Shelley wrote after that trip, "and so far surpasses all conception that it requires an effort of imagination to believe that they do indeed form a part of the earth." Other writers who came here after Shelley include Charles Dickens, Mark Twain, Robert Louis Stevenson, Sir Arthur Conan Doyle, Paul Theroux, Thomas Mann, Jean-Jacques Rousseau, Henry James and Ernest Hemingway. And the list of cultural figures associated with the mountains does not stop at writers: Wagner and Mahler came here to compose, Turner and Ruskin to paint, Leni Riefenstahl and David Lean to make films, and Freddie Mercury and Deep Purple to make pop records. In fact the cultural history of these mountains is as rich and diverse as the views from the Jungfraujoch terrace, and almost as formidable as the north face of the Eiger itself.

It is appropriate at this point to consider the precise parameters of the region this book aims to cover. Although it is clear that the Jungfraujoch lies at the heart of the Alps, the fringes of the region are less distinct; where, for example, do the Alps become sub-alpine foothills? And should these areas merit inclusion in a book that purports to survey a region known as the "Alps"? In some places the edges of the mountain range are clear: above Chiasso, the most southerly town in Switzerland, rises the 1,804m Monte Generosa, a bald rocky peak from whose summit the views stretch in one direction into the heart of the Alps, and in the other over the flat expanse of the plain of the River Po. Chiasso is clearly where the Alps both begin and end. Hundreds of miles to the north-east, Neuschwanstein Castle in Bavaria overlooks a crashing river that plunges from a craggy gorge into a region of gently rolling forested hills—again marking one of the region's clearest boundaries between mountain and plain. But in other places the edges of the range are less distinct: where, for example, do the thyme-scented limestone hills of Provence become what most would consider to be the Alps? There is no clear marking point: the land simply rises until, travelling north from the Mediterranean, it is obvious that the countryside around Briançon or Grenoble befits the term "Alpine", whereas that to the south does not. Similar problems are faced around Lake Geneva: the eastern part, overlooked by peaks of over two thousand metres, clearly has an Alpine setting, but the scenery around the lake shore flattens out as one travels west, and Geneva itself could not really be considered an Alpine town. Nor could a number of other cities that lie beyond the fringes of the mountains: from Munich, Turin, Zurich and Milan, the Alps are clearly visible on the near horizon, but are not really within touching distance. Other cities lie at the exact point where the mountains end: like Chiasso or Neuschwanstein, the cities of Lucerne, Salzburg, Bergamo and Lausanne turn their heads both ways, towards adjacent high mountains and over flatter countryside that barely rises to form what could be termed "foothills".

Notwithstanding these difficulties of definition, this book aims to cover the entire mountain region that stretches from Grenoble and the shores of Lake Geneva eastwards as far as the Austrian regions of Carinthia, Styria and the Lake District near Salzburg. The Dolomites are considered part of the range, but the hills of Provence and those of Lower Austria between Vienna and Styria are not; Innsbruck, Grenoble, Lucerne and Lausanne are all considered Alpine towns, but Geneva, Zurich, Munich and Turin are assumed to lie outside the range. To the north-east, the Alps stretch into southern Germany, and in the south-east a part of the range forms a corner of Slovenia; but Switzerland, France, Italy and Austria are the countries that include the most substantial amounts of Alpine territory. The highest part of the mountains, the Mont Blanc Massif and the Bernese Oberland, lie in the west, and as one travels east along the spine of the mountains, past the Matterhorn and into the Austrian Tyrol, the peaks gradually become lower and less spectacular, although the scenery and culture is still firmly "alpine". But away from the highest parts of the range, the places covered by this book are necessarily subjective: it is impossible to arrive at a definition of the Alpine region any other way.

Whatever the true boundaries of the region, the position of the Alps at the centre of Europe has also brought an eclectic collection of historical figures to the mountains: Napoleon, Charlemagne, Julius Caesar and Adolf Hitler have all come here, to witness the fulfillment of their imperial ambitions. Pioneers in the fields of tourism, scientific research, winter sports and mountaineering have also left their mark, along with Christian missionaries, wealthy merchants, mining entrepreneurs, railway engineers, and peasant farmers, generations of whom have worked the rough soil of the Alps and husbanded herds of sheep, cows and goats among the lonely slopes above communities such as Wengen and Grindelwald. Over time both popular and intellectual imagination has cast the mountain range as, variously, an abode of devils and dragons, a tourist paradise, a testing gound for human strength and stamina, and a romantic wilderness. In fact the Alps seem to speak in a myriad of different voices, all of which can be heard in this book, providing a clamour of opinions and impressions of one of the most written-about, visited and fought over parts of the globe. Indeed, the cultural net of the Alps is spread so wide that it might be prudent to begin an investigation of the historical legacy of these mountains in another part of Europe entirely.

Part One
Landscape

Oh there is gorse on Ditchling Beacon
All golden in the sun.

The English poet Alfred Norman wrote these lines in 1917. He was describing the steep hill that rises to the north of Brighton, whose summit views stretch in one direction to the English Channel, and in the other over a patchwork of woods and fields scattered with tiny villages built of grey stone. Norman goes on to describe the "sweeping slopes of Downland" and walking with a "skylark for companion/The sea-wind for a friend." His description, though perhaps rather purple, perfectly captures the Englishness of this Sussex scene: on a fine Sunday afternoon in spring, when the rays of the sun poke through the scudding clouds and bathe the countryside in continuously changing patterns of soft light, the place is populated by dozens of walkers, who sit on low stone walls, out of the wind, hugging their thick coats around them and drinking from thermos flasks extracted from car boots. They will have spent their afternoon crunching chalk and flint underfoot, walking along the paths that run along the ridge of the South Downs, of which the 248m-high Beacon is one of the highest points; from here the spine of hills stretches west and east, the bald grassy crests dotted with occasional trees bent and bowed by the fierce winds that sometimes buffet this exposed place.

Ditchling Beacon is owned by the National Trust, and was given to the charity in memory of a Second World War fighter pilot who was shot down near here during the Battle of Britain. ("Thank you for being responsible dog owners" reads one of their signs.) But despite the Englishness of the scene, there is a link to the Alps, which lie five hundred miles to the south: Alfred Norman certainly did not know this, and many of the walkers who tramp along the chalk paths of the Downs at weekends probably do not know it either: that the South Downs were formed by the same mighty tectonic processes that pushed up the Alpine

ranges of central Europe some sixty million years ago. These tremendous forces created geological ripples that travelled hundreds of miles and buckled and crumpled the land into more humble hill ranges, such as those of southern England. But these links have only recently been established: when the Battle of Britain was being fought over the South Downs, any geologist who suggested that their formation was in any way linked with that of the Alps would have been laughed out of his laboratory.

"Wriggling rock conundra"

The geologist Richard Fortey indicates that Lochseiten, in the Sernft Valley of central Switzerland, provides the key to understanding the forces that created the Alps. "For this region of the earth's surface is where everything is topsy-turvy," he writes in *The Earth: an Intimate History*. "Where great slabs of rock may be flipped over like badly-tossed pancakes, and where a mountain of a height to challenge the most experienced alpinist may be no more than the tip of a vast geological fold. It is a place where nature has apparently relished stirring up the strata on such a scale as to make wriggling rock conundra to torment the minds of scientists." The place, he contends, is "one of geology's holy places".

These "wriggling rock conundra" that have so perplexed scientists consist of contortions in the earth's surface of such magnitude as to fold whole sections of rock up and over themselves. At Lochseiten, a dark, grey slaty rock known as flysch, which was formed from layers of mud on the sea floor that have since been hardened and compressed, underlies a rock known as the verrucano, consisting of pebbles stretched and elongated through being exposed to the high pressures and temperatures that only exist deep within the earth's crust. A short distance away at Engi, flysch was once quarried, and sent by a succession of rafts all the way down the Rhine to Rotterdam. In the nineteenth century the Swiss palaeontologist Louis Agassiz visited the quarry at Engi and found fossils of creatures in the flysch that he had never seen before. He thought he had discovered some new species unknown at that time to science. But he hadn't. The fossils were of familiar species of sea fish that had been contorted and mangled out of all recognition by the subsequent movement of the rock in which they had died.

Lochseiten offers two geological riddles: firstly, how did a rock that was over two hundred and fifty million years old (the verrucano) end up *on top of* a rock (the flysch) that is only twenty-eight million years old; and secondly, why are there fossils of sea creatures in rock so far from the sea, and at such a high altitude ?

Until the twentieth century, no-one dared think that mountain ranges were the product of massive, continental-scale movements of the earth's crust. A variety of ideas had existed before then as to how mountains had come into being. (The Greeks thought that they were thrown up from the earth's interior by the mythical titans.) One influential early thinker on this subject was an Anglican churchman and philosopher named Thomas Burnet. Treated to a ten-year sabbatical by his Cambridge college, Burnet took to acting as a chaperone to young aristocrats as they undertook journeys of enrichment to the classical ruins of Italy. One of these was the Earl of Wiltshire, with whom Burnet crossed the Simplon Pass in August 1672. Like all seventeenth-century thinkers, Burnet knew that the conventional view of the Alps was that they were dangerous and repellent, an obstacle on the journey south, and not worth considering in their own right. But at the summit of the Simplon Pass he noticed something odd: he found the mountains beautiful. "There is something august and stately in the air of these things that inspires the mind with great thoughts and passions," he later wrote. "They fill and overbear the mind with their excess and cast it into a pleasing kind of stupor and imagination." His interest in the possible formation of the mountains inspired a book full of disturbingly new ideas, *The Sacred Theory of the Earth*, which was written in Latin and given a first print run in 1681 of a mere twenty-five copies.

Ten years later the book appeared in English and received wide attention. Burnet considered himself "inquisitive into the works of God" and claimed that a lot of the thinking about geology up until then had been wrong. At that time it was believed that the world was six thousand years old (in 1650 James Ussher, Archbishop of Armagh, had determined that the exact moment of creation was 9am on Monday 26 October 4004 BC), and that the earth had not changed since being formed; and yet Burnet identified two difficulties with this—firstly, that mountains were absent from the Biblical account of creation, and secondly, that the Flood could never have covered the highest mountains of the world, even with forty days of continuous rain. So *The Sacred Theory* suggested radical answers to these problems: the earth, Burnet postulated, was smooth following creation, with no hills or mountains: "a mundane egg", he called it, with "not a scar or fracture in all its body, no rock, mountain nor hollow cavern". All the rivers flowed from the poles to the tropics, where they evaporated; and the earth revolved in such a way as to make the Garden of Eden enjoy a perpetual spring. There was water in the centre of the earth, on which the land floated. Over time, Burnet said, the sun desiccated the crust and it began to crack and fracture, and in doing so let out the waters of the Flood. This catastrophic event led to the crust being broken and buckled and when the waters eventually receded the chaotic aftermath was "a world lying in its rubbish... wild, vast and indigested heaps of stone... the ruins of a broken world."

So the Alps which he had crossed with his young charge in 1672 were, like all mountains, the residue that remained after the Deluge: fragments of the earth that had been swirled around and piled up by the immense waters of the Flood. This was why mountains were not mentioned in Genesis. They were not part of God's plan. They were part of his punishment.

Burnet's theories divided intellectual opinion of the day. His ideas were well received in the pages of the *Spectator* magazine, and Samuel Taylor Coleridge considered turning *The Sacred Theory* into a blank verse epic. But others were horrified: Burnet lost his fellowship at Christ's College, Cambridge, and his career as a senior churchman was over. However, his book had at least set the scientific ball rolling in suggesting that mountains had a geological past distinct from that of the rest of the earth; in short there was, Burnet's ideas suggested for the first time, a *reason* for them being there.

Later theorists began to build and expand on the kernel of ideas that formed the backbone to Burnet's book. The French naturalist Georges Buffon (1707-88) suggested in *Natural History* that each of the days of creation was in fact an epoch, which, added together, made the earth 75,000 years old. In the 1770s the Swiss mountaineer and scientist Horace-Bénédict de Saussure wrote that mountains were the result of some sort of subterranean explosion—another definite step in the right direction. In *Theory of the Earth*, published between 1785 and 1799, the Scottish geologist James Hutton postulated that the landscape we see at any one moment is a mere snapshot in a continuous series of cycles: a single frame in a roll of cinema film, to use a modern metaphor. Mountains were not permanent, he said; they rose by forces not understood, and were cut down by erosion; sea shells found at the tops of mountains, embedded in the rock, did not arrive there by means of the Biblical Flood, they were there because the tops of mountains were made from former sea floor. Hutton's ideas were developed further by another Scottish geologist, Charles Lyell, whose *Principles of Geology* (1830-3) was as radical and as popular as *Origin of Species*; in fact Darwin had a copy of Lyell's book in his luggage as he set off from Plymouth on the *Beagle* in 1831, and Lyell's text was to guide the development of the science of geology during the rest of the nineteenth century.

It was shortly after Lyell's great work had been published that two Swiss geologists, Arnold Escher and Albert Heim, began to undertake detailed examination of the rocks in their home country, searching for the geological Holy Grail that would cast light on the formation of the Alps. "No one would believe me... they would put me in an asylum," Escher later wrote, casting doubt on his own radical idea that some sort of massive geological compression had occurred here, creating the buckling and folding he (and earlier workers such as Agassiz) had observed in places such as Lochseiten. Escher's student, Albert Heim, the author of the three-volume *Geologie der Schweiz*, painstakingly constructed models of the Alps whose detail even included pinhead-sized sparrows sitting on the top of clock towers. He used the models as teaching aids for his students, and they are still kept to this day, in his old university department in Zurich. Heim supported Escher's idea of the Alps being caused by massive geological forces of folding and compression. But, although things had come a long way since Burnet, and Heim and Escher were correct in their assertion that the Alps were in fact some sort of huge geological fold, the exact explanation for the formation of the mountains still proved as elusive as ever.

"Badly-made lasagna, buckled in the cooking"
The breakthrough finally came in 1915, and from an unlikely source. Alfred Wegener was a German meteorologist who turned his thoughts to geology and suggested, in *Origins of Continents and Oceans*, that the

continents somehow moved around and that this shifting of the world's land masses accounted for phenomena such as mountains and ocean basins. His ideas were initially rubbished by the scientific community, and Wegener went back to his weather studies, eventually freezing to death in 1930 in a blizzard in Greenland. But over the course of fifty years the theory of continental drift was gradually accepted, and was confirmed in the 1960s when geologists discovered that new crust was continually being created on the ocean floor of the mid-Atlantic, proving that the tectonic plates into which the earth's crust was divided were in a state of constant motion—just as Wegener had suggested. It was eventually accepted that the Alps had been formed by two of these plates pushing together, the African plate and the Eurasian plate; as these two gigantic tectonic structures collided, mountains were forced to rise, making the Alps one part of a broad mountain range (the Carpathians) stretching from Morocco to Turkey and including chains such as the Pyrenees, the Massif Central, the Tatras in Slovakia and the Atlas in Morocco.

This is where the South Downs (and other European ranges such as the Jura) come into the equation: they are the result of tectonic "ripples" that spread away from the principal centre of crushing in the Alpine region. And these processes are still continuing: the formation of the Alps began 65 million years ago and the mountains are still rising; in terms of geology they are babies, far younger than ancient, noble chains such as the Scottish Highlands or the Appalachians, which were once as high as the Alps but which are now being worn down to nothing by wind, rain and ice—a fate that, in time, will eventually befall the Alps.

Using Wegener's theory of plate tectonics, the complex story of the formation of the Alps begins to become clear. Around six hundred million years ago the climate of this region was hot and humid, and the undulating countryside was covered with lush sub-tropical swamps and forests; the trees that once grew in these swamps now form the coal seams that are mined in places such as La Mure and Briançon in the French Alps (in the nineteenth century coal was even worked from a mine next to the Hofkirche in Lucerne). Fast forward three hundred and fifty million years and the area was a vast shallow sea, at the bottom of which layers of sand and clay built up—forming the sandstone and shale of today. Limestone, which derives from the skeletons of tiny tropical sea creatures, was also laid down during this era. This rock forms the Dolomites in northern Italy, which were named after a French geologist, Dolomieu, who was the first to identify the unique magnesium-rich character of Dolomite; it also forms the great limestone plateaus of the French Alps, including the Vercors and the Chartreuse near Grenoble, and further south the plateau of the Haute Provence region. These high plateaus are dissected by precipitous gorges such as the Grand Canyon du Verdon in Haute Provence, which was cut down by the River Verdon as the land later rose, while under the surface of these plateaus wind hundred of kilometres of subterranean caverns, such as the Grottes de Chorance in the Vercors, replete with spectacular stalactite and stalagmite formations.

Then, at around the time of the extinction of the dinosaurs, the Eurasian and African plates collided and the folding and compression began. The old sea floor of the previous era was lifted up, and then buckled and twisted like some giant geological roller-coaster, leaving fossils of sea creatures and marine plants stranded on some of the highest peaks. Besides Lochseiten, where Louis Agassiz had been so confused by the fossils he saw in the flysch, the effects of these events can be seen in a number of places in the mountains. Near Trento in the Dolomites there are curious rock formations known as the Pale di San Martino, which are made from a distinctive pale rock that was once part of a coral reef in a tropical ocean. Near Digne, in the very south of the French Alps, a strange fan-shaped feature in the landscape known as the Vélodrome is the result of the compression and twisting of layers of sandstone into a complete semi-circle; in some parts of the sandstone here it is possible to see the fossilized footprints of birds which once walked on the damp sand of the former tropical beach, while a fossilized ichthyosaurus, a fish-like reptile nearly five metres long that once swam in these warm seas, can be seen in a museum close by. At the summit of the San Bernardino Pass in Switzerland (2,066m) a grey, slaty rock known as gneiss, which was once buried a hundred kilometres down inside the earth, has been exposed in outcrops next to the road over the pass. In the village of Pianazzo, situated in a deep valley above Bellinzona in Switzerland's canton Ticino, in the southern fringes of the mountain range, a small river flowing at the bottom of a rocky chasm marks the exact spot where the Eurasian and African plates meet.

According to Richard Fortey, the fault line along which the river flows is the location of the "aperture that spun out those gobs of tectonic pasta that extend a hundred kilometers to the north." From the centre of Pianazzo, which consists of no more than a few villas strung out along a road, a steep path runs down through dense woodland, buzzing with cicadas and heavy with the scent of horse chestnuts, to a single-span pedestrian bridge that crosses the Mobbio river and so, in a sense, links Europe and Africa. The buckled rocks that stretch hundreds of miles north from here, forming the heart of the Alps, are in Fortey's words "no more than the desperate scrambling of the earth away from the encroachment of the inescapable giant [the African continent]...The whole Carpathian chain curves away from the oppressor." (One of the most famous mountains in the Alps, the Matterhorn, is a spectacular result of this process: the upper segment is actually a part of "Africa" that has been thrust bodily over "Europe".)

Fortey goes on to liken the whole process of the formation of the Alps to the folding of a tablecloth: "if you should place your hand flat onto the table and push forward, the cloth will begin to rise into folds... Push more and the folds will flop over and the rearmost fold will progressively override those before it, producing a stack of folds... Alpine mountains might be seen as badly-made lasagna, crudely layered and buckled in the cooking."

"A terrible noise that frightens the neighbourhood"

As the Alps rose, so they were worn down, by the forces of water, wind and—in particular—by moving ice. In the past there were vast glaciers in the Alps, tens of kilometres long, which gouged out wide, straight, steep-sided valleys such as those of the Rhône and the Inn, and created finger-like lakes, such as Como, Maggiore, Geneva, Lucerne and Lugano. Nowadays the glaciers have retreated to the upper parts of the mountains, but those that remain are still formidable; the most spectacular of all is the Aletsch, whose source can be seen below the Jungfraujoch and whose massive frozen form winds twenty-three kilometres south towards the Rhône valley, where it can be seen at Bettmeralp above Brig. Other glaciers long popular with both tourists and scientists include the Pasterze, whose source is below the Grossglockner, the highest mountain in Austria; the Rhône glacier,

whose melt-waters provide the source for that river; and the clutch of cascading ice flows near Chamonix in the heart of the French Alps, including the Argentière glacier and the Mer de Glace.

In former times, the way that glaciers worked, and what exactly they were, remained a mystery to scientists, and the enigma surrounding these rivers of ice made them seem just as alluring and forbidding as the high peaks in whose shadows they formed. The Mer de Glace, famous because of the dramatic, twisting curve it makes as it creeps down from the Mont Blanc massif into the forested Arve valley just north of Chamonix, has been popular with tourists and scientists for nearly three centuries. In 1741 two Englishmen climbing in the region, William Windham and Richard Pococke, visited the glacier and commented on the huge fissures in the surface of the ice that could swallow crystal hunters whole and preserve their bodies perfectly in an icy tomb for decades. (They were two of the more eccentric Alpine travellers: Pococke had just returned from a tour of Egypt and Palestine and at one point while out on the mountain dressed himself in a turban, kaftan and sandals, not surprisingly exciting interest from local shepherds.) Twenty years later, de Saussure described the rippling surface of the same glacier as "a sea which has become suddenly frozen, not in the moment of a tempest but at the instant when the wind subsided, and the waves, though very high, have become blunted and rounded." (The Alpine enthusiast Albert Smith, who in the 1850s staged an entire London stage show about his ascent of Mont Blanc, begged to differ when he came to the glacier in 1838: "the story that the Mer de Glace resembles the sea suddenly frozen in a storm is all nonsense," he wrote. "From Montenvers it looks rather like a magnified ploughed field.") By 1785 there were three inns in Chamonix catering for the fifteen hundred tourists who arrived annually; souvenirs on offer in the town included jars of locally-produced honey, and crystals found by local farmers high in the mountains.

One visitor, in 1779, was the German playwright Johann Wolfgang von Goethe, who was intent on "walking on the ice itself and considering these masses at close hand." Climbing the Montenvers, the rocky outcrop which overlooks the Mer de Glace, he came upon a remote wooden cabin known as the Château de Folie which had been erected by an Englishman named Blaire as a private wine cellar and bar for his friends. Just over thirty years later, the poet Percy Shelley came here with his wife Mary; they took care to tread carefully through the ice caverns that had been carved into the glacier, after they were told that two Dutch tourists had fired a pistol inside one of them and were hit by a falling boulder. Another writer who came here later on in the same century was Mark Twain, who wrote in *A Tramp Abroad* (1880) that the walls of the ice caves "emitted a soft rich blue light that produced a lovely effect" and that the whole tunnel possessed an almost ethereal "tender blue radiance".

Many glaciers over the border in Switzerland are just as impressive as the Mer de Glace—though none is as famous or as accessible. In 1673 an Englishman named Muraltus published a letter about the Grindelwald glacier in the *Philosophical Transactions* of the Royal Society; his description of this glacier below the Eiger was accompanied by a rough illustration of what he had seen. He described how the glacier grew "by increments that make a great noise of cracking. There are great holes and caverns… when the sun shineth, there is seen such a variety of colours as in a prism." He also wrote of the "terrible noise that frightens the whole neighbourhood" when the ice cracks and bends in the summer heat, and went on to describe the glacier's surface, which is "not smooth and level, but has deep swales and swelling elevations, and sometimes has the look of a tossing sea whose turbulent billows were frozen hard in the instant of their most violent motion." He also mentions the formidable crevasses, the gashes and fissures on the glacier surface (which result from the ice literally ripping and tearing as it moves) that are like the "icy jaws of death". John Russell, in his 1950 book *Switzerland*, wrote about the Rhône glacier, but chose not to use the stormy-sea analogy when describing its surface; instead Russell observed that it "had the texture of the tongue (ridged, slimy and scaly) of some prehistoric monster." In *A Tramp Abroad*, Twain provides a tongue-in-cheek account of a visit to another Swiss glacier, the Gornergletscher above Zermatt. Knowing enough about glaciers to understand that they moved, he went onto the ice, and "chose a good position to view the scenery as we passed along." Finding that he did not go anywhere, he opened his guidebook to see if there was a timetable of glacier movement (there wasn't—but Twain swore that there would be one in Bradshaw's, the well-known public transport timetable of the day).

Of course, the Gornergletscher *was* moving—but at a very slow pace. (In fact you could say at a glacially slow pace). Although early scientists who investigated glaciers realized that they moved, the precise mechanism for this movement remained mysterious for many centuries. De Saussure thought that heat from the earth's interior caused the lowest part of the glacier to melt, and the ice slipped along on a layer of meltwater. Then in 1837 Agassiz, who had been so foxed by the elongated fish fossils he had found at Lochseiten, came up with the radical suggestion that ice had once covered all of Europe, from the poles to the Alps, and much of the scenery of the mountains was the result of past movement of glaciers. His ideas were initially scorned by the nineteenth-century scientific community. "A long and stupid hypothetical dissertation on geology, drawn from the depths of ignorance," was how the Rev. Adam Sedgwick of the British Association greeted Agassiz's theories when listening to a paper of his in Dublin. Sir Roderick Murchison, President of the Royal Geographical Association in London, wrote that if one accepted "Agassiz's idea that his deepest valleys of Switzerland were once filled with snow and ice, I see no stopping place".

But Agassiz knew he was right, and went to huge lengths to prove his theory: to aid him in his studies he established a tiny cabin on the Unteraar glacier in the Bernese Oberland, which he dubbed the Hotel des Neuchâtelois (named after his home town). The cabin had flat stone slabs on the floor, a curtain over the entrance, and niches cut into the ice serving as a kitchen. From this superbly-situated lair Agassiz was able to investigate glacial processes at close quarters. At one point he even witnessed at first hand the creation of a crevasse on the glacier surface. "I heard… a sound like the simultaneous discharge of fire-arms… the glacier actually trembled… a crack opened between my feet and ran rapidly across the glacier in a straight line," he later wrote. Eventually he published his findings in a book entitled *Etudes sur les Glaciers* (1841), which was rumoured to have been written in a single night. The following year he was in Britain on a lecture tour, propounding his theory of ice ages, and startling his sceptical audiences with the notion that as recently as fourteen thousand years ago ice had extended over huge areas of Europe.

Agassiz was right about ice ages but wrong about glacial movement. He thought that glaciers moved by a process of dilation, by which freezing water expanded in crevasses and this somehow pushed the whole structure along. However, glaciers actually move on a thin film of melt-water created by friction between the rock and the moving ice, which warms the rock and melts the ice to create a lubricant. But, more than this, ice also flows; it has a plastic consistency that allows it to be compressed and stretched, so that crevasses can close up and completely engulf any rocks that have fallen into them. These ideas were expounded in the 1840s by another eccentric glaciologist, a dour Scot named James Forbes, who saw glaciers as having an almost spiritual essence. Forbes walked hundreds of miles through the French Alps in the course of his research, engaging in solitary commune with nature and running away from any tourists whom he saw. In *Travels through the Alps of Savoy* Forbes wrote that "a glacier is an endless scroll, a stream of time upon whose stainless ground is engraven the succession of events, whose dates far transcend the memory of living man." Forbes, who ended his career as Rector of St. Andrew's University in Scotland, was a huge influence on John Tyndall, a railway engineer turned natural scientist, who in 1860 wrote one of the standard works on glaciology, *The Glaciers of the Alps.*

By the end of the nineteenth century glaciers were becoming more and more understood, thanks in no small part to workers such as Agassiz, Tyndall and Forbes. But there were still some grey areas of research. In the Glacier Garden in Lucerne there is a complicated machine called the Glacial Mill, built in 1896, which purports to show how potholes formed beneath a glacier; water cascades down onto a rock surface and turns a huge stone, whose continual motion supposedly carves out the pothole. Although the model still works the theory is obsolete. Potholes were actually created by thousands of small stones, not one big one, endlessly churning around in tight spaces beneath the ice. The impressive pothole in the Glacier Garden, a few steps away from the machine, is nine metres deep and was created by water moving at speeds of up to two hundred kilometres per hour beneath the Reuss Glacier, which covered the area during the last ice age.

Although the builders of the Glacial Mill were wrong in their theory of pothole formation, other effects of glaciers were more accurately understood by the end of the nineteenth century. It was agreed that these heavy, cumbersome masses of ice were so powerful that, over successive ice ages, deep valleys had been carved such as the spectacular Lauterbrunen Valley in central Switzerland, where seventy-two waterfalls tip down sheer vertical sides of a thousand metres to the lush, undulating valley floor. Another of these so-called "U"-shaped valleys is that of the River Rhône, where towns such as Martigny and Sion sprawl across its wide, flat bottom, while roads wind up its steep sides to access ski resorts such as Crans Montana. Rocky outcrops on the valley floor, like those at Sion, provide defensive sites for castles, while the grey-green Rhône flows along the centre of the valley, draining what remains of the present glacier that is located miles up the valley at Gletsch (1,759m). (Like all glaciers, the Rhône shrank when the last ice age ended, its melting front retreating back up the valley that it had carved for itself; and in recent decades most Alpine glaciers have shrunk even further, as the world's temperature increases through global warming.) In the highest areas of the mountains, moving ice cut back at different angles to form extraordinary pyramid-like peaks, such as the Matterhorn (4,478) whose distinctive profile rears up above the resort of Zermatt. "The monarch... is peculiarly steep, and is also most oddly shaped. He towers into the sky like a colossal wedge," Mark Twain wrote of this famous peak. "The Matterhorn stands black and naked and forbidding, the year round, or merely powdered and streaked with white in places, for its sides are so steep that the snow cannot stay there. 'Grand, gloomy and peculiar' is a phrase which fits it aptly."

In the lowland areas, where the glaciers moved away from the mountains and onto the flat plains such as the Po valley in northern Italy (which was smothered by an ice sheet hundreds of metres thick during the Ice Age), depressions were gouged out by the moving ice, later to be filled with water and to become the long, narrow, twisting lakes that characterize the fringes of the Alps. The croissant-shaped Lake Geneva is the biggest of these, containing eighty-nine trillion litres of water; liquid takes an estimated seventeen years to travel from Villeneuve at one end of the lake to Geneva at the other, from where it flows on down the Rhône through France to the Mediterranean. Over a hundred families still earn a living from fishing for perch, trout and pike on the lake, but otherwise it is given over to tourism, with dozens of boats crisscrossing each day between famous resorts such as Lausanne, Vevey, Montreux, Évian and Geneva itself. On the other side of the mountains, Lake Bled on the edge of the Julian Alps in Slovenia is one of that country's most popular tourist destinations, thanks to the placid fairy-tale lake with its island, its castle and its background of snow-capped mountains.

The most famous Alpine lakes, however, are those on the southern fringes of the mountains, such as Maggiore, Como, Lugano and Garda, which form a region known as the Italian Lake District. In the nineteenth century these areas became hugely popular with tourists from northern Europe, and a Murray's *Handbook* of the day described their character as being "soft and smiling; blessed with a southern climate, their thickets are groves of orange, olive, myrtle and pomegranate; and their habitations villas and palaces".

Glaciers also produced some smaller-scale features as they carved their way through the landscape. Some, like the Pyramides d'Euseigne near Sion, are quite odd; the formations here consist of jagged, bare needle-sharp points that appear to have rounded boulders balanced at the top of them; the boulders are actually pieces of caprock that were protected from erosion by being harder than the rocks underneath them. The Piramidi di Erosione near Cislano, just east of Lake Iseo in the Italian Alps, are similar, and like the formations near Sion are a popular tourist attraction. In Lucerne's Glacier Garden there is a rock whose surface is riddled with scars and pockmarks that indicate that a glacier once passed over it. Mark Twain wrote in *A Tramp Abroad* that these scars and scratches showed "the rasped and guttered track which the ancient glacier had made as it moved along upon its slow and tedious journey." (Glaciologists actually know these features as striations; they were caused by jagged pieces of rock, held within the ice, scratching the surface of the rock over which the glacier was passing.) Glaciers also deposited huge boulders in odd places, known as erratics; one is the Pope's Stone, an 8,500-ton lump of rock which lies close to the village of Gignese near Lake Maggiore. Another field of erratics is Pierre Grosse, on the approach to the Col Agnel in the French Alps. Once it was thought that features such as these were the result of the Biblical Flood, which had somehow shifted huge boulders hundreds of miles; but they were in fact dumped by melting glaciers, and are just one more instance of how the Alpine landscape of today is almost wholly controlled by the ice movements of the past.

"The smoking blueness of Pluto's gloom"

As the ice receded from the valleys and lowlands ten thousand years ago, it left only the highest reaches of the mountains permanently covered in snow. Below the snowline and the remaining glaciers plant life re-established itself, and soon there were animals too, feeding from trees and flowers that had managed to secure a foothold on the rocky slopes.

Many of the most distinctive Alpine flowers are found only at high altitudes. At Flimerstein in the Lauterbrunnen valley there are meadows covered in gentian flowers, a species of lily coloured the most intense blue imaginable; D. H. Lawrence described the gentians here as "darkening the day-time, torch-like with the smoking blueness of Pluto's gloom." Another plant that thrives in high altitudes is the beautiful alpenrose, a shrub which yields pink and red flowers each summer, bathing the upper slopes of the mountains in vibrant colour. The most famous of all alpine flowers, however, is the edelweiss, which grows particularly well in limestone areas up to an altitude of 3,400m; it is prized largely because of its rarity, and can often be found growing on

exposed grassy cliffs above glaciated valleys. Twain wrote this half-affectionate, half-mocking paean to the cult of the "ugly Swiss favourite" in his satirical travelogue *A Tramp Abroad*: "Its name seems to indicate that it is a noble flower and that it is white. It may be noble enough, but it is not attractive, and it is not white. The fuzzy blossom is the colour of bad cigar ashes, and appears to be made of a cheap quality of gray plush. It has a noble and distant way of confining itself to the high altitudes, but that is probably on account of its looks... Everybody in the Alps wears a sprig of edelweiss in his hat. It is the native's pet, and also the tourist's." Edelweiss can be found as low as 1,700m in areas usually characterized by extensive reaches of grassy meadow (and known specifically as "Alps"—which slowly became adopted as the name for the mountains themselves).

Below the meadowland it is warm enough for thick forests to thrive. These mostly comprise conifers: fir and spruce in the heart of the Alps, and pine in the warmer areas further south, the latter gradually giving way to holm oak and Aleppo pine, and also pistachio trees and olive groves, all of which buzz with the familiar Mediterranean sound of cicadas in summer. Areas of the southern French Alps also contain *garrigue*, vast expanses of rocky limestone moor dominated by thistles, gorse, lavender, thyme, and rosemary, interspersed with short dry grasses.

A number of artificial gardens have been established in the Alps over the last hundred years or so, often growing many plants that are not native to the region. Lake Maggiore is particularly well-known for its exceptionally mild climate, and in the 1930s a retired Scottish soldier, Captain Neil McEachern, created on its shores one of the best-known sub-Alpine tropical gardens, the Villa Taranto at Verbania. Here there are twenty thousand species of plants including Amazonian lilies, lotus blossoms, Japanese maple and a sacred tree from India, all laid out around fountains and pathways. Other similar gardens are the Hruska Botanical Gardens at Gardone on Lake Garda, the Jardins de l'Europe beside Lake Annecy, and the Alpinum Juliana in Slovenia's Trenta valley, which has more in the way of Alpine rather than tropical flora.

The most distinctive animals to make their home in the high parts of the Alps are red deer, the smaller and more timid roe deer, and marmots, a rodent which R. L. J. Irving described as "jolly little fellows in thick fur coats, about the size of a rabbit" in his book *The Alps*.

Marmots dig deep burrows and hibernate for up to six months a year, and issue a shrill, high-pitched alarm whistle when they sense danger—one strident cry for a golden eagle or bird of prey, or a series of cries for a mammal such as a fox. The ibex, a stocky wild goat, is another common animal in the Alps, the male famously using its horns to establish dominance during the mating season. Chamois are smaller and not unlike antelopes; the chamois hunter in Schiller's play *William Tell* complains that his prey "never turns to feed... till they have placed a sentinel ahead, who pricks his ears whenever we approach, and gives alarm with clear and piercing pipe." There are also blue hares, which live in high alpine pasture and change colour with the seasons (white in winter, grey in summer), and lynx, a form of wild cat that stalks the slopes in search of dear and marmot. King among Alpine bird species is the golden eagle, which builds its nests in inaccessible rock ledges high in the mountains, and feeds on grouse, mountain hair, and marmot and ibex carcasses.

Some of these animals can be seen in specialist zoos, such as the Alpenzoo in Innsbruck, whose cages, situated on a sunny plateau above the city with fine views over the Tyrolean Alps, rattle with the movements of grumpy-looking bears, lynx, and ibex, and also a colony of nimble, tree-climbing pine martens. Away from this and other zoos a number of conservation parks have been established out in the wild, such as the Swiss National Park in the far east of that country, where bearded vultures, kestrels, ravens, woodpeckers, grouse, deer, marmots, and chamois, in addition to edelweiss, gentians and other flowers, survive in relative peace in an isolated area of the Alps that sees few tourists.

In the past the Alps have been home to a number of animals which have since become extinct, including cave lions, panthers and wolves. Many of these and other animals were once hunted for food or sport. In the Tyrol the sport of *Gamsstechen*, where chamois would be impaled on pikes up to five metres in length, was championed by the Habsburg Emperor Maximilian I in the late fifteenth century. King Vittorio Emanuele II of Italy also enjoyed hunting in the Alps and converted a medieval castle near Aosta, the Castello di Sarre, into a hunting lodge, whose collections of ibex horns and chamois skulls now confront visitors on guided tours. With the emphasis increasingly on conservation, in the 1920s Emanuele's former hunting grounds became the Gran Paradiso

National Park, which now abounds in golden eagles, ibex and chamois colonies. Animals are also being deliberately re-introduced into many areas of the mountains: bearded vultures were reintroduced in 1993, after being decimated through the Alps during the nineteenth century but surviving in areas such as Corsica and the Pyrenees, from where the current population was taken; these formidable birds feeds off chamois and ewe carcasses, diving for bones and then dropping them on rocks to break them into smaller pieces. Another successful re-introduction has been the moufflon, a wild sheep introduced from Corsica into the Queyras region of the French Alps in 1973. Brown bears and golden eagles have also been introduced into Slovenia's Triglav National Park, which covers the highest part of the Julian Alps. After centuries of deliberate and non-deliberate human destruction of the Alpine environment it is good to see that such positive steps at conservation have been taken in so many areas. But these measures are too little, too late once it is realized that the destruction of the environment probably began ten thousand years ago. It was then that humans gradually colonized the mountains after the ice had gone, finding a new home among the animals they started hunting, the trees they began cutting down for wood and fuel, and the edible plants they started gathering for food.

Part Two
History

In the Beginning: Ötzi the Ice Man

He is kept in a large box, whose walls are made almost entirely from blocks of ice. The only light in the box comes from two bare bulbs set in the ceiling, which emit a dull and ghostly indigo glow. The figure inside the box is little more than four foot tall, and is completely naked. But, considering he is more than five and a half thousand years old, he is looking in remarkably good condition.

"Ötzi" the Ice Man is the most tangible link we have with the Alps in prehistoric times. The body of this Neolithic man was found by two German climbers, Erika and Helmut Simon, in September 1991, while they were walking on the Similaun glacier in a remote, high part of the Alps, right on the Italian-Austrian border. They noticed an obviously human form protruding from the ice and, thinking they had stumbled on the aftermath of a tragic climbing accident, they reported their discovery to the police when they reached the next mountain hut. For three days Austrian police and mountain rescue workers worked at freeing the body from its icy resting place. When a local Tyrolean mountaineer, Reinhold Messner, visited the scene and pronounced the body to be over three thousand years old, the press and media suddenly realized that something interesting was afoot. The subsequent airlifting of the corpse from the mountainside by helicopter was seen around the world on television.

Subsequent testing of the body by archaeologists at Innsbruck University revealed what many had already suspected: that this was an anthropological find of major importance. Carbon dating indicated that the body dated from around 3,500 BC; its natural burial in an icy tomb had prevented decay from setting in, and it was clear that the man was dark haired, blue eyed, sported charcoal tattoos, and according to an examination of the contents of his stomach, had just eaten a meal consisting of ibex. He wore well-made shoes, and on his head was a hat

made from bearskin. The sheaves of wheat found embedded in his clothes suggest that he came from a farming community, and his clothes were fashioned from goat hide, so these farmers must have kept domesticated animals. The artefacts the man was carrying also excited considerable interest: they included a rudimentary rucksack made from animal skins and mounted on a wooden frame, really not much different from the backpacks carried by the hoards of inter-railers who cross the Brenner Pass each summer by train, close to where Ötzi was making his own journey across the mountains.

Who was he? The man had charcoal with him, to make a fire. He was probably planning to be in the mountains for several days. Perhaps he was a trader, crossing the Alps to sell produce, taking the high route to avoid passing through hostile territory; or maybe he was a shepherd, taking his animals to summer pasture (pollen in his stomach suggests that he made this, his last journey, in the spring). Then in 2001 came another major revelation: the man had an arrowhead embedded in his shoulder blade, and there was blood on his clothing that was not his own. Had he received some sort of ritual punishment, meted out for a transgression? Or was this wound inflicted during a period of tribal unrest in what must have been a violent, lawless time? The truth is, we will never know. But Ötzi's clothes and belongings have given scientists an immense insight into prehistoric life in the Alps.

That name, "Ötzi", is derived from the Ötztal valley above which the man was found. Nowadays Ötzi resides in a museum in Bolzano, a small city in northern Italy on the southern approaches to the Brenner Pass. This in itself is a little odd, because it was the Austrians who lifted him off the mountainside; but a careful cartographical examination of the exhumation spot revealed that it was ten metres into Italy, so the Italians kept Ötzi once the preliminary scientific examination was over. This took some years, as did the international wrangling over Ötzi's future; but eventually, in 1998, he was packed into a frozen food transporter in Innsbruck and taken across the Brenner with a police escort (a shadowy Austrian nationalist group had threatened to destroy the body if Ötzi ever left Austrian soil). Now his resting place is an ice box, because he will decay if his body does not remain constantly frozen; a piece of glass little bigger than a TV screen allows visitors to the Bolzano Museum of Archaeology to get a glimpse of him. Not that Ötzi seems to take much notice of the attention. One of his hands is clenched firmly into a fist, while the other arm is slung awkwardly over his neck and shoulders; his torso his shrunk to almost nothing, but the fingers and toes and knees and teeth are all very distinct. Most strikingly of all, the head is pointing upwards, giving Ötzi an air of aloofness, as though he is keeping all his remaining secrets to himself.

In addition to giving a vivid insight into the life of prehistoric man in the Alps, the town of Bolzano itself is also emblematic of more recent events of Alpine history. Set at the confluence of the Adige and Rienza Rivers, Bolzano occupies a narrow plain that is sunk below rocky, forested ridges that rise, even to summer, to peaks whose summits are dusted in snow. Almost every valley-side bluff overlooking the plain is occupied by a squat medieval castle. Arrangements of impregnable-looking grey squared towers, surrounded by battlements and walls, seem to be everywhere; when you spot one, you see two more, across the valley and further down it too, and at different levels of the hillside. The number of castles around Bolzano attests to the political volatility of this area throughout the Middle Ages—and before, too, as many of the castles are built over the foundations of Roman forts that stood on the same strategic outcrops. Meanwhile, Bolzano itself leads a notoriously schizophrenic existence: all the street names are in both German and Italian, and the town has a distinctly Germanic feel to it, as this is the South Tyrol, which has long been the subject of intense Austro-Italian political squabbling. Nowhere else in the Alps has been quite so fought over—and to the south of the Bolzano is Rovereto, where some of the most significant and fiercely-fought battles of the First World War took place. But all of this—both the medieval castles and the remnants of the First World War trenches that cross the Italian mountainsides—form only the more recent chapters in a story that has for centuries been hard and bloody. The history of the Alps consists, for the most part, of constant fighting between the different ethnic, linguistic, religious and national groups that have occupied the mountains over the millennia; only two men, Augustus and Charlemagne, have united the whole of the region under one ruler (although Napoleon came close as well), and for thousands of years the fate of the mountains has been one of fragmentation, invasion, rebellion and war.

Pre-Celtic Times

Alpine communities had already been flourishing for thousands of years at the time of Ötzi's last journey over the mountains. Ten thousand years ago, as the ice melted from the Alpine valleys to leave just the mountain tops permanently covered in snow, Paleolithic communities began to appear on the shores of the region's major lakes, while other groups found shelter in caves. The Grottes de Choranche in the Vercors, near Grenoble, has yielded considerable evidence of occupation by prehistoric cave dwellers, while in the Mondsee region of the Austrian lake district, nineteenth-century archaeologists uncovered waterside dwellings that were mounted on stilts to keep them dry (the so-called "Mondsee Culture"). Other places with particular evidence of prehistoric habitation include Ville-Vieille, near Queras in the French Alps, which has a seven-metre standing stone (now broken) called Pierre Fische, and Aosta, in north-western Italy, where evidence has revealed a large necropolis dating from around 2700 BC that was used for religious rituals and "sown" with human teeth as part of a ploughing ritual of consecration. But, as tangible evidence of Alpine pre-history, all of these pale beside the extraordinary rock carvings in Italy's Val Camonica, created by early communities thousands of years before Celtic and Roman times.

Situated north-west of Lake Garda, the Val Camonica is a valley typical of the Dolomites. The valley floor is deep but not flat, and is peppered with picturesque villages whose stone-and-wood houses, with their characteristic red tiled roofs set in a confusion of different heights and angles, seem to be a relic of a bygone era. Away from the villages, the valley sides are covered in vineyards and thick woodland; above the tree-line grass soon gives way to near-vertical, tooth-like jagged rocks, pale and strangely benign-looking in the sunshine. On summer afternoons it is often baking hot; the distant mountains at the end of the valley appear as dark shadows, shimmering in the dull blue haze, while the villages, with their narrow cobbled streets twisting past heavy stone churches and ancient thick-walled barns, are silent during the afternoon siesta, which is observed as closely here as in any other part of Italy. From one of the villages in the Val Camonica, Nadro, a path runs through thick woodland to emerge next to a series of flat, dark rocks on which appear some of the best-known carvings of the whole valley; in fact the archaeological remains here are of such importance that they have been designated a UNESCO world heritage site.

The rocks, smooth, black, bald intrusions that have already been sliced through with geological cracks and fissures, are covered with designs depicting people, huts, weapons, animals and trees. The designs are not coloured (these are carvings, not paintings) and are little more than shallow indents in the rock surface. But they still remain distinct, even after thousands of years of exposure to the heat, rain, snow and wind of the mountains. The images are cartoon-like in their simplicity: one design shows a man running, with a shield in one hand and a spear held aloft in the other; another design shows two eight-inch-high figures fighting a duel. But many of the other designs are confusing. (Some might be early forms of writing, using alphabet-like symbols.) And these rocks, at Foppe di Nadro, are just one set of carvings: there are over two hundred thousand individual carvings spread over the Val Camonica, most of them dating from the time of the Camuni tribes, who lived here from 5000 BC until the Roman incursions. (Some of the carvings have also been dated to the pre-Camuni era, and to the Middle Ages.) In Naquane, situated between Nadro and Capo di Ponte (the main town of the Val Camonica), is a rock whose carvings depict a religious ceremony attended by priests, along with a burial in which the deceased is surrounded by weapons and tools; elsewhere on the rock surface here, a blacksmith is shown hard at work, a sure sign that these designs were made during the Iron Age.

The Celts and the Coming of the Romans

Celtic peoples began moving into the Alps from around 1000 BC, gradually replacing tribes such as the Camuni, who had fashioned the Val Camonica carvings. The most powerful Celtic tribes to settle in the Alps were the Helvetii and the Rhaetians, who lived in what is now Switzerland; another tribe, the Allobrogi, settled between the Rhône and the Isère in modern-day France. Under Celtic rule the economics and culture of the Alps underwent decisive change. Many place names in the region are derived from the Celtic, because these towns and villages were founded by the newcomers; Lucerne was probably a Celtic town, its name derived from the Celtic *lozzeria*, meaning "a settlement on marshy ground". But the Celtic era in the Alps is remembered today by much more than place names.

The principal economic initiative of the Celts was mining, particularly for salt, and many of the salt mines established in areas such as the Salzkammergut, near Salzburg, are still being worked to this day. Two towns in this area which had flourishing salt mines in Celtic times were Hallein and Hallstatt. In the nineteenth century, the works manager of the mine at Hallstatt, Johann Georg Ramsauer, who was also an amateur archaeologist, uncovered a major find from Celtic times: he discovered more than a thousand graves, some of which contained pottery, jewellery, swords and daggers. The discoveries made it clear that a major Celtic community, grown rich and powerful through the control of salt mining and trading, had flourished here from around 800 BC onwards. A similar community was in existence in near-by Hallein, where the prized exhibit in the town's museum is a *Schnabelkanne*, or beaked jug, found in a princely grave near that town's mine; it is decorated with a lion-like beast which is possibly the Celtic god, Taranis.

As the Celts were establishing themselves through much of the Alps, the might of Rome was growing in the Italian peninsula to the south—so much so that Roman expansionism was seen as a threat by many rulers in Europe and around the Mediterranean. One of these threatened regimes was that of Carthage, whose military commander, Hannibal, famously crossed the Alps with forty thousand men (and many elephants) in 218 BC, on his way to do battle with the burgeoning Empire. (He defeated the Romans at Trasimene in Perugia the following year, and in so doing concluded the second Punic War.) Supposedly the pass Hannibal's army used to cross the mountains was the Great St. Bernard, although there is no evidence for this, apart from it being the most widely-used route for trans-Alpine trade at the time (in 390 BC a Gaulish army had definitely passed that way, later defeating the Romans in north-western Italy and establishing the province of Cisalpine Gaul). A plaque fixed to a rock on another pass, the smaller Col Agnel, says *it* was the pass used by Hannibal, and R. L. J. Irving maintains that there are no fewer than five different passes claiming to be the one that Hannibal crossed.

Whichever pass he used, Hannibal's feat was clearly an extraordinary military triumph—the sort of boy's-own adventure saga of which legends are made. Not surprisingly, the story of his advance over the Alps proved alluring to classical writers. One, the Greek historian Polybius, recounted it in vivid and gory detail, writing that after journeying through the mountains for several days, the Carthaginians "at last reached a place where it was impossible for either the elephants or the pack-animals to pass, owing to the extreme narrowness of the path… and the soldiers once more became disheartened and discouraged. Hannibal encamped on the ridge, sweeping it clear of snow, and next set the soldiers to work to build up the path along the cliff, a most toilsome task…" Once he had got all his forces together, including the elephants who were in "wretched condition from hunger", Hannibal marched everyone down the pass in three days until they reached the plains of northern Italy. According to Polybius, the whole march from New Carthage (modern Tunis) took five months, and the crossing of the Alps a total of fifteen days. Another writer, the poet Silicus Italicus, penned a fanciful verse epic about the second Punic War, in which he described the dreadfulness of the mountain crossing: soldiers, he wrote, were tormented by tremendous avalanches, and a violent wind that "strips the men of their shields and rolls them round and round, and whirls them aloft in the clouds." According to Silicus, the frostbite was so bad that many soldiers were forced to leave their arms and legs behind in the snow.

Over time, however, not even armies with elephants were able to halt the expansion of the Roman Empire, and the Alps gradually became part of the *Pax Romana*. In 121 BC the Celtic Allobrogi tribe recognized Roman superiority, and in 58 BC at Bibracte in France, a Roman army under Julius Caesar defeated the army of the Helvetii; over the next hundred years the Rhaetian tribe in eastern Switzerland was also conquered and subdued. In 15BC the Romans turned their attention to what is now Austria, occupying the country south of the Danube, subduing the tribe of the Brigantes but naming a new town, Brigantium (modern Bregenz on Lake Constance) in their honour. In this and other places a Romano-Celtic tradition gradually arose after occupation, with new gods, customs and architectural styles that had antecedents in both cultures.

One area where this is seen to best effect is Carinthia, in the extreme east of the Alps in what is now the Austrian-Slovenian border region. On the slopes of the Magdalensburg (1,058m), near Klagenfurt, is a grassy area scattered with the remains of a Celtic town that was later occupied by the Romans. The Celts had come here in the first century BC, and their community had grown rich through gold, amber and iron ore mining; but the town was occupied by the Romans in the following century, and soon had the familiar trappings of Roman towns grafted onto it, such as a forum and baths. Close by, and in a similar manner, the old Celtic town of Noricum was subsumed into the Roman Empire and reborn as Virunum in around 10BC. A beautifully preserved mosaic, now in the regional museum at Klagenfurt, has been unearthed from here, showing Dionysus surrounded by near-naked satyrs; the presence of Medusa at the corner of the design was there to ward off guilt-bearing spirits, as the mosaic would probably have decorated a room where the order of the day would have been feasting, entertainment and debauchery. The Romans, with their characteristic taste for grand architecture, hedonism and baths, had clearly arrived in the Alps.

Roman Remains

There are Roman remains scattered all over the Alpine region, but the town with the most reminders of the Roman era is unquestionably Aosta in north-western Italy. Today this elegant town, set in verdant mountain countryside, is known as the gateway to the most spectacular region of the Italian Alps: the chic ski resort of Courmayeur nestles a little further up the valley, beneath high snow-capped mountains that can be clearly seen from the centre of Aosta. Lying as it does at the southern approach to the Great St. Bernard Pass, Aosta's tradition of controlling major routes across the highest parts of the Alps stretches back thousands of years, and was enhanced when the Mont Blanc road tunnel, whose eastern portal lies immediately beyond Courmayeur, was opened in 1965. Recognizing its strategic importance, the Romans took control of the town from the Celtic Salassi tribe in 25 BC, and set about endowing it with their monuments. To honour the Emperor Augustus, a very handsome triumphal arch, the Arco di Augusto, was constructed (now somewhat marooned in the centre of a roundabout); also in the Emperor's honour the town was renamed Augusta Praetoria, from which its modern Italian name is derived. Aosta was primarily a military

town, and its old Roman walls and defensive gateways are still very much in evidence, as is the old entrance to the town, the Porta Praetoria, a set of parallel triple-arched gateways now partly buried through the build-up of mud and soil over the centuries. (Nevertheless the arrangement of the gateway is still very clear: chariots used the large central arch, while pedestrians had to make do with the smaller arches that flanked it.) Close to the Porta Praetoria are the remains of a theatre—its grand arcaded façade, pierced with arched windows, still intact, but with its stage mostly gone—and also an amphitheatre, once capable of holding twenty thousand spectators, but which has now virtually disappeared, apart from some of the external walls that now form part of a nunnery.

Aosta's most famous relic of the Roman age, however, is on a smaller scale than any of these monuments: it is an elegant single-span hump-back bridge, built over the Buthier river, which was constructed sturdily enough to be in use every day by pedestrians two thousand years later. All that is missing from the bridge is the water underneath it: the river has changed its course over the centuries, and now flows close by. All the bridge crosses these days is a scruffy patch of grass.

On the northern approaches to the Great St. Bernard Pass, Aosta's "twin" city is Martigny, a fairly mundane Swiss town whose apartment blocks and light industrial complexes scatter the flat floor of the Rhône valley. Here, not surprisingly, are more Roman remains. Nestling at the base of steeply wooded slopes on a quiet suburban street in the town's eastern fringes is a small and rather neglected amphitheatre, now the arena for the Combat des Reines, a festival held every October when local farmers show off the "Queen of the Herd", a title disputed by specially-trained cows fighting each other through locking horns. The amphitheatre is later than Aosta's, dating from the second to fourth century AD; nearby, the knee-high foundations of a temple to Mercury form the centrepiece of the stylish modern building housing the Fondation Pierre Gianadda, a fashionable museum and art gallery. One of the museum's exhibits is a striking bronze head of a bull from the second century, while outside, remains of Roman baths are scattered around the museum's outdoor café and sculpture park.

Many Roman travellers would have passed through both Martigny and Aosta on long-distance journeys across Europe; there are still clear traces of the old Roman road at the very summit of the Great St. Bernard Pass (running above the modern roadway and customs houses), and at Bourg St. Pierre on the Swiss approach to the pass is a Roman milestone dating from around 310AD. (There was a Temple to Jupiter at the summit of the pass in Roman times, and the route was known in Latin as the *Summa Poenina*, in deference to the Celtic god Poenn who was worshipped in the Martigny region.)

The old Roman road from France leading towards Martigny and the St. Bernard Pass went along the northern side of Lake Geneva and through the city of Lausanne. In Roman times this settlement straggled along the lake shore (rather than rising in steps above it as it does now), but all that remains of Roman *Losonna* these days are some knee-high walls and a couple of sad-looking column stumps, all grassed over in a public park. There are sign boards showing where the forum and the basilica were, but it is hard making any sense of the place, and the site is now given over to joggers and dog-walkers, a forgotten part of this lakeside city well away from the yachts and the fashionable hotels.

Beyond Martigny, if Romans were heading on along the Rhône valley and not crossing over the Alps to Italy, they would have passed through Sedunum, meaning "Place of Castles": this is now Sion, still home to two mightily impressive fortresses, one of which, the Château de Valère, has massive Roman foundations walls and may stand on the site of what was once a Roman temple. Just beyond Sion, Sirrum Amoenum translates as "Sierre the agreeable"—a reference to it being the driest, sunniest town in Switzerland, famed nowadays for its pinot noir reds, the product of a wine-making tradition which probably started during Roman times.

Elsewhere in the Alps place names are the lasting legacy of Roman rule. Curia Rhaetorium, the garrison town which controlled the Julier and Splügen passes, is now Chur (and at the summit of the Julier Pass are some column stumps of a former Roman temple); Parthanum, in the Bavarian Alps, is now Partenkirchen; Trento in the Dolomites was Tridentum, while Rovoreto, to the south, was Ruboretum; the town of Sesto Calende, on the southern tip of Lake Maggiore, got its name from the days when a Roman market was held here on the sixth days after Calends, while a Roman general named Titus Labenius led an expedition against the Gauls from a town on the same lake that was later named Laveno in tribute to him. In the French Alps, the town of Grenoble was named after the Emperor Gratianus, while Annecy derives its name from a Roman villa, the Villa Aniciaca—and so it goes on, with dozens of other possible examples.

Roman rule did not end suddenly in the Alps; rather, it was a case of the gradual withdrawal of imperial forces from various parts of the mountains following a sustained onslaught from stubbornly aggressive northern tribes. As the Romans left, the western parts of the Alps were occupied by Bergundian (Latin-speaking) tribes originating from what is now France, while the Alemanni tribes from Germany moved into the eastern Alps, sacking Aventium, the Roman city in lowland Switzerland which governed their province of Helvetia, in 277 AD.

These migrations established the main linguistic division of the Alps that are apparent today: the areas occupied by the Bergundian tribes eventually became French-speaking, while the area settled by the Alemanni peoples roughly correlates with German-speaking regions of Switzerland and Austria. The Romans finally withdrew from the Alps during the early decades of the fifth century, encouraging yet more migration from the north. But they left behind them something much more important than a few place names and some noble but slowly collapsing monuments: the most important legacy of the Romans, Christianity, was to shape the history of the Alps, and of Europe, for much of the following two thousand years.

The Beginnings of Christianity

In the year 287, during the rule of the Emperor Maximilian, a Roman soldier named Maurice was ordered to serve in the Imperial army on a campaign that would involve him fighting against Christian insurgents in Gaul. But Maurice was himself a Christian, and refused to obey his military commanders; Maximilian, seething with rage, had the soldier's entire garrison slaughtered in retribution. In the years that followed, Maurice's tomb, situated below a steep cliff on a dark and wooded section of the Rhône valley between Martigny and Lake Geneva, became a place of pilgrimage for his fellow believers. Their visits were secret at first, as early followers of Christianity faced death if they were discovered practising their faith; but after 313, when the Edict of Milan allowed Christians to worship freely in the Roman Empire, the tomb became a public shrine. In around 390 Bishop Theodore of Martigny had the first church built over the site, and in 515 the Bergundian King Sigismund founded a monastery next door. By then the tomb of St. Maurice was a popular place of pilgrimage, not least because it was on the road leading to the Great St. Bernard Pass, which ensured a steady flow of passing traffic.

Over the ensuing centuries, more churches came and went on the site, many destroyed by the cascades of boulders which regularly tumbled from the huge slab of grey cliff rearing above the site of the tomb. The current abbey and the adjacent monastery are hemmed in between this forbidding cliff and the main road along the valley floor; the complex incorporates buildings dating from different eras between the fourth century AD and the 1940s. The abbey itself is entered through a strikingly modern doorway on which is listed, each in the appropriate language, the names of dozens of different martyrs from different countries; in the abbey treasury are gifts brought by pilgrims through the ages, including some left by Eucher, the fifth-century

Bishop of Lyon, and a fine gold jug encrusted with precious stones that was reputedly given by Charlemagne in the year 800. Over time the cult of St. Maurice has spread around the world: thousands of churches are dedicated to him, and two countries, Mauritania and Mauritius, are named after him. And his legend remains potent to this day: once a year, on 22 September, the saint's relics are paraded around the streets of St. Maurice by monks, in an elderly casket with a pointy lid; and all year round pilgrims are drawn to the abbey church in their droves, just as they have been for sixteen hundred years.

The story of St. Maurice, and the sanctification of his burial place, provides a fine synopsis of the first thousand years of Christianity in the Alps, from its earliest stirrings as an underground movement during the Roman era, through to the foundation of the great Alpine monasteries in the later Middle Ages. Besides Maurice, a number of other martyrs emerged from Roman legions serving in the Alps: one story concerns Felix and Regula, deserters from a legion stationed in the Valais, who were martyred in Zurich and are buried under the city's Fraumünster church. Then came Constantine's edict, and with it public demonstrations of conversion: in the Défilé de Pierre Ecrite, a deep gorge near Sisteron (Roman Segustero) in the French Alps, a Latin inscription on a rock records the conversion of Dardanus, a prefect of Gaul, to Christianity during the fifth century AD, and the subsequent construction of the first road through the gorge.

Conversions were less common among ordinary civilian folk, who remained true to their pagan beliefs. At around the time of Dardanus' conversion missionaries began to come to the Alps, such as the brothers Giulio and Giuliano, who were sent from Rome to preach the gospel in the wild area around Lake Orta in the Italian Lake District. Giuliano founded a church at Gozzano, south of the lake, while Giulio lived as a hermit on an island in its middle, undeterred by the locals who maintained that the place was inhabited by dragons and serpents. (The site of Giulio's cell is now occupied by a Romanesque basilica built in the ninth century; the church holds a bone belonging to one of the monsters killed by Giulio when he first came to the island, while the saint's ashes are kept in an urn in the crypt.) Giulio and Giuliano were missionary pioneers, and by the last decades of the Roman occupation of the Alps the process of conversion was well underway. Christian churches sprouted up all over the region: on the floor of the medieval Santa Maria del Tiglio church in Gravedona on Lake Como is a mosaic floor from the church that was established on this site during the fifth century, while in another part of the mountains, excavations underneath the magnificent Romanesque cathedral of Chur have revealed the remains of a much earlier church dating from the time of Asinio, who was made the city's first bishop in the year 451. But by this time, as we have already seen, the Roman era in the Alps had drawn to a close, and a long era of political uncertainty, underscored by the steady growth of Christianity, was sweeping over the region.

The Holy Roman Empire: Castles, Dukes and Princes

In AD 600 the Alemans and Bergundians, who had filled the vacuum in central Europe left by the Roman withdrawal, were conquered by a newly dominant political force, the Franks. This powerful group of Germanic tribes, who had risen to prominence as fierce foes of the Romans, was to dominate the politics of Europe for centuries: at the height of their power the Franks ruled much of what is now Germany, France, northern Italy and the low countries, as well as the Alps, from their capital at Aachen in northern Germany. In 507 Clovis, King of the Franks, converted to Christianity, and so established the most powerful Christian Kingdom of early medieval Europe, a forerunner to the Holy Roman Empire.

During the early centuries of Frankish expansion an alliance was forged with another Germanic tribe, the Bavarians, who pushed into the eastern area of the Alps while the Franks gained control of the western parts. Like the Franks, the Bavarians introduced feudalism and Christianity to the areas they conquered. During the eighth century they founded a number of monasteries in Austria, including one at Mondsee near Salzburg, whose church was used in the wedding scene in *The Sound of Music* over a thousand years later. Later on still, the Bavarians pushed out the Slavs from their Duchy of Karantanija (Carinthia) which they had established in what is now the Austrian-Slovenian border region. An unusual exhibit in the Landesmuseum in the Carinthian city of Klagenfurt dates from this era. It is the top of an old Roman column, fashioned into a smooth and broad-topped stool, which is known as the *Fürstenstein*, or Prince's Stool. This was used in public ceremonies

confirming the power and authority of German-speaking rulers over the Slav-speaking peasants who remained here after the Bavarian advance. The use of the column is an indication that the Romans, and their reputation for law and order, were still highly revered; the Frankish and Bavarian tribal leaders must have been keenly aware of the long political shadow that Roman rule still cast over Europe, even as they set about establishing a new post-Roman political order.

While the Bavarians were facing down opposition from the Slavs in the eastern part of the Alps, the Franks were up against a very different foe in the west. The Saracens were sea-farers from North Africa, who indulged in piracy on the high seas and bouts of military expansionism on land, making frequent incursions into Italy and southern France. After the Saracen victory at the Battle of Poitiers in 732 groups of these Arab speakers remained behind in Europe, and according to tradition some settled as farmers in the valleys of the Alps. (They gained a political foothold too: in the early tenth century the King of Italy, Hugh of Provence, was forced to hand over guardianship of a number of Alpine passes to the Saracens after their military exploits grew even more successful.) According to legend, the remote Val d'Hérens near Sion, in the heart of the Valaisian Alps, was one area that was settled by the Saracens during these centuries. The patios spoken in this valley today is as guttural as Arabic, and the people who live in the shadows of its deep rocky slopes are dark-skinned and dark eyed, suggesting a possible Mediterranean ancestry. Elsewhere in the Valais, the people of the town of Isérables are known as the *Bedjuis*—which some have suggested is derived from "Bedouin"—while the Allalinhorn Peak near Saas Fée might derive its name from Allah.

Stories concerning the Saracens abound in other parts of the western Alps too: close to Sisteron in the Alpes de Haute-Provence are a group of rocks known as the Pénitents de Mées, which according to local legend were formed when a group of monks fell in love with the beautiful Arab girls whom a local lord had brought back from his campaign against the Saracens. St. Donat punished the monks for their sinful lust by turning them into stones as they walked in procession along the River Durance. All of this is, of course, rather fanciful, but the legends do at least cast some light on how confusing was the era that settled over Europe in the centuries following the withdrawal of the Romans; not for nothing were these times known as the "Dark Ages".

Gradually, however, a period of political stability emerged out of the gloom, and the Alps (and much of the rest of Europe) became a mosaic of dukedoms and princedoms, most of which were at least nominally under the control of the Holy Roman Emperor. The first holder of this rather nebulous title was the legendary Charlemagne (Charles the Great) who, already King of the Franks, was crowned "Patricius Romanorum"—Protector of Rome—by the Pope on Christmas Day in the year 800, by way of a "thank you" for saving the Papal States from the Lombards six years earlier. His coronation took place in St. Peter's in Rome, and to reach that city from Paderborn in northern Germany Charlemagne, with his magnificent entourage, had to pass over the Alps; a series of medieval murals in the church of Santo Stefano at the village of Carisolo, near Trento in the Dolomites, record that part of his procession took him through the Campiglio valley. (He returned to Germany via another Alpine route, over the Great St. Bernard Pass.) During the centuries that followed, the Holy Roman Emperor became the most important political figurehead in Europe (second only to the Pope). But with communications difficult and local rivalries and egos running high, it was not surprising that aristocratic families became powerful rulers throughout the Alps, theoretically subservient to the Emperor but actually too busy covering the mountains with their castles to give much attention to what he said.

One superb example of a medieval Alpine fortress dating from this time is the Château de Gruyères, located in wild and remote countryside to the north of Lausanne, on the fringes of the Bernese Oberland. The castle here was occupied between 1080 and 1554 by nineteen successive counts of Gruyères. The castle's austere battlements and squat, irregular set of towers are picturesquely framed by the steep peaks towering behind it; all around are thick, steeply wooded slopes, which rise from the lush meadowland where the cows, which produce the famous Gruyère cheese, graze. The castle was destroyed by fire in 1493 and rebuilt in luscious style as a palatial residence rather than a fortress, a fate which befell many Alpine castles as more settled times emerged out of the political quagmire of the Middle Ages. This rebuilding ensured the castle's survival, and nowadays the tiny village of Gruyères which nestles beneath its walls is swamped by over a million visitors a year, turning the attractive cobbled main street into a mass of souvenir shops (mostly selling the usual Swiss kitsch of cowbells and cuckoo clocks, although the odd souvenir cheese board is thrown in for good measure too).

Other castles in French-speaking Switzerland have had a slightly different history: the one at Aigle, which dates from the thirteenth century, was used as a prison until 1972, and is now a wine museum, while the austere Château de Valère, one of two castles which rise ominously above Sion on natural rocky outcrops in the centre of the broad Rhône valley, has the world's oldest playable organ (dating from 1390) and is itself built on ancient Roman foundations. Across the Great St. Bernard Pass in Italy is another area famed for its bloodshed and castle building: dozens of castles were built in the Middle Ages by the Challant family along the valley of the Dora, west and east of Aosta. The one at Verres was the very first Alpine fortress to install a toilet, while the Challants' palatial residence at Issogne boasts an arcaded courtyard decorated with vivid frescoes depicting a bustling medieval high street. In the same valley, the Castello de Fenis near Nus was built by the Fenis branch of the same family; it consists of a fairy-tale cluster of turrets and towers, and also has some fine Gothic frescoes, including one on which St. George rescues a damsel in distress from a dragon, while saints holding curling scrolls inscribed with pious sentiments look on. But none of these can compete with castles around Bolzano, the northern Italian town where Ötzi has his icy residence. From the battlements of the Schloss Hocheppan, situated in the hills near the town, it is possible to see over thirty castles and fortresses, occupying bluffs overlooking the broad valleys that converge at Bolzano and lead up towards the Brenner Pass. Most are now in ruins, or have been converted into fancy restaurants, but their brooding presence among the vineyards and pale limestone crags is a reminder of the centuries during which this area was the arena of a bloody feud between two powerful aristocratic clans, the Counts of Eppan and the Counts of the Tyrol.

One important ingredient poured into the already complex political cocktail of medieval Europe was a new type of ruler, the Prince-Bishop. These rulers enjoyed the patronage of the Holy Roman Emperor and wielded both secular and religious authority, making them hugely powerful within their own territorial borders. One of the first Prince-Bishoprics was Salzburg, established by a Frankish monk, St. Rupert, in the year 700. The Bishops of Salzburg soon established territorial control over an area that stretched as far south as Carinthia and included many hitherto heathen valleys of the eastern Alps, considered ripe for conversion. Wealth and power came from the salt mines at Hallein and as the Middle Ages progressed, the Prince-Bishops of Salzburg became some of the most powerful in the region. In the eleventh century an austere fortress was built on a craggy hill at Werfen in the southern part of the territory by the Prince-Archbishop Gebhard von Felsenstein, as a bulwark against the encroaching Bavarians; the Hohenwerfen Fortress is one of the most spectacularly situated in the Alps, a tremendous sight visible from trains on the main line running south from Salzburg into the heart of Austria. Elsewhere in the region, other powerful Prince-Bishops were the rulers of Brixen, who gained control of the area around the town of Bled in the Julian Alps in 1004; in the chapel of Bled Castle is a mural dating from this time which depicts Emperor Henry II conferring the property of Bled on the first of them, Bishop Albuin.

In the Alps of the Valais, the skyline of medieval Sion, already dominated by the Château de Valère, was transformed in 1294 by the powerful Prince-Bishop Boniface de Challant who built his own castle, the Château de Tourbillon, on a hill adjacent to the one occupied by the earlier fortress. The place is now a ruin, following a fire in the eighteenth century, and its appealing mix of rubble and picnic tables, collapsed crenellations and rocky paths makes it popular with local families and day-trippers. Trento, in northern Italy, was also ruled by a powerful dynasty of Prince-Bishops; the most noted was George of Liechtenstein, who governed between 1391 and 1407 and endowed Trento with one of the most extraordinary legacies of all the Alpine Prince-Bishops—a series of frescoes that adorn the inside of one of the lookout towers in the Castello del Buonconsiglio. In intricate detail, the frescoes depict the ordinary lives of peasants and nobles in each month of the year, with snowball fights in January and haymaking in May; they are counted as one of the most notable examples of Gothic art in Europe.

Liechtenstein: the Last Remaining Princedom

Mention of the Liechtenstein family brings the story around to the tiny mountain state which bears that name and is sandwiched between Austria and Switzerland on the east bank of the Rhine, in the heart of the Alps. The Principality of Liechtenstein is the one remaining legacy of the complex canvass of dukedoms and princedoms that once made up the Holy Roman Empire. The von Liechtensteins were a powerful family of medieval nobles whose ancestral seat was at Mödling, near Vienna. In the twelfth century one of the von Liechtensteins, Hugo, gained control of this Alpine territory through inheritance, but for centuries control of the area was passed from family to family until 1699 when Johann Adam Andreas von Liechtenstein purchased the Lordship of Schellenberg to obtain a position on the German Imperial Diet of Princes. Schellenberg was the northern, flatter part of what eventually became the Principality; in 1712 the same Count purchased the Lordship of Vaduz, now the capital, and the Principality of Liechtenstein was born. Liechtenstein's independence from Europe's two emerging nineteenth-century superpowers (Germany and Austria) was recognized in 1866, and its current ruler is Prince Hans Adam II von und zu Liechtenstein, a direct descendant of twelfth-century Hugo and seventeenth-century Johann Adam Andreas.

Covering an area the size of Manhattan Island, the place counts itself as the world's fourth-smallest country, and lives off farming, banking, the printing of postage stamps and the bus-loads of tourists who are drawn here without really knowing why. There is an "open border" agreement with Switzerland dating from 1923 and the Swiss Franc is the national currency, but the principality is resolutely independent, only joining the United Nations in 1990 and (like its western neighbour) showing no sign of wanting to throw in its lot with the European Union. The seat of government is the severe medieval castle which glares over Vaduz from a steep hillside, its towers and turrets framed against a stunning backdrop of mountains (the principality's highest peak is the 2,570m-high Naafkopf). The population of 32,000 people is governed by the last remaining hereditary monarch in Europe who wields any real authority (although his decisions must be ratified by the elected parliament); Liechtensteiners live mostly in Vaduz, a sprawling collection of apartment blocks stretching from the castle to the banks of the Rhine, and in small villages and hamlets that pepper the Unterland, a lonely area of thick forest and rolling hills in the country's tapering northern part. In truth, however, there is not really a lot to Liechtenstein apart from novelty value: the mountains are good for skiing and hiking, the castle looks impressive and the designer shops in Vaduz might appeal to some, but really the place is no different to any medium-sized town lying across the Rhine in Switzerland. Its importance lies only in its throwback to an old and forgotten political order: the current ruler is the last survivor of all the Princes, Prince-Bishops, Prince-Archbishops, Dukes and Kings who once ruled the medieval mosaic of proto-states that once covered the entire Alpine region.

Savoy and the Dauphiné

One powerful kingdom within the Holy Roman Empire was that of Savoy, a political entity that had its origins in the old Frankish kingdom of Burgundy; by the time of the powerful feudal lord Humbert I the Whitehander, who ruled Savoy in the eleventh century, the territory covered the area of the western Alps between Lake Geneva and the Isère River. Humbert was the founder of a powerful dynasty, whose fortunes nonetheless ebbed and flowed; in the early fourteenth century the Savoyards hit on hard times and the territory was divided, its southern part being sold to the King of France. This area became known as the Dauphiné, from the French word *Dauphin,* itself deriving from the nickname "Dolphin" that the English mother of Count Guigues III had given her younger son, Humbert, under whose auspices the sale was organized (from then on the heir to the French throne was also known by this title). In 1339 Humbert founded a university in the new Dauphiné capital, Grenoble; one of the oldest universities in Europe, it is now a well-known centre from the study of Alpine geography and geology, and for research into nuclear science.

Meanwhile, the Savoyards to the north were acting as guardians to a number of increasingly busy Alpine passes, whose taxes charged to traders made the ruling family very wealthy. During the tail-end of the Middle Ages a succession of powerful and charismatic rulers held court at the Savoyard capital of Chambéry and restored the prestige of the dynasty after the loss of the Dauphiné: Amadée VI (1343-83) was known as the "Green Count" because of the colours he wore when taking part in tournaments; Amadée VII (1383-91) was known as the "Red Count" from the blood shed during his frequent battles; while Amadée VIII (1391-1440) had the title Duke of Savoy conferred on him by the Holy Roman Emperor, and brought the city of Geneva and the Piedmont region of northern Italy under Savoyard control.

As Savoyard territory expanded further and further east, the capital was moved in 1563 from Chambéry, in the heart of the French Alps, to Turin, on the north Italian plains; fifteen years later the famed Holy Shroud from Christ's crucifixion, which until then had been in Savoyard hands and resident in the church of Saint-Chapelle in Chambéry, was moved to its current resting place in Turin Cathedral. Over the ensuing centuries, Savoy was occupied a number of times by French forces (particularly in the seventeenth century, and then later on by Napoleon) but it did not become fully a part of France until 1860. At that time it was still ruled by the dynasty which Humbert I had founded in 1034, and in fact the House of Savoy became the oldest ruling house in Europe, its end not coming until 1946 when the last King of Italy, the Savoyard Umberto II, was forced to abdicate. When Umberto died in 1983 he was buried in the Abbaye Royale de Hautecombe, a former monastery on the shores of the Lac du Bourget, which has been the burial place of many members of the House of

Savoy since medieval times; earlier incumbents laid to rest here include Boniface, a thirteenth-century Archbishop of Canterbury who was a member of the Savoy family, and Béatrix de Savoie, whose four daughters respectively became Queens of England, France, and Sicily, and Empress of Germany. The heavily restored church, sitting on a rocky promontory of the lake, is a testament to the enduring legacy and power of the Savoy clan; these days it is the home of an interdenominational Christian group called the Chemin Neuf, who took over the chapel and monastery after the last Benedictines left in 1992, and who spend much of their time showing round the hordes of visitors who come here on boat trips from the popular resort of Aix-les-Bains, which lies just across the water.

In contrast to Savoy, the Dauphiné enjoyed rather less glamorous history—although it bred two noted military figures. The first was Pierre Terrail, born in 1476 in the Château de Bayard near Pontcharra, just north of Grenoble. Pierre was born into a family of knights and soldiers and while still a boy became famed for his fearlessness and his riding prowess. At the age of thirteen he moved away from the Dauphiné and became a page boy to Charles I, Duke of Savoy; soon after he was at the court of King Charles VIII of France and at the age of sixteen he took part in his first proper tournament, defeating one of the finest jousters in the kingdom. His career as a brilliant soldier and politician led to his appointment as lieutenant-general of the Dauphiné in 1515; he died on the field of battle in 1524, meeting the same fate as had all his male ancestors. By then he was an almost legendary figure, the last and arguably the greatest embodiment of the values of heroic knightly conduct and military honour that formed the medieval code of chivalry: throughout the centuries since his death he has been celebrated as the *cheavalier sans peur et sans reproche*. Parts of his old castle at Pontcharra remain and are now a museum dedicated to his life.

The second figure associated with the Dauphiné is Sébastien le Prestre de Vauban (1633-1707), a brilliant military strategist and architect who directed fifty-three sieges, and whose bridges, buildings, canals, harbours, and citadels are scattered over the mountains of the southern French Alps. During the late seventeenth century Vauban built twelve fearsome castles between Antibes and Briançon, on the orders of Louis XIV who wanted to protect the French territory of the Dauphiné from Savoyard attack. One of Vauban's most noted works is the huge defensive fortress at Briançon (itself the highest town in Europe, situated at an altitude of 1,321m), which towers over the Durance from a rock previously fortified by the Romans and Celts. (An army ski school was established in the fortress in 1904, and the place is still in military use.) Another castle was constructed at Colmars, which came under siege from the Savoyards in 1690; Vauban built the fortress in his familiar star-shaped design, with soldiers in each wing able to defend the wings either side of it. On Mont Dauphin near Briançon Vauban created one of his mightiest constructions, a fortified military settlement governing the approach to the Col de Vars that was in army hands until 1980, whereupon it was transformed into a centre for arts and crafts workshops. Vauban also built castles in many other French border regions, including Alsace, Flanders and the Pyrenees, and his work reflects the growing military might of France during the century that culminated in the rule of Napoleon.

The Château de Chillon

However, none of Vauban's grandiose and forbidding constructions come anywhere close to the fame and beauty of the most celebrated castle of the French-speaking area of the Alps. Built on a narrow promontory of land on the northern side of Lake Geneva, the Château de Chillon is one of the best preserved medieval castles in Europe. In her novel *Hotel du Lac* Anita Brookner describes the place as a "...dour, grim, rebarbative silhouette, a corrective to the dazzle of water"—but it is also a romantic place, seemingly floating on the lake, its turrets shimmering in the mist and framed by the high peaks of the Savoy Alps which rise on the lake's southern shore. There are traces of Bronze Age settlements on this site, but the first fortress built here was a Roman construction, whose purpose was to extract tolls from traders heading along the road that ran along the lake's northern shore up to the Great St. Bernard Pass. In the early Middle Ages the property was in the hands of the wealthy and powerful Bishops of Sion, who passed it on to the rulers of Savoy in 1150. In the thirteenth century Peter II of Savoy turned the place into a princely residence where the nobility of Savoy indulged in lavish entertainment and water-side debauchery. Even so, the castle's defensive role was retained, and this duality of function is still

clear today: the dark, dank dungeons and strong walls are still intact, but the rest of the castle features beautifully-decorated rooms with wonderful views over the lake, set around irregular cobbled courtyards and covered wooden walkways that run along the walls. Although many of the palatial rooms were extensively renovated in the sixteenth century, the kitchen still has its original ceiling and pillars dating from Peter's rebuilding of the fort in 1260, and the small, dark, vaulted chapel bears traces of frescoes from the same era.

During the early sixteenth century, when the House of Savoy was squaring up to the ever-growing power of the Habsburgs, the castle took on the role of prison and a garrison centre. The most famous prisoner held here was the scholar François Bonivard, who angered the Savoyards by inciting the people of Geneva to form an alliance with the Swiss confederation against Savoy. His dungeon is really a wide, vaulted passage, gloomy on account of the high, thin windows, and dank through the nearness of the lapping waters; a line of seven sturdy columns hold up the roof vaulting (Bonivard was chained to the fifth).

In 1536 the Bernese army took control of the fortress from the Savoyards and released Bonivard, who by that time had been held for six years; the Bernese then used the building as a depot and armoury and a residence for their bailiffs, and in 1798 passed it on to the Canton of Vaud. The turn of the nineteenth century marked the start of the great era of Alpine tourism, and two visitors to the castle at this time were the English poets Byron and Shelley, who were taken round in 1816 and were told the story of Bonivard by a tourist guide; Byron went back to his hotel and retold the tale his famous poem "The Prisoner of Chillon". Of the dungeon itself, Shelley wrote that he had never seen "a monument more terrible of cold and inhuman tyranny," while Byron famously carved his name onto one of the pillars.

The poem made Byron, and the Château de Chillon, famous in Europe and America. Mark Twain visited the place in 1880 and put a characteristic tongue-in-cheek twist on the story that Byron had told. "Bonivard's dungeon was a nice, cool roomy place, and I cannot see why he should have been so dissatisfied with it," he remarks sardonically. "It has romantic window-slits that let in generous bars of light, and it has tall, noble columns, carved apparently from the living rock; and what is more, they are written all over with thousands of names, some of them— like Byron's and Victor Hugo's—of the first celebrity. Why didn't he amuse himself reading these names? I think Bonivard's sufferings have been overrated." Twain also commented on the "swarms" of tourists ("what was to hinder Bonivard having a good time with them?") and to this day the castle is one of the most popular and iconic tourist attractions in the western Alps, with a multitude of foreign tongues echoing around its dingy dungeon and resplendent palatial rooms (the information guide is available in twenty languages, including Catalan and Lithuanian, although most visitors seem to be English or Japanese). The walk to the château from Vevey is particularly pleasant, along the lakefront promenade shaded by verdant tropical foliage. Only up close does the castle disappoint, as it is almost pushed into the lake by the railway and road that squeeze along the narrow ledge between the defensive walls and the mountainside—offering a very different prospect to the one painted by J. M.W. Turner in the early nineteenth century, when the castle was the only building visible on a lake shore otherwise covered by woods and fields.

The Viscontis and the Venetians

To the east of the Italian territory controlled by the Savoy family was an area that gradually came into the hands of an equally powerful medieval dynasty, the Viscontis of Milan. Their ascendancy began in the eleventh century, when the family obtained the hereditary title of Viscount of Milan; in 1262 Ottone Visconti was appointed Archbishop of Milan, and by the early fifteenth century much of northern Italy (except the area around Turin) was under Visconti control. Castles dating from this time are scattered all over northern Italy, including a number in the southern, Italian-speaking part of the Alps. The town best-endowed with Visconti castles is Bellinzona, a handsomely-situated settlement that occupies the valley of the River Ticino as it sweeps down to the Italian plains from its source near the Gotthard Pass; the place is overlooked by no fewer than three separate medieval castles, all built or controlled by the Visconti clan. Bellinzona came under control of the family in 1242, and the first of the fortresses, the Castelgrande, dates from this time. It is situated on a rock overlooking the centre of town known as the Monte San Michele (the forbidding White Tower is the only part of the original castle that remains). Another wealthy Italian family, the Rusconi of Como, built the second of Bellinzona's three castles, the Castello di Montebello, in the early fifteenth century, linking the two fortresses by a line of fortifications strung across the valley. In 1479 the Sforza family, close relatives and successors of the Viscontis, refortified this and the earlier castle and built a third castle, the Castello di Sasso Corbaro, on a high hillside overlooking the town; they wanted to stop the incursions of the Swiss confederates who had recently defeated Milanese troops at the Battle of Giornico. But all was to no avail: unlike the Savoyards, the Viscontis were unable to hang onto their possessions, and by 1500 their dynastic time was up; Ticino came under Swiss control and northern Italy became the arena for a new set of dynastic squabbles. The three castles in Bellinzona now form a UNESCO world heritage site, and are given over to use as museums, galleries, and restaurants, with their lawns carefully tended and their battlements restored. (Another noted Visconti castle is at Locarno, the Castello Visconteo, which was also badly damaged during a Swiss attack, this time in 1513; it is now the site of the town's archaeological museum.)

At constant loggerheads with the Viscontis was the Venetian Republic, whose tentacles were reaching into the Alps by the second part of the fifteenth century. On one occasion, in 1439, the Venetians even dragged their warships to Torbole at the northern end of Lake Garda and launched them onto the water to meet the Milanese fleet; the boats were rolled along on tree trunks and even had to be hauled over a low pass, the San Giovania (320m). One of the cities in the possession of the Venetians was Bergamo, close to Milan, whose extraordinarily beautiful Old Town is built over one of the last ripples of the southern Alps as the mountains plunge gracefully into the flat plains of the Po valley. One of the principal monuments from this time is the beautiful Cappella Colleoni, a chapel built onto the city's Santa Maria church in the 1470s by Bartolomeo Colleoni, a Bergarmo mercenary who twice captained Venetian forces against the Milanese. Both the interior and exterior of the chapel are opulent and extravagant, fashioned from pastel-coloured marble sculpted into miniature arcades, balustrades and twisted columns. Deeper into the mountains, the Venetians also fought the

Tyroleans for control of Trento, capturing the city in the Dolomites in 1487. The gilded lion of St. Mark, symbol of the Venetian Republic, can be seen in this city, in Bergamo, and also in the old town of Rovereto, south of Trento, which five centuries later was to play a crucial part in the Alpine theatre of the First World War.

The Rise of the Habsburgs

As the Viscontis fought for control in the Italian-speaking part of the Alps, and the power of Savoy and France grew in the French-speaking areas, an even more commanding political force was exerting itself in those areas of the mountains where German was the principal language. The politics of central Europe were to be dominated by the Habsburgs for nearly seven hundred years, from the rise of the dynasty in the thirteenth century to its demise after the First World War. In the later Habsburg era the Alpine regions of the empire were thought of as little more than remote backwaters, a world away from the sophistication and imperial glory of Vienna. But that was not so in the Middle Ages, for in the late fifteenth century one of the most famous Habsburg emperors, Maximilian I, chose to make the city of Innsbruck, in the heart of the Alps, his imperial capital, endowing it with by far the most impressive collection of monuments of any Alpine city.

Habsburg power dates from the year 1273, when a little-known count named Rudolf of Habsburg was proclaimed Holy Roman Emperor by the German Electors; the decision was soon ratified by the Pope, and news of Rudolf's elevation finally reached him while he was busy besieging Basel. (The position of Holy Roman Emperor had, even by then, ceased to mean much in terms of actual power; but the Emperor was vested with a quasi-mythical authority and the title was to remain in Habsburg hands until Napoleon abolished it in 1806). Rudolf's ancestral home was Habichtsburg Castle, situated at the confluence of the Aare and the Rhine on what is now the border between Germany and Switzerland. Over the decades following Rudolf's election his family secured control of much of what is now lowland Austria; then in 1363 Duke Rudolph IV inherited the Tyrol from his sister Margaretta, and for the first time part of the Alps was in Habsburg hands. In the 1380s Duke Leopold III held his court in Innsbruck, but it was the decision of his grandson, Maximilian, to make Innsbruck a glorious imperial capital that has given the city the rich architectural legacy (and swarms of tourists) for which it is famous today.

Innsbruck is one of the great cities of the Alps. Occupying a flat plain, scoured out by an enormous glacier, it is hemmed in on its northern edge by an immense wall of rock, the Nordkette, whose craggy grey face looms ominously over the city. A ten minute walk away from the ancient heart of Innsbruck is the lower station of a funicular railway, whose cabins cross the Inn on an elegant cantilever bridge and then grind and bump steeply up the lower slope of the Nordkette, forming the first stage of a three-part journey which ends at a cable car station at Hefelkar (2,334m), from where, not surprisingly, there is an extraordinary view over the city and the surrounding mountains. To the south, the lower slopes of the Patscherkofel (2,246m) are dominated by the silver scar of the ski-jump built for the 1976 Winter Olympics. It is said that Innsbruck is the only city in the Alps where office workers can take to their skis during their lunch hour. But of course the Habsburgs were not interested in any of this, nor were they concerned about the wonderful scenery surrounding their capital. They were much more interested in what was *under* the mountains than what they looked like—namely, the extensive silver deposits at nearby Schwaz, which would help make their burgeoning empire rich.

Maximilian I became Habsburg Emperor in 1493 at the age of thirty-four. Paintings of him as a young man show that he had the perfect youthful appearance for a figure known throughout his life for his chivalrous ways and courtly bearing. So confident was he of his credentials that Maximilian actually wrote an autobiography, *Weisskönig,* as an example to future princes, illustrating it with woodcuts showing his gallantry and his love of culture, learning and sportsmanship. Given this, it is not surprising that he was also known as a colossal egotist: he is supposed to have divulged a private fantasy to his daughter Margaret that he would one day be both Holy Roman Emperor and Pope, thereby uniting Christendom under one head.

Maximilian's most famous legacy in Innsbruck is the Goldenes Dachl. This is a sloping gold roof which covers a narrow balcony in the centre of the city, from where members of the imperial court could overlook the entertainments taking place in the square below. Built in the 1490s, the balcony is adorned with a series of reliefs showing

Moorish dancers performing before Maximilian and his second wife Bianca Maria Sforza. She is shown holding an apple that would have been thrown to the dancers to show appreciation; Maximilian's first wife, the adored Maria of Burgundy, who died after falling off her horse while flying her falcon near Bruges, stands behind them, like a watchful spirit. (The reliefs are replicas; the originals are in a museum in Innsbruck.) Nowadays the irregular cobbled square below the roof forms the heart of the city's café culture, a gathering point for fruit sellers, mime artists, and tourists (this must surely be one of the most photographed roofs in the world); but it is not difficult to imagine the noise and stench of the medieval throng five hundred years ago, and the cacophony of music and dancing and entertainers. The crowds, jammed in tightly between the high buildings, must have been curiously eyeing up their imperial rulers as much as watching the entertainment on offer—which was clearly diverting, judging by the one of the balcony reliefs, which depicts a dancer actually bent right over backwards, in an extraordinary feat of balletic elasticity.

A stone's throw away from the Goldenes Dachl, Innsbruck's well-trodden tourist trail leads to the Hofkirche, the church where Maximilian built a typically ostentatious cenotaph for himself. The huge black sarcophagus is overlooked by twenty-eight life-sized statues of earlier European rulers; Maximilian's father, Frederick III, had proved (at least to his own satisfaction) that he was a direct descendant of King Priam of Troy, and the figures represented in the Hofkirche are all the presumed spiritual—or actual—ancestors of the Habsburg dynasty. The motley group assembled here includes King Arthur, the semi-mythical king of the Britons, Clovis, the fifth-century king of the Franks, and Theodoric, the sixth-century king of the Ostrogoths. The ostentation is all the more hollow when one realizes that Maximilian is actually not even buried here; in 1519 he was refused entry to Innsbruck by the city burghers who thought his soldiers would not pay their bills, and the ruler was eventually buried near Vienna.

Habsburg expansionism continued relentlessly over the three centuries following Maximilian's accession. Maximilian himself brought the Bavarian town of Kufstein, further upstream along the River Inn, into the family fold in 1504 by bombarding it into submission with a cannon called "Weckauf" (which means "wake up") situated on the

banks of the river. The Bavarians got their own back in 1703 when they occupied Maximilian's old fortress for a year after climbing in through the windows using ladders. (To this day the town is situated right on the border between Germany and Austria.) In the same year the Tyroleans defeated invading Bavarians at the Battle of Landeck, fought in the western Tyrol, enhancing their reputation as fearless military warriors; their victory is commemorated by the Annasäuler Monument in Innsbruck, which takes the form of a slender column surmounted by the Virgin Mary. (The Tyroleans have always been proud of their military might and as early as 1511 signed an agreement with the Habsburgs that they would be responsible for defending their own borders but would not be expected to serve elsewhere in the Empire—an arrangement that lasted until 1918. The famed Schützen rifle associations are the most obvious manifestation of this military prowess; although now officially disbanded, the associations still attract a loyal amateur following, and weddings or processions in the rural Tyrol often feature men dressed up in military regalia to celebrate what amounts to a "national" Tyrolean identity.)

Innsbruck was to remain a prominent Habsburg centre during the dynasty's glorious heyday, even though the imperial capital was moved to Vienna in the late seventeenth century. In the middle of the following century, over the spot where Leopold III had first held court in the Middle Ages the Empress Maria Theresa built a large rococo palace, the Hofburg, which is still crammed with lavish apartments and monumental wall paintings depicting the glories of Habsburg history. (Nowadays the Hofburg's white and yellow courtyard makes a good venue for summer open-air concerts; it is often reached by tourists clopping through Innsbruck on a horse and carriage.) But during this time the Habsburgs also encountered fierce opposition to their expansionism. The greatest threat was from the Turks: the Ottoman Empire, expanding relentlessly around the Eastern Mediterranean, was also pushing its tentacles through the Balkans, threatening Vienna in 1529 and then again in 1683. Earlier a number of castles had been built in the south-eastern (now Slovenian) Alps to ward off the Ottoman threat; one of the most striking is the impressive Kluže Fortress, built in 1613 on a steep rock face overlooking the sixty-metre deep Koritnica Gorge, in the shadow of Mount Rombon (2,208m). The Ottomans were at last beaten back after a series of decisive battles fought during the second part of the seventeenth century, principally the Battle of Szentgotthàrd (1664). But the Habsburgs were not always as successful as they were against the Turks; their biggest defeat, which came some four centuries before the triumph at Szentgotthàrd, involved a clash with a seemingly much more humble foe—and resulted in the creation of an entirely new country within the heart of the Alps.

A Man, a Boy, an Apple and an Arrow

The scene is a gravel-strewn town square in Switzerland. A tall, sturdily built man, with bushy beard and deep-set eyes, wearing clothes made from thick animal-skins and carrying a formidable cross bow, stands confronting a well-drilled phalanx of guards and pikemen. He is clearly outnumbered, but he is standing firm; the black-robed figure who sits astride a magnificent horse garlanded with gold tassels seems to be berating him to no effect. Then, from the crowd of villagers that have gathered behind the soldiers, a young boy around twelve years of age appears, dressed simply in sandals, dark trousers and a loose white tunic fastened at the middle with rough twine. He stands next to the man, who is fully a head taller than him, and is clearly his father. The lad is handsome in a blond, blue-eyed, Teutonic sort of way, and lets the man place a comforting hand on his shoulder, as both of them adopt an expression of cool, steely defiance.

The scene is very tense: neither side wishes to lose face. Then a command is given by the hectoring horseman. The boy is led over to a tree that grows outside a ramshackle peasant's house; the soldiers stand him up against it, and place an apple on his head. The crowd falls silent and the boy stands motionless. The bearded man raises his crossbow, aims at the apple, and fires: the arrow pierces the apple dead-centre, and the crowd of villagers gasps and surge forward. The apple is presented to the man on the tasseled horse, whose moustache and black feather-plumed hat seem to quiver in anger and frustration. He is the representative of the Habsburg Empire and he knows that imperial Austrian might has just been mocked by a man with a good aim and a trusting son. This rebellious pair now unashamedly embrace each other in front of the seething crowd, who begin to press round them, nervous of what will happen next.

Exactly the same act of heroism and derring-do will happen the following day, too, as this is the open-air production of Friedrich Schiller's play *William Tell*, performed every evening during the summer in a specially-built open-air theatre just outside Interlaken. The play involves a vast cast of over two hundred performers, all of whom are amateurs drawn from local villages; their home town—perhaps Interlaken, or Thun, or Grindelwald, or Lauterbrunnen—is listed in the programme next to their name. And the familiar thespian mantra (never work with children or animals) is cheerfully and robustly ignored; the cast includes dozens of children, some of whom are barely old enough to walk, while at regular intervals teams of finely-clad horses gallop across the stage, raising clouds of dust and gravel, while the opening of the play involves the appearance of some real Alpine cattle, cowbells swinging from their necks, being led up to high pasture. In fact, using the words "play" and "stage" in this context seems a mite uncharitable: this is a spectacle, rather than a mere theatre production, and the stage, open to the sky, encompasses wooded glades, medieval houses, streets winding up towards a church, and a half-built castle covered in scaffolding. The audience—or should one say spectators—sit in a covered area of seating, so if it rains, they stay warm and dry under their rented blankets, while the actors and animals are soaking wet.

Schiller's slice of folkloric melodrama has been performed in this manner every year since 1912; some of the older cast members must have been involved in dozens of productions. Although the play is in German, a brochure handed out to members of the audience recounts the story—which, in any case, is not difficult to follow: a mean Austrian turns up in an Alpine town and demands that the populace pay respect to their new Habsburg overlords. One local farmer and hunter, William Tell, does not want to lower himself to such expressions of servitude. A challenge is thrown down. Tell wins and escapes; the mean imperialists are beaten off and a new country called Switzerland is formed.

The legend of William Tell, and his determination to stand up for the rights of his people in the face of aggression from a powerful neighbour, seems to be the very embodiment of Swissness. No matter that Tell probably never existed, or that even if he did, the stories associated with him are likely to be little more than just that—stories. Swiss people still flock in their thousands to the places on the shores of

Lake Lucerne associated with his name and with the foundation of their country. One of the locations is the Rütli Meadow, a narrow strip of Alpine pasture overlooking the lake, where the document confirming Swiss nationhood was drawn up and signed; the other is the pretty town of Altdorf, located a short distance away across the water, where the spirit of the nationhood and self-determination won at Rütli was vigorously and legendarily defended by William Tell.

The Creation of Switzerland

Altdorf and Rütli form part of the historical and spiritual heartland of Switzerland, which lies on the southern shores of the Vierwaldstättersee, literally "the lake of the four forest cantons" but better known to English speakers as Lake Lucerne. This lake is a very curious shape: on a map its multiple branches and twisting arms makes it resemble a huge ink blot, or perhaps a squashed insect. The part of the lake furthest away from Lucerne seems so distant from the bustle of the resort and the lake's western arm that it has acquired a name of its own: the Urnersee. It is one of the most dramatic stretches of water in Switzerland, its steeply wooded banks often shrouded in swirling mists, and its coastline, pockmarked with rocky peninsulas and tiny bays, often battered by waves from fierce storms. The Urnersee has none of the sprawling development that characterizes the flatter shores of the lake around Lucerne; it is darker and quieter, and often the only sound to break the silence is the rumble of trains along the busy line that hugs the lake's eastern shoreline, taking rail traffic from Zurich south towards Andermatt and the Gotthard Pass. The main settlement on the Urnersee is Flüelen. This unremarkable town takes over three hours to reach from Lucerne, travelling by one of the myriad of passenger ships that crisscross the lake in the summer season (even by train the journey takes an hour). Few of the tourists who board at Lucerne are going all the way to Flüelen, however; most are heading for the more popular lakeside stops of Brunnen or Weggis or Vitznau, which are chock full of lakeside restaurants and hotels. For those who are travelling the entire length of the lake there is time enough to soak up the history of Switzerland's foundation while indulging in a leisurely on-board meal.

The four cantons that give Lake Lucerne its German name are Uri, Schwyz, Nidwalden and Obwalden. They count themselves as the four original founding cantons of Switzerland. Much of their territory is wild and mountainous, especially that of Canton Uri, whose deep forested valleys are home to tiny, remote farming communities. But in the year 1220 these communities suddenly found themselves sitting on a potential gold mine. The riches were not in the ground, but in the form of tax revenues that could be levied on goods and people crossing the Gotthard Pass, which was opened to regular traffic when the Schollenen Gorge, near the summit, was finally bridged by engineers. Lucerne was the natural point of departure for those using the new pass; from there, travellers went by boat to Flüelen (a road along the Urnersee, known as the Axenstrasse, was not built until 1865) and thence by track to Andermatt, the last settlement before the final push over the barren and rocky summit of the pass itself. After it opened the Gotthard quickly became one of the most heavily used of all Alpine passes, popular with traders travelling between Italy and Germany.

Not surprisingly the Habsburgs looked on this potential gold mine with greedy, imperialistic eyes. In 1291 Rudolf of Habsburg bought the city of Lucerne from the Abbey of Murbach, with the intention of channelling the wealth from travellers into imperial coffers. But Rudolph died suddenly on 15 July of the same year, and the civic leaders of the four cantons, worried about the uncertain political situation, decided to sign a pact of mutual assurance and co-operation in the face of the perceived Habsburg threat. On 1 August at Rütli the cantonal leaders put their name on a document which is now seen as heralding the very beginning of the Swiss nation. In fact, the signatories to the Rütli document called themselves *Eidgenossen*, meaning something like "comrades bound by oath into a co-operative", and this word is still used today as a synonym for the people of Switzerland.

The mutual assurances of co-operation and consultation stressed in the Rütli document are widely perceived as being key Swiss attributes to this day, as is the determination to defy occupiers and outside influences which brought the cantonal leaders to Rütli in the first place. In the popular imagination the Rütli oath sets down on paper the very essence of "Swissness". The reality, however, is rather different. Rather than proclaiming the foundation of a new state, the Rütli document is merely an agreement of mutual military assistance, indicating, in NATO-style terms, that an attack on one canton will be seen as an attack on all four of them:

> Be it known to every one, that the men of the Dale of Uri, the Community of Schwyz, as also the men of the mountains of Unterwald, in consideration of the evil times, have full confidently bound themselves, and sworn to help each other with all their power and might, property and people, against all who shall do violence to them, or any of them. That is our ancient bond.

This all seems rather dry, and it is not surprising that Schiller gave the signing of the document rather more of a historical resonance in the scene of his play *William Tell* that is based on Rütli: "Shall we four cantons… together stand, in victory and defeat, in life and death?" asks Werner Stauffacher, one of the men of Schwyz, his pen poised to make its mark on the historic parchment. "We are all one heart, one blood, one race… we are all one people and will act as one… we, the genuine race of ancient Swiss, have kept our freedom from the first till now, never to princes have we bowed the knee."

Schiller was using a good measure of dramatic licence in his play. Amidst all the legend and hyperbole surrounding these events, there is no evidence that in the late thirteenth century outright animosity existed between the four cantons and the Habsburgs, still less that the cantonal leaders wanted to lay the foundations for a new state. In fact, some historians even doubt that anything actually happened at all on the damp and often rain-drenched patch of sloping grass above the Urnersee. Why would such an obviously important document, sceptics argue, be signed in the middle of a field? Other historians play down the importance of the document allegedly signed at Rütli, maintaining that the alliance it forged was just one of many such agreements made between cantons around that time; it is surprising, they say, that the charter signed across the water at Brunnen in 1315, which was of clear military and political significance, made no mention of this earlier charter—so perhaps the importance of the Rütli document has been wildly exaggerated, and the Confederation of Switzerland grew organically, rather than from one single event that can be dated and located so precisely.

Nevertheless, the Rütli document has been devoutly and solemnly preserved through the generations. Nowadays it is displayed in a specially-built museum in Schwyz, the town to the north of Lake Lucerne which gave its name to the people of this region (the Schwyzers) and eventually the whole country. (The canton has also provided the national flag of Switzerland: the familiar bold symmetrical cross was displayed on the Coat of Arms of Canton Schwyz in 1240, although it was not adopted as the flag of the Swiss Confederation until 1848.) The actual parchment, nestling in its own case behind bullet-proof glass, is smaller and more humble than one might expect: the size of a piece of A4 paper, it is charred at the edges and bears evidence of numerous folds. The cramped writing, however, is beautifully clear, the ink rust coloured against the dull cream of the parchment. Three round and rather battered seals are attached by ribbons to the bottom edge; the fourth, that of Schwyz itself, was consigned to historical oblivion at some unknown time in the document's long and revered existence.

The Rütli Meadow itself, meanwhile, has attained the status of a place of national pilgrimage. It can be reached by a steep path that leads up from one of the landing stages on Lake Lucerne, or alternatively by a twisting track from Seelisberg, the nearest village. Although the place is very busy every 1 August, when it is the focus for the celebrations surrounding the Swiss National Day, for much of the time it reverts to being the quiet stretch of open meadow that it was over seven centuries ago when the cantonal representatives met here. There is a flagpole, and a view down through the trees to the misty lake, but not much more. When I came, I was the only one here, and the only sounds were the flapping and slightly bedraggled flag, and the singing birds, and the hammering of the raindrops in the trees (the area around Lucerne is famous for its seemingly perpetual rain). The lake was invisible, beneath a veil of low grew cloud, and every so often came the toot of an invisible boat on the lake, or the whine and grumble of a train over on the far side of the water, grinding its way up to the Gotthard. One final touch: just a few steps away from the flag pole is a working farm, appropriately complete with neat piles of firewood outside, and cows in its sheds adorned with ringing cowbells.

One ingenious way of focusing Swiss national attention on the meadow, as well as emphasizing the unity of the confederation, is through a long-distance footpath, the Weg der Schweiz, which starts at Rütli. Inaugurated in 1991, to commemorate the seven hundredth anniversary of the founding of the state, the path, which runs around the Urnersee to Brunnen, is divided into sections representing the twenty-six cantons—in the order that they joined the confederation (from the original four, in 1291, to Jura, which joined in 1979). Each canton has been allocated a length of path proportionate to its population (it works out as five millimetres of path for each Swiss citizen); the shortest section is that representing Appenzell Innerrhoden, which is a mere seventy-one metres. To walk the entire length of the path takes two days (or one *very* long day); the up-and-down nature of the path, which includes sections both along the lake shore and high above it, soon becomes tiresome to all but the most dedicated walker.

William Tell

William Tell, the bearded huntsman from Altdorf, embodies in one person the national consciousness of Switzerland; no other country has a folk hero quite like him. The story of Tell's spirited defiance of Habsburg aggression unfolds in various settings around the Urnersee, including Altdorf itself, close to Flüelen on its southern shore, and a number of rocky, remote locations along the water's edge. Like all good yarns, the story of William Tell (at least in Schiller's hands) has both a hero and a villain, and the figure who raises boos and catcalls from the audience is Hermann Gessler, an Austrian parachuted into the region by the Habsburgs to make the locals toe the imperial line. In Schiller's play, Gessler remarks of the Swiss that "their tongues are all too bold… I will subdue this stubborn mood of theirs, and crush the soul of liberty within them," while the Austrian foreman in charge of building a new castle for Gessler sums up the Habsburg attitude by calling the Swiss "a worthless race… and fit for nothing but to milk their cows and saunter idly up and down the mountains." Tell hates the Austrians, and seeing their new castle being built, he points to the mountains and refers to them as the "house of freedom God hath built for us… the mountains cannot awe the mountain child."

The story opens with an event sure to upset the already tense political situation in Altdorf. Gessler orders a pole to be raised in the centre of the town square, on top of which he places one of his hats. The intention

·1307·

· WILHELM TELL ·

behind this provocative piece of dictatorial whimsy is that all who pass by the pole have to bow their heads to the hat, to show deference to Gessler and the bullying Habsburgs. Schiller has the town Crier of Altdorf inform the citizens of their new civic duty in these words:

> Ye men of Uri, ye do see this cap!
> It will be set upon a lofty pole
> In Altdorf, in the market place: and this
> Is the Lord Governor's good will and pleasure...
> And all shall reverence it with bended knee,
> And head uncovered; thus the king will know
> Who are his true and loyal subjects here:
> His life and goods are forfeit to the crown,
> That shall refuse obedience to the order.

The reaction of the citizens to this order is predictable. "A petty farce," one townsperson remarks. "No freeborn man with stoop to such disgrace," they mutter. Tell, of course, takes his opposition to the pole one stage further: he dares to walk past it without bowing. And to punish Tell for his defiance, Gessler presents him with one of the most famous forfeits in history.

If Tell manages to shoot an arrow through the apple placed on his son's head, he will be released and allowed to live. If he fails, he and his son will die. Tell puts one arrow in his quiver and one in his crossbow. Of course, the arrow that he fires pierces the apple, leaving the trembling boy beneath unscathed. Gessler asks Tell what the arrow in his quiver is for; Tell replies by saying that if the first arrow had hit the boy, the second would have been for Gessler. For his impertinence Tell is sentenced to be imprisoned at Gessler's castle at Küssnacht near Lucerne. But during the journey there, across the lake, a terrible storm blows up, and the oarsman asks Gessler to release Tell from his bonds so that the rebel farmer can steer the boat to safety. Tell, predictably, steers the boat towards the shore and leaps out of it onto a flat rock, before casting the boat back onto the stormy lake. Tell later heads for Küssnacht and kills Gessler as he is walking to his castle.

Not surprisingly, bearing in mind its epic sweep and mountainous setting, Schiller's play presents considerable problems for a director. Its vast cast includes forty-eight named characters (men, women and children), along with assorted workmen and monks, and the list of *Dramatis Personae* finishes with the daunting words "horsemen and many peasants". (No wonder the open-air performance at Interlaken is on such a huge scale.) Beyond the problems of casting, the play's stage directions also raise practical problems. The piece opens with a boy rowing around the Urnersee in a fishing boat, with a background of "green meadows, the hamlets, and farms of Schwyz, lying in the clear sunshine"—which sounds like a challenge for scenery painters and backdrop artists. At various points in the action, Schiller's stage directions require the sounds of cowbells and hunting horns, while at one point the lighting designer has to contend with direction that "the stage is dark, but the lake and glaciers glisten in the moonlight." Shadows of clouds are seen sweeping over scenes, a castle is constructed on-stage, and one scene is played out against "a meadow surrounded by high rocks and wooded ground", while other scenes feature babbling brooks, and, on one occasion, the appearance of a rainbow over the lake, its colours reflected in the water's glistening surface.

If the story of William Tell sounds a little too neat, it is probably because it never happened. The legend is a descendent of similar Norse legends, reconfigured with an Alpine setting out of a need to embody Swiss liberty in one single, heroic figure. It was not until 1477 that William Tell's patriotic deeds first appeared in writing, in the form of an epic song about the founding of Switzerland; the story was later popularized by French revolutionaries, who also hated the Habsburgs. Schiller wrote his play in 1804 after Goethe, who had travelled through Switzerland, told him the story of William Tell. It is Schiller's play, and to a lesser extent the opera by Rossini, which was first performed in Paris in 1829, that has ensured the enduring popularity of the legend. But true or not, the legend still strikes a patriotic chord with many Swiss. Tell remained a potent symbol during the Second World War, as the Swiss sought to maintain independence from Nazi Germany, and later on in the twentieth century his shadow loomed large over decisions not to join the United Nations and the European Union.

To this day, Altdorf and other places associated with the story of William Tell are regarded by Swiss people with quiet but genuine reverence. One of the most striking monuments connected with the legend is close to the Rütli meadow, but only visible from a boat on the lake: it is a twenty-five metre obelisk, known as the Schillerstein, which rises from the thick covering of trees on the bank; the inscription, dating from 1859, is picked out in gold letters and reads "to Friedrich Schiller, the chronicler of Tell". On the opposite shore of the lake is another virtual place of pilgrimage, the Tellsplatte, a piece of flat rock where Tell is supposed to have escaped from Gessler during the storm; nearby is the Tellskapelle, a small chapel built in 1880 whose frescoes depict the life of Tell. It is a beautifully situated building, hidden in a wooded glade well away from roads, with one of its sides completely open to the lapping lake. The murals depict Tell (tall, strong, bearded) defying Gessler (small, mean-looking) as his son (blond curly hair, bold blue eyes) holds up the apple pierced by an arrow; another mural is a dramatic portrayal of the near-shipwreck, with Tell heroically dragging himself ashore as the rest of the party crash around on the water in the tiny boat.

Meanwhile in Altdorf itself is the Telldenkmal (Tell monument), built in 1895 in the Rathausplatz, the main square where the apple-shooting incident is supposed to have happened. The monument shows Tell raising his eyes to the sky while his son accepts his father's protecting arm and gazes trustingly up at him. They stroll, together, across a tilted slab of rock, in front of a tall tower adorned with murals. But all in all, Altdorf is very low-key; there is no Tell kitsch on offer, no china figurines or souvenir arrows, nothing, in fact, but a few restaurants bearing the hunter's name and, in Bürglen, just up the hill, a tiny chapel dating from 1582 built over his the place of his birth, with a small museum close by.

Perhaps surprisingly, few foreigners come here; most of the visitors are Swiss, giving themselves a taste of their heritage, and the subdued nature of it all means that there is no tourist circus to drown the symbolic importance of all the places associated with the legend. Many leave the area by taking in a final view from the terrace outside the church at Bürglen, which comprises a typically Swiss scene: spread out in the foreground is the pretty town of Altdorf, while beyond it is the narrowing valley of the Reuss, providing a route for the road and railway that head up towards the Gotthard Pass. Passing this way in 1845, crossing the Gotthard from Italy, Charles Dickens wrote that the area around "William Tell's town... is the highest sublimation of all you can imagine in the way of Swiss scenery. O God! What a beautiful country it is!" Perhaps it is appropriate that the country's earliest political stirrings took place in surroundings that so typically and readily concur with our modern idea of what Switzerland ought to be.

Switzerland after William Tell

It would take more than a maverick hunter with a good aim to end the Habsburg interest in what was to become Switzerland. In fact, it took a full-scale battle—won by the Swiss confederates at Morgarten, near the Urnersee resort of Brunnen, in 1315. Morgarten was the natural culmination of the events that were set in motion at Rütli and by all the other cantonal alliances signed at the end of the thirteenth century, and was the first in a series of fourteenth-century battles fought by the nascent Swiss state as it struggled to hold onto its independence. The spark that set the fighting off at Morgarten was a boundary dispute between the town of Schwyz and the powerful monastery of Einsiedeln; the Habsburgs moved in to protect the monastery, while the King of Bavaria sided with the cantons. (The attack by Schwyz forces on the monastery was famously recorded in a poem by an Einsiedeln monk named Rudolf von Radegg.) After losing the battle, Ludwig of Habsburg conceded more privileges to the cantons, and it seemed that the future of the confederacy as an independent political entity was becoming more secure.

But then in 1332 the powerful city of Lucerne joined the confederation, upsetting a fragile political balance and making the Habsburgs edgy again. Up until then the confederacy had essentially comprised a loose collection of remote farming communities. Now one of the region's principal market towns was also muscling in on the rebel act. Fearing trouble from a more powerful and emboldened confederacy, Habsburg agitators set about trying to undermine the city's new political allegiance.

An unusual legend dates from this time, which concerns the presence of pro-Habsburg conspirators in Lucerne. The story goes that a young boy overheard a group of plotters talking one day in Lucerne's marketplace, known as Unter der Egg. The boy was caught, and instead of being killed by the conspirators, was forced to promise to tell no living soul what he had heard being discussed. The boy then ran to the Guildhall where he knew the confederates were meeting. Ignoring the politicians, he turned to the stove in the corner of the meeting hall and told it everything that he had heard. Of course—as the boy intended—the confederates heard him and were able to thwart the plot. But the boy had kept his side of the bargain: he had spoken to the stove, not the men, who he made sure just happened to be in the room at the same time. The ancient stove in question, with its bent and blackened heavy iron door, is now kept in the corner of a fairly ordinary pizza restaurant in the Weinmarkt, Lucerne's cobbled central square. Unter der Egg itself, where the boy overheard the would-be conspirators, is a few steps away, overlooked by a huge seventeenth-century Rathaus. Its market tradition remains to this day, and every Tuesday and Saturday morning fish, flowers and fresh produce are sold from stalls set up under the Rathaus' deep arcades, which provide a cobbled, shady and sheltered market area overlooking the River Reuss.

Lucerne was the first town that was properly Swiss. It had always been a prosperous trading centre, controlling the approaches to the Gotthard Pass. Now its new political role encouraged the city fathers to build new fortifications, many parts of which can be walked along today. The start of the so-called Musegg fortifications is marked by the Nölliturm, a defensive gateway on the river bank; more towers and gates punctuate the walls at regular intervals as they climb over a low hill overlooking the town. The strength and durability of these defences reflects Lucerne's wealth and importance in medieval times, as does the Chapel Bridge (the Kapellbrücke), whose origins date back to 1333, the year after the city threw in its lot with the confederates. This bridge is very much the symbol of Lucerne, an elegant covered walkway built entirely from timber, resting on stone supports and angled around the octagonal stone Wasserturm in the middle of the River Reuss. This tower has served at various times as a lighthouse, a prison and a meeting room. Tragically, in August 1993, a small boat moored alongside it caught fire, and the flames spread, burning almost the entire medieval bridge into the water. The destruction made headline news around the world, as the bridge was counted as being one of the most important medieval monuments in Europe. Today, the bridge that thousands of tourists wander across is a faithful reconstruction of the medieval original; the point on the bridge where the wood changes colour marks the place where the old and new structures meet. The 1993 fire is commemorated by a plaque positioned close to where the boat that started it was moored. And those who walk across the bridge still pass under the famous series of triangular panels that fit underneath its roof at various intervals along its length. These were painted between 1599 and 1611 and depict events from Lucerne's history, including a picture of the city as it was when the panels were made, with the bridge clearly visible, and the twin-towered Hofkirche in the background, surrounded by a cluster of houses beside the lake. The other panels show William Tell, St. George and the Dragon, and (ironically) the devastation wrought by the great fire of Lucerne in 1340. But, not surprisingly, many of the original panels were destroyed in 1993, and those that hang there now are modern facsimiles.

It took two further battles after Morgarten, at Sempach in 1386, and Näfels in 1388, for the Habsburgs to finally give up their claims to confederate lands. Thereafter the Habsburgs concentrated on winning new territory for their Empire in northern Germany, where they were having better luck defeating the locals, while the confederacy grew steadily, absorbing more cantons such as Zurich in 1351 and Bern two years later. Already the confederacy was taking on the character of modern Switzerland, with Alpine cantons rubbing political shoulders with those occupying lowland areas beyond the mountains (today, around a third of Swiss territory is lowland, with large cities such as Bern, Basel, Zurich, St. Gallen and Schaffhausen standing well away from the mountains that so define the country to outsiders).

In 1476 the state became multi-lingual, when the French-speaking town of Aigle (now in the Valais canton) voted to join Canton Bern. Less than thirty years later, the country added a third linguistic group to its territory, as the confederates moved south to occupy and control the southern approaches to the Gotthard running through the Italian-speaking Ticino, which joined the confederacy after the Treaty of Arona in 1503. Switzerland finally gained complete independence from the Holy Roman Empire after victory was secured against Maximilian I at Dornach in 1499. During this period of expansion, political and social rights were conferred on both the land-based peasantry and the city-based workers, to the extent that by the beginning of the fifteenth century the country was being run as a nascent democracy at a time when most of Europe was still being ruled by despotic kings, princes and bishops.

The expansion of the confederacy suffered a setback in 1515 when the Swiss forces were defeated by the combined armies of the French and the Venetians at Marignano. After this no new cantons were to join the confederacy for almost another three hundred years. However, various alliances were formed between Swiss cantons and neighbouring states and cities, such as the pact between the city of Geneva and Cantons Bern and Fribourg forged in the sixteenth century (Geneva had previously been part of Savoy, and the Dukes of Savoy tried and failed to retake Geneva for themselves in 1602). Shortly after defeat at Marignano the confederacy declared its neutrality. This was first put to the test during the Thirty years War (1618-1648), which tore Europe apart but left Switzerland unscathed. The end of this bloody conflict was marked by the Treaty of Westphalia in 1648, which formally recognized Swiss neutrality for the first time. Meanwhile the Rütli meadow had become an important political focus, used by cantons for formal meetings and agreements, and in 1780 a French philosopher and abbot, Thomas-François de Raynal, made a suggestion to Canton Uri that a ten-metre-high obelisk should adorn the site—a proposal which came to nothing.

Although the Swiss state was by then a confident political entity, it was not powerful enough to resist the only major full-scale invasion the country has ever suffered, when the forces of Napoleon invaded in 1798 and declared the Helvetic Republic under French political auspices. After the Napoleonic wars, the country again declared its neutrality, and in July 1940 when a Nazi invasion seemed possible, the Swiss Commander in Chief General Guisan and the entire Swiss officer corps gathered on the Rütli Meadow to solemnly and ceremonially reaffirm this commitment. But this is to race ahead somewhat. Between the Battle of Marignano and Napoleon's invasion the country underwent a series of hugely divisive civil wars, caused by the same destructive arguments that wrenched apart whole swathes of Europe during the same era: those disagreements all centred around religion, and Switzerland, with its protestant reformers in Geneva and Zurich and its largely Catholic rural peasantry, found itself in the thick of things.

Missionaries and Monasteries

It has already been noted that Christianity had been introduced into the Alps by the Romans, and that the religion gained in strength during the time of the great Frankish Empire established following the Roman withdrawal. But conversion of the common people from pagan belief was still a high priority for the Church in the very early Middle Ages, and from around AD 600 onwards hundreds of missionaries came to the Alps, some of whom founded monastic communities that continue to function to this day.

Perhaps surprisingly, a number of these missionaries came from the British Isles. One of the earliest was an Irish monk named Columban, who came to Bregenz on Lake Constance in 610. He established a monastery whose site is now occupied by a Gothic church now containing the relics of another Irish monk, Gallus, with whom Columban was travelling. (The place where Gallus had established his own hermitage, around thirty kilometres west of Bregenz, is now occupied by the large lowland Swiss city of St. Gallen.) Another Irish monk, named Virgil, succeeded St. Rupert as the second Bishop of Salzburg in the eighth century. Under Virgil's leadership, the Bishopric was expanded to include many Alpine valleys south of the city; on the very southern fringes of the Bishopric, along what is now the Austrian-Slovenian border region, there were Slavic speakers, and Virgil decided to send a monk named Modestus to Christianize (and Germanize) these peoples. Modestus concentrated on the area around Klagenfurt, and in the hills north of that city he founded a church, the Wallfahrtskirche, on a low peak which rises above the village of Maria Saal. The current church here, which is largely fifteenth-century, is built partly of old Roman gravestones from the nearby classical-era city of Virunum; the inscriptions on the stones can be seen around the church portal. Inside, the high altar, with its statuettes of the Madonna and Child, is the focal point of a church that is still a popular pilgrimage centre twelve centuries after its foundation.

Some of the British monks who came to the Alps at the time of Bishop Virgil brought with them the cult of St. Oswald, the King of

Northumbria, who had been canonized for promoting Christianity in the north of England. The Pfarrkirche St. Oswald, in the ski resort of Seefeld in the Tyrol, is one of the many churches dedicated to him; Oswald's death (in battle, fighting the Welsh) is depicted on a series of frescoes in the church. (After this initial wave of new churches it was to be another five centuries before another church with English connections was founded in the Alps. This unusual building is at Avrieux, on the road up to the Mont Cenis pass in Savoy, where two English families connected to the Archbishop of Canterbury, Thomas Becket, founded and dedicated a church to him  shortly after his murder in 1170. A diptych in the church dating from 1626 tells the story of the saint's life and death.)

As the Middle Ages progressed more and more monasteries were founded in the valleys of the Alps. These religious houses soon gained a tradition of sheltering travellers from the robbers, dragons and other threats that were known to lurk amid the peaks and crags. By 1500 most of the emerging monastic orders were represented in the region. The monastery at Lucerne was founded by the Benedictine monks of the Abbey of Murbach in Alsace in the middle of the eighth century; nowadays the city's great Hofkirche, founded in the twelfth century, sits on site of this first monastery, and is dedicated to the French bishop St. Leger, who was blinded with a drill by a political enemy. Another Benedictine foundation, the Kloster Ettal, was founded near Oberammergau in the Bavarian Alps in 1330 by Ludwig der Bayern in gratitude for having survived his pilgrimage to Rome; it still draws tens of thousands of pilgrims each year, who come to honour the marble Madonna that Ludwig brought back with him from Italy. (Above the abbey's Gothic portal is a tympanum showing the crucifixion, with Ludwig and his wife looking on.) Around sixty monks still live at Ettal, running among other things a boarding school, a publishing house, a hotel and a distillery.

Elsewhere, monasteries were founded by the Cistercians at Stams in the Tyrol and at Mehrerau near Bregenz on the shores of Lake Constance, the latter famous for its striking winged altar in the abbey church. The Augustinian order was active too, founding monasteries at Interlaken and in the mountains of Savoy at the village of Abondance; although both are now defunct, their abbey churches remain. The large grassy patch of parkland in the centre of Interlaken, the Höhematte, marks the place where the monks once put their cattle out to pasture, while the town's *Schloss*, dating from 1747, incorporates some of the old monastic buildings including the former abbey church. The church of the Abbaye d'Abondance, some twenty kilometres from the southern shore of Lake Geneva, boasts two galleried cloisters dating from the fourteenth century, and a fifteenth-century painting of the *Wedding at Cana* which shows details of daily life in Savoy at the tail end of the Middle Ages.

Many religious houses grew rich and powerful. The Benedictine monks of the monastery at Engelberg in the Swiss Alps, founded in 1120, were political masters of the whole valley, which remained independent of the Swiss Confederation until 1803, when the area was finally absorbed into the Canton of Nidwalden. (The monastery remains unusually influential: nowadays it has offshoots as far away as Oregon and Missouri.) As with many other monasteries, the buildings at Engelberg are eighteenth-century rather than medieval, the original structure having been destroyed by fire. This is also true of another monastery of the same religious order at Benediktbeuern in the Bavarian Alps. One of the oldest monasteries in the region, it was founded in 739, but all its present-day buildings date from over a thousand years later. The abbey church, the Basilika St. Benedikt, is a noted example of early Italian Baroque, stuffed full of elegant white stucco rising to a ceiling painted with colourful and typically effusive designs. Outside the abbey, the monastery consists of spacious, elegant courtyards surrounded by green and cream arcades. In one of these buildings, in the year 1803, a remarkable manuscript was discovered containing a series of thirteenth-century humorous and erotic poems probably written by Goliards—defrocked monks, minstrels and wastrels. The poems were later set to music by a German musicologist named Carl Orff (1895-1982) who called his piece *Carmina Burana*. This secular cantata has been mightily popular ever since its world premier in Frankfurt in 1937. In particular, *Carmina Burana* is a popular staple with English choral societies, whose members possibly remain blissfully unaware that the poems, written in a mixture of Latin and medieval German, are vivid accounts of such cheerfully debauched activities as sex, gluttony, drinking, and gambling.

Benediktbeuern is old but architecturally not impressive; however, several Swiss monasteries are spectacular in their own right—perhaps the best example being the monastery at Einsiedeln, nestling amidst green mountain pastures and thick forests east of Lucerne. The site has been an important site of pilgrimage for hundreds of years (the earliest recorded pilgrims came here in 1337 when they were given a letter of safe passage by Tumb von Neuburg, a knight from the Vorarlberg). A quarter of a million devout believers are still drawn to the place every year. The first glimpse the pilgrims have of the monastery is extraordinary—a giant, four-storey Baroque complex looms behind an expansive courtyard, which itself is flanked by a circular arrangement of arched colonnades; no wonder John Russell called this "the most exhilarating edifice in the country" in his 1950 book, *Switzerland.*

The origins of the monastery here dates back to the time of St. Meginrat, a hermit who withdrew to the wild forests of these parts in the year 828; he lived in peaceful seclusion until 861, when he was murdered by two brigands who were later executed on the rack in Zurich. Seventy years after Meginrat's death the Provost of Strasbourg Cathedral allowed a Benedictine Community to establish itself on the site of his cell (the present building is the sixth to occupy the site of Meginrat's altar). There is a famous story that when the Bishop of Constance was asked to consecrate the abbey church, on 14 September 948, he heard a voice ringing through the building that Christ himself had already consecrated it; the Pope declared this to be a miracle and issued a papal bull blessing the site as a place of pilgrimage.

The main focus of Einsiedeln's pilgrimage activity is the Black Madonna, a fifteenth-century wooden statuette of the Virgin Mary kept in the Lady Chapel in the centre of the nave; the figure has over fifty robes that are changed in accordance with the ecclesiastical year. As for the rest of the church, the bulk of it is pink rococo, with silver organ pipes decorated with gold cherubs, and an altar fashioned from a black and gold sarcophagus in which the relics of St. Meginrat are housed. Outside the complex is the Well of Our Lady, whose fourteen spouts spurt fourth spring water from the same source that originally drew Meginrat here.

The monastery has attracted the curious, as well as pilgrims, for hundreds of years. In 1776 William Coxe, the author of *Sketches of the Natural, Civil and Political History of Switzerland*, came here and witnessed a "pavement continually covered with prostrate sinners rapt in meditation and happy to have attained the end of their pilgrimage." The historian Edward Gibbon had been shocked a few years earlier by the

> profuse ostentation of riches in the poorest corner of Europe; amidst a savage scene of woods and mountains, a palace appears to have been erected by magic; and it was erected by the potent magic of religion... the title and worship of the Mother of God provoked my indignation.

Perhaps Gibbon should have tried to seek inspiration in the scenery that surrounds the monastery; both it and the village of Einsiedeln sit in the bottom of an enormous green bowl, surrounded by wooded slopes leading up to craggy mountains. The monks of the monastery have always been dedicated to working on the surrounding land, although with arable agriculture an impossibility in this region of barren rocky slopes, the brothers have had to resort to animal husbandry, and have become noted breeders of horses.

Although not a place of pilgrimage as such, there is one Alpine monastery that serves as the "mother house" of a whole monastic order. The Couvent de la Grande Chartreuse, the original monastic foundation of the Carthusian order, is situated in a deep, remote wooded valley in the mountains near Grenoble. It was founded in 1084 when, according to legend, Bruno, the Bishop of Grenoble, had a vision alerting him to the imminent arrival of seven travellers who wished to lead a solitary life. The travellers duly arrived on Bruno's doorstep and he took them to an isolated area known as the Desert de Chartreuse, so founding both the monastery and the Carthusian Order (which is named after the region). In the twelfth century one of Bruno's successors laid down the Carthusian rulebook, which has never been altered since, and by the Renaissance there were over two hundred religious houses; now, worldwide, their number has dwindled to seventeen monasteries and five convents. Carthusians lead a life of silence and solitude, meeting each other for a Sunday meal and three times a day in church. The monks can often be seen working in the fields around their monastery in Chartreuse, but they also maintain a distillery where various liquors are created using a formula kept secret since 1605 (the strongest is 71 degrees proof).

These days, like Einsiedeln, the Couvent de la Grande Chartreuse attracts a steady stream of visitors. These modern-day tourists are following on the heels of the poet Thomas Gray and the writer Horace Walpole, two eighteenth-century men of letters who visited the monastery in 1739 and were some of the earliest travellers to seek out this remote but beautiful spot (unlike today's tourists, they were actually allowed inside the buildings). Gray wrote of reaching the monastery by negotiating a narrow road that ran under a "monstrous precipice, almost perpendicular, at the bottom of which rolls a torrent", and that the monastery itself "concurs to form one of the most solemn, the most romantic, and the most astonishing scenes I ever beheld." The place, he wrote, was of "wonderful decency", and he noted that the community of one hundred monks had three hundred servants to minister to them! In those days, two of the monastic brothers were allowed to break their vow of silence so that they could serve travellers, and Gray recalls that the pair were given cheese, butter, grapes, egg, and fish; he went on to admit that the monastery would "awe an atheist into belief" and that had he been born in the Middle Ages he might have been attracted by the monastic life (although he and Walpole politely refused to take up the monks' suggestion that they spend a night in one of the cells). Another English poet who was similarly awed was William Wordsworth, who came here in 1790 and wrote of its "awful solitude" in his poem *The Prelude*; his sister Dorothy later remarked "I do not think that any one spot made so great an impression on his mind… in his young days he used to talk of it so much to me."

The Monastery at the Summit of the Great St. Bernard Pass

There are other monasteries in the Alps which are older, or larger, or more impressive than the foundation at the summit of the Great St. Bernard Pass; but there are few that are as celebrated. The religious community that makes its home on the bleak, rocky summit of one of the busiest routes over the Alps was established around a thousand years ago by King Canute of Denmark and King Rudolph III of Burgundy, who were dismayed by the threats to trans-European trade caused by Saracen attacks on those using the pass; the Saracens were removed and Bernard, Archdeacon of Aosta (923-1008), was invited to found a monastery at the summit to protect future travellers. Bernard, who hailed from Menthon on the shores of Lake Annecy, had already founded one hospice, at the top of the Petit St. Bernard Pass, on whose summit he is supposed to have personally torn down a Roman statue of Jupiter; now he was given an opportunity to found a second monastery, and on doing so a second pass, the Great St. Bernard, was named after him. (After founding the two religious communities, Bernard spent the rest of his life ministering in the mountains, and in 1923 he was named patron saint of the Alps by Pope Pius XI.)

Over the years following its foundation the monastery grew rich through gifts made by travellers grateful for a safe haven as they crossed the dangerous pass. The road over the summit was increasingly busy as it formed part of the famed Via Francigena (Franconian Way), a long-distance route linking northern Europe with Rome which made use of a number of old Roman roads and is believed to have been operational from around the seventh century onwards. In particular, the road was used by pilgrims travelling from Canterbury to the Holy City: from the English Channel the route passed through Arras, Rheims and Besançon before passing over the Vosges to Lake Geneva and Lausanne; the travellers would then pass through the pilgrimage centre of St. Maurice before heading through Martigny and over the pass to Aosta, with the final leg of the journey to Rome itself passing through Piacenza and Siena. (In the year 990 Sigeric, Archbishop of Canterbury, made this journey to collect his pallium of office from Pope John XV; on the way back he kept a diary, describing the journey by mule over the St. Bernard Pass and the hospitality of the monks.) By 1177 the monastery owned land all over Europe (including a property at Hornchurch in Essex); at around this time the monks also began to keep packs of dogs trained to help in the rescue of travellers in difficulty, the animals famously carrying reviving barrels of beer around their necks. The first written mention of these dogs came in 1708; by then a distinct breed had been created, a cross between a mastiff and a Great Dane. (Dogs are still kept by the monks to this day, though they serve no purpose other than to be cooed over by tourists.)

Although at the time of writing the religious community here consisted of only four brothers, the monastery is still permanently active, housed in two buildings dating from 1560 and 1898; during the winter monks brave huge snowdrifts and months of below-freezing temperatures. Although the pass has recently been eclipsed by the road tunnel running underneath it, and by busier routes such as the Simplon rail tunnel and the Mont Blanc road tunnel, for hundreds or even thousands of years this was the busiest route over the Alps. Nowadays the route is not cleared of snow in winter (and there are still isolated snow patches at the summit in August), but in summer the place is filled with bikers and day-trippers, who shop at the stalls (featuring row upon row of cuddly St. Bernard dogs), look at the kennels and buzz round the monastery church before heading back down into Switzerland or Italy.

The tourists have been making a beeline for the monastery for over two hundred years. A nineteenth-century guidebook to the Alps published by John Murray indicates that the monastery had a drawing room for the use of overnight guests, which was "hung with many drawings and prints, presents sent by travellers in acknowledgement of the kind attentions which they have received from the brethren... a piano was one of the presents thus sent, by a lady." The same book cannot resist a dig at the chapel services, which display "tawdry ornaments of Catholic ceremony and worship [that] weaken the impressive character of the establishment and its devotees." By and large, however, the guidebooks were enthusiastic about the place, although some travellers were clearly not taken with it: the Alpinist Edward Whymper, who in 1865 led the first successful conquest of the Matterhorn, wrote of his trip to the pass, "I have not had any day so devoid of interest and barren of incident, neither have I walked over so uninteresting a road"; he dismissed the scenery as "commonplace." The artist William Brockedon, who came here in 1825, was also unimpressed by the place, but for different reasons. He wrote that he was appalled by the discovery of a morgue attached to the hospice, where the bodies of the unfortunate people who have perished in these mountains have been placed, left with their clothes on, to assist the recognition by their friends, if they have any... the bodies are seen in the postures in which they have perished. Here they have 'dried up and withered'... some of the bodies presented a hideous aspect; part of the bones of the head were exposed and blanched... several bodies were standing against the wall, upon the accumulated heaps of their miserable predecessors, presenting an appalling scene.

The most famous writer to have visited the monastery was Charles Dickens, who made a number of journeys in France, Italy and Switzerland. He came here in 1846 on an expedition from Lausanne and provided a memorable description of the pass in a letter to his friend (and later his biographer) John Forster. "I wish to God you could see that place," he wrote of the summit of the pass itself:

A great hollow on the top of a range of dreadful mountains, fenced in by riven rocks of every shape and colour: and in the midst, a black lake, with phantom clouds perpetually stalking over it. Peaks, and points, and plains of eternal ice and snow, bounding the view, and shutting out the world on every side: the lake reflecting nothing: and no human figure in the scene. The air so fine, that it is difficult to breathe without feeling out of breath; and the colour so exquisitely thin and sharp that it is not to be described... [There is] nothing of life or living interest in the picture... No vegetation of any sort or kind. Nothing growing, nothing stirring. Everything iron-bound and frozen up.

Regarding the monastery, Dickens described it as "a most extraordinary place, full of great vaulted passages... and presenting a series of the most astonishing little dormitories where the windows are so small (on account of the cold and snow) that it is as much as one can do to get one's head out of them." Of the monks themselves, Dickens was interested to talk with one of them, who could speak English and had recently been given a copy of *The Pickwick Papers*, but said of the community as a whole that they "are a lazy set of fellows... rich, and driving a good trade in innkeeping." Like Brockedon, he also discovered the morgue, finding some of the bodies of travellers "horribly human, with distinct expressions on the faces," while others merely "presented a heap of skulls and fibrous dust."

Saints and Pilgrims

The Alps abound in pilgrimage centres; some of them, like Einsiedeln, have monasteries attached, but not all of them do. Many are in remote locations that proved appealing to medieval ascetics. One of the best-known of these is Monte Verna, just outside Varallo in the Italian Alps, which was the remote location chosen by St. Francis of Assisi for forty days of fasting and prayer in 1224. The location features some impressive rock formations and a century after St. Francis prayed here a set of stories called *The Little Flowers of St. Francis* recalled that "it was revealed to him that those clefts [in the rocks]... had been miraculously made at the hour of the passion of the Christ when according to the gospel, the rocks were rent asunder." Two hundred years later, in 1486, Bernardino Caimi, a local friar, created a series of forty-five chapels in the hills here, featuring three-dimensional tableaux of painted statues and frescoes depicting the life of Christ in vivid and terrifying detail. The sensationalism and spectacle was an effort to reach out to the illiterate at a time when heresy was rife in these remote valleys: in the scene depicting the Massacre of Innocents, the floor is lined with dead babies, while other chapels show crazed flagellators and a realistically blood-spattered Christ. These days the place attracts families, pensioners and nuns in their droves, as do the other *sacri monti* in the Italian Alps at Varese, Domodossola and Arona, and still more throughout Spain, Portugal and France.

As for other the other hermits whose remote mountain retreats have become places of pilgrimage, one of the most popular is Hemma of Gurk, who founded a long line of churches and abbeys in Carinthia in the eleventh century, and is buried in one of them, the Benedictine convent church of Gurk. The century before, Wolfgang, the Bishop of Regensburg, had sought a rural lakeside retreat in the Austrian Alps; the lake where he did so now carries his name, the Wolfgangsee. The Pfarrkirche in the town of St. Wolfgang was built over the site of his hermitage and is famous for its multi-pinnacled Gothic high altar, built by Michael Pacher in the 1470s. At exactly the time as Pacher was at work, a Franciscan monk, Bartholomeo, established a hermitage on the hillside above Locarno, at a spot where he saw an apparition of the Virgin; the church, the Madonna del Sasso, is a popular site of pilgrimage and one of the main tourist attractions in Locarno (nowadays reached by a funicular which rumbles up the mountainside from the centre of the lakeside resort).

Apparitions of the Virgin have provided the impetus for the foundation of other pilgrimage sites, such as the basilica of Notre-Dame de la Salette, situated at an altitude of 1,770m in a striking mountain setting near Grenoble, where hundreds of thousands of pilgrims are welcomed each year to the spot where the Virgin Mary appeared to two local children in 1846. Meanwhile, at the foot of the Bavarian Alps at Steingaden the Wieskirche houses the Statue of the Scourged Saviour, a wooden effigy of Christ that seemed to ooze tears in June 1738 during evening prayers; the statue is now part of the high altar, and attracts a million visitors a year. (The popularity of pilgrimage centres has not always been welcomed by local residents. At Puimoisson, in the very south of the French Alps as they sweep towards Provence, is a church that once was in the hands of the Knights of the Hospital of St. John of Jerusalem. In the sixteenth century the remains of two saints were uncovered in the church, and pilgrims began flocking to the place, until the locals lost patience with the unending stream of visitors and secretly reburied the relics elsewhere—where they remain to this day.)

Religious Strife
The Reformation, inspired by the revolutionary teachings of figures such as Martin Luther and Jean Calvin, led to centuries of religious strife across Europe. However, the radical ideas associated with the new religion, and the resultant political changes, emanated primarily from the cities; more isolated areas of the continent such as the Alps did not feel the stress as much as lowland areas with their larger, concentrated populations and the consequent opportunity for new ideas to travel fast and for opposition to the established order to quickly develop.

Although most parts of the Alps remained Catholic during the Reformation (and are still largely Catholic to this day), two cities on the fringes of the region, Zurich and Geneva, became known as radical hotbeds of Protestant ideology during the early sixteenth century. In Zurich the preacher Huldrych Zwingli (1484-1531) opposed clerical celibacy and Papal authority; his ideas spread to Bern and Basel but made little impact in the rural Swiss cantons (Zwingli himself was killed in battle at Kappel during a brief war inspired by religious differences). On Zwingli's death the mantle of religious dissent passed to Jean Calvin, who turned his home city of Geneva into a "Protestant Rome" after his expulsion from the Sorbonne and his arrival there in 1533. Within a decade the new religion was edging along Lake Geneva's northern shore to Lausanne: a new university was founded in that city in 1540, and soon became a centre of radical Protestantism, while at the same time Lausanne's magnificent cathedral lost its statuary, paintings and stained glass, marking the beginning of an era when the ornamentation of Catholicism was removed from many churches throughout newly Protestant Europe.

By the middle of the sixteenth century the new faith was winning converts among the business and political communities in a number of Alpine towns, particularly those in Switzerland and Austria. Openly espousing Protestantism in lowland Swiss cities such as Basel, Schaffhausen or Bern was no problem, but in many other places dissent was not welcomed by ruling authorities, and Protestants were dealt with swiftly and brutally. In the Tyrol the silver miners of Schwaz briefly embraced Protestantism and in 1525 their religious differences spilled over into an open revolt, which was also underpinned by political resentment at Habsburg control. Archduke Ferdinand I was forced to engage mercenaries to put the uprising down; its leader Michael Gaismair fled to Venice, and Ferdinand quickly purged the Tyrol of Protestants. Nowadays the region is one of the most devoutly Catholic parts of Austria.

Schwaz, however, was an exception, and most mountain areas remained largely Catholic, with their remote communities naturally suspicious of new ideas. Even so, some Alpine valleys proved ideal hideaways for dissenters eager to hide from the long arm of Catholic law. One of these places was near Badgastein in the Austrian Alps where local Protestants once gathered for clandestine prayer meetings in a cave, the Naturhöhle; the chamber they used was known as the "Fledermaus-Dom", which translates as "Bat Cathedral". Similar secret hidey-holes can be found in many other Alpine valleys. But nowhere in the high Alps is more associated with dissent than the area around La Vallouise, a remote valley near Briançon. In the twelfth century this wild and isolated area had been the hiding place of the Vaudois (or Waldenses), a breakaway church whose founder, a merchant named Pierre Valdo (or de Vaux), believed that salvation depended on the renunciation of all worldly possessions. Catholic authorities became suspicious of the group's beliefs, and Pierre Valdo was branded a heretic and excommunicated in 1184. But his followers continued to live in their remote hideaway until a vicious campaign in 1488, led by the Catholics of Grenoble, led to the destruction of the community; the valley of the Gyronde, in particular, was devastated and became known as the Val Pute, or bad valley. The whole area was later named Valouise (Val Louis) in honour of the French King Louis XI, who brought the persecutions to a close, although the area emerged again as a centre of dissent in the seventeenth century, when it became the hide-out of French Huguenots. (By that time there was a clandestine network of Protestant communities living in remote locations all over the Alps. One group of Italian Protestants who were hiding out in the remote Val Pellice near Turin even managed to make contact with Oliver Cromwell, who paid for the construction of a dam to protect their community from flooding.)

Despite the efforts of rulers in fervently Catholic places such as Bavaria and the Tyrol, Protestantism made significant inroads into European religious life and as the Geneva printing presses turned out more and more radical texts (including in 1560 the first methodically-organized English Bible), the Catholic Church decided to stage a fight-back. The counter-reformation was initiated by a series of conferences held in the beautiful Romanesque cathedral at Trento in the Dolomites between 1545 and 1563. The deliberations of the so-called Council of Trent proved inspirational to many European rulers, and those such as Duke Albrecht V (1550-79) and Wilhelm the Pious (1579-97) of Bavaria played a leading role in stamping out the new faith during the second half of the sixteenth century. But the counter-reformation needed a vanguard of forward troops, and these came in the form of the Jesuits, a religious order founded specifically for missionary and teaching work by St. Ignatius Loyola in the 1530s. Jesuits were welcomed by rulers in many parts of the Alps, including Savoy and Habsburg Austria, where they worked at grass roots level, inspiring ordinary people to embrace Catholicism through re-invigorating Catholic traditions and forms of worship. One such tradition established by Jesuit missionaries was the practice of constructing ornate and detailed Christmas cribs and nativity scenes, complete with scenery and painted backdrops, which was introduced into the Tyrol; it was thought that this rich mix of theatre and colour would provide an appealing counterweight to the dourness of Protestantism. (The practice caught on and the craft of crib-building is still practised to this day in villages such as Thaur near Innsbruck.) Jesuits also played an important role in influencing changing fashions of church architecture. The Domkirche in the Carinthian capital of Klagenfurt is outwardly a stern, unadorned structure, resulting from its foundation in the early sixteenth century when most of the city rulers were Protestant; but inside there is effusive and colourful Baroque decoration, inspired by seventeenth-century Jesuits as a means of strengthening the traditions of the old faith. In the same region, at Millstatt, the eleventh-century Benedictine abbey was given to the Jesuits by Emperor Ferdinand II in 1612 as part of the same process of re-Catholicization; once again the church is full of ornate Baroque decoration encouraged by the religious order.

Another way in which the Catholic Church tried to reinvigorate the ways of the old religion among the people of post-Reformation Europe was through its encouragement of the performance of passion plays. The most famous of these theatrical and religious extravaganzas is the passion play staged at Oberammergau in the Bavarian Alps, which has been performed (more or less) every ten years since 1634, when the first performance celebrated the departure of the Black Death from the town. The play consists of a dramatic presentation of the Passion of Christ, an epic production involving a cast of over two hundred and fifty adults and children and takes all day to perform. The piece has changed over the centuries: scenes depicting Jews as horned devils have been quietly removed, while women were allowed to perform for the first time in 1990 (previously Mary had been played by a man). In the year 2000 non-Germans and non-Catholics could join in, so long as they hailed from the village of Oberammergau, where a huge modern theatre, some of which is open to the sky, is now used for performances. (Away from the performance season, Oberammergau is a quiet town, whose tourist shops and houses painted with scenes from fairy tales such as Hansel and Gretel retreat into a quiet Alpine slumber.)

At least two other towns in the Alps stage similar plays: every five years, at Einsiedeln in central Switzerland, the monks from the town's monastery direct six hundred locals in a performance of a religious drama called *The Great Theatre of the World*, which was written by the Spanish dramatist Pedro Calderón de la Barca and received its premiere in Madrid in 1685; meanwhile in Škofja Loka in the Slovenian Alps the *Skofjeloški Pasijon*, written by a local friar in 1721, is performed every two years on Good Friday. The piece features Hell, the Crucifixion, the Last Supper and Judgment Day; it was performed in 1999 after not being seen for over two and a half centuries, but in fact has more of the characteristics of a festival or procession than a performed play.

By the turn of the seventeenth century Protestantism had become a potent political force, and for over two hundred years Europe was wracked with conflicts stemming from religious differences. The wars of religion in France saw fierce fighting in the French Alps and the besieging of towns such as Sisteron and Castellane; in 1598 the Edict of Nantes granted freedom of worship to French Protestants, but this edict was famously revoked in 1685, when eight thousand French troops were sent into the Vallouise region in an attempt to remove the Protestant dissenters who were hiding where the followers of Pierre Valdo had gathered four centuries before. In Switzerland, Catholic cantons formed alliances with Spain and France, while the Protestant ones threw in their lot with sympathetic German princedoms and with the Protestant Netherlands. Civil war between Catholic and Protestant cantons dragged on over the latter part of the seventeenth century, ending in a Protestant victory following fierce battles at Villmergen in 1656 and then again in 1712.

In the mid nineteenth century civil war erupted again in Switzerland, when ultra-Catholic Lucerne, whose government had asked the Jesuits to run the city's schools in 1841, was at the heart of the Sonderbund, a group of rebel (and largely Alpine) Catholic cantons including Schwyz, Uri, the Valais and the Unterwalden. Their war against the lowland cities of the Confederacy in November 1847 led to defeat for the Sonderbund. The new constitution drawn up the following year provided a balance of power between Protestant and Catholic cantons, an arrangement that still forms one of the cornerstones of Swiss federalism to this day.

Napoleon and the French Revolution
The French Revolution, that great fulcrum of European history, has some of its roots in Alpine France. On 7 June 1788 the regional assembly in Grenoble was closed in a fit of absolutism by the French King, Louis XVI. The people of Grenoble did not take kindly to this diktat from Paris, and when the troops turned up to close the *parlement* the citizens climbed onto the roofs of buildings and pelted the soldiers with tiles. Meanwhile, rebel members of the Grenoble *parlement* met in the nearby town of Vizille. They were in belligerent mood and called for all the regional assemblies throughout France to gather so that a discussion on the political future of the nation could be opened. The meeting in the Château de Vizille, on the outskirts of the small Alpine town, is now considered one of the opening salvos of the French Revolution; not surprisingly the castle is now home to a museum documenting the vital role it played in the build-up to the momentous events that soon began unfolding in Paris.

There is another link between the French Revolution and the Alps—and it is a surprising one. Denied much opportunity to take part in military action on their home turf, Swiss soldiers have famously taken to adopting defensive roles outside the country (an example is the troop of soldiers known as the Swiss Guard that still defend the Pope). In 1792 seven hundred Swiss soldiers were killed in Paris, defending the French royal family from the revolutionary mob, and they are remembered by a unique sculpture in Lucerne known as the *Löwendenkmal* or lion monument. This moving sculpture, dating from 1821 and depicting a lion wounded by a spear draped over a shield, is carved into a vertical rock face which overlooks a verdant area of greenery (and a small duck pond) just north of the town centre; the designer was the Danish sculptor Bertel Thorwaldsen (1770-1844) and the actual carver was a stonemason from Constance named Lucas Ahorn. In *A Tramp Abroad* (1880) Mark Twain memorably calls it "the most mournful and moving piece of rock in the world... [The lion's] attitude is noble. His head is bowed, the broken spear is sticking in his shoulder, his protecting paw rests upon the lilies of France."

After the French Revolution most European wars took the form of squabbles between empire-builders rather than battles for religious supremacy. In the 1790s French troops pushed eastwards from the

revolutionary motherland, spreading not a new religious faith, as the Jesuits and Protestants had done two centuries earlier, but a new and radical political creed. Savoy, at that time part of the Kingdom of Sardinia and still ruled by the Savoyard dynasty, was occupied in 1792. Next came northern Italy, which brought French forces into conflict with the once-mighty Venetian Republic. French troops stormed the old Venetian stronghold of Bergamo, on the southern fringes of the Alps, in 1796, and local revolutionaries declared the place an independent city-state under French protection. By way of celebration, the city's Piazza Vecchia, which Stendhal called "the most beautiful place on earth", was transformed into an open-air ballroom, and in true revolutionary spirit the dancing was opened by an aristocrat partnering a butcher. The stone lions around the fountain, which were the proud symbols of the old Venetian Republic, must have been growling with despair as they watched.

In 1799 a young Corsican named Napoleon Bonaparte, formerly a general in the French army, seized political power in Paris after orchestrating a successful coup. He was keen to spread the revolutionary message even further than Savoy and Italy, and in particular wanted to square up against two sworn enemies of France, England and Habsburg Austria. The French navy was kept busy on the first campaign, in the eastern Mediterranean and then later off Cape Trafalgar; meanwhile Switzerland was a natural jumping-off point for an attack on Vienna and, encouraged by pro-revolutionary demonstrations in Zurich, the country was invaded in 1798. As in Bergamo and other parts of northern Italy, a new Republic was declared, supposedly independent but actually under the control of revolutionary France. Two years later Napoleon marched with an army of forty thousand across the Great St. Bernard Pass from the new Helvetic Republic into the Republic of Cisalpine Gaul, the grand name given to French-controlled north-western Italy. On their march between the two territories the troops famously treated the villages and the monastery along the route of the pass with imperial contempt. Army records show that they consumed 21,724 bottles of wine, a tonne and a half of cheese, and 800kg of meat, much of it purloined from local villages; moreover, they did not pay the hospice bill of 40,000 Francs. (In 1850 the monks finally received part of the money owing to them, and in 1984 President Mitterrand made a token payment to the monks and the inhabitants of the area, by way of much-delayed compensation and acknowledgement of the damage caused.) Napoleon crossed the pass on the back of a mule but apparently said nothing about the beauty of the scenery; his wife Joséphine, on the other hand, was so taken with the place that she later invited a Swiss farmer and his wife, along with seven cows and a bull, to live with her in a mock-Alpine chalet on the outskirts of Paris.

In 1803 the Swiss cantons rebelled against the French puppet regime installed in Bern, and the Helvetic Republic collapsed. Through the so-called "mediation" agreement, Napoleon allowed the return of cantonal government to Switzerland, although the country remained under nominal French control; and between 1800 and 1808 the general's forces set about endowing the country with a legacy rather more positive than the unpaid bill at the St. Bernard monastery—a new and brilliantly engineered road over the Simplon Pass, which opened up an entirely new trans-Alpine trade route.

Meanwhile, French forces were busy pressing east to confront the Habsburgs. Here Napoleon conducted one of his most successful campaigns, defeating the Austrians decisively at Austerlitz in Moravia in 1805. The King of Bavaria proved to be a firm and trusted ally of Napoleon during this time and was given the Tyrol as a reward for his loyalty. But in 1809 the Tyrol rose up against Bavarian rule. The principal rebel upstart was an innkeeper, wine merchant and cattle dealer named Andreas Hofer, who was born in the tiny mountain village of Pfandleralm in what is now Italian south Tyrol. Under Hofer's command, the insurgents defeated the Bavarians on Bergisel Hill just outside Innsbruck, and even managed to install a provisional government in the Hofburg palace in the city before being forced out by superior forces of Germany and France. Hofer, who was later executed in Mantua on the orders of the French, is still something of a national hero in the Tyrol (which has always seen itself as being very separate from the rest of Austria). His tomb in Innsbruck's Hofkirche consists of a stark white representation of the bearded hero, with a wreath in red and white at his feet reading simply "Das Land Tyrol"; it is a simpler and much less pompous affair than the tomb of the Emperor Maximilian, which is in the same church (and, if you remember, completely empty).

The legend of the battle of Bergisel is also remembered elsewhere in Innsbruck, in a building beside a churning reach of the River Inn called the Rundgemälde. This houses an enormous circular panorama depicting the bloody battle, all chaos and flags and fighting, with oompah marching music and a grandiose commentary booming over the speakers; it was unveiled in 1896 when these bold, shameless displays of patriotism were all the rage in Europe. As for Hofer's attempted rebellion, it fell apart after Napoleon gained control of Vienna in 1809; the French general made the Austrian Emperor, Francis I, cede the Tyrol to France, although Austria later regained control of the territory after the French defeat at Leipzig in 1813.

Alpine France also boasts reminders of Napoleon's brief but dramatic domination of European politics. On his return to his homeland after his first period of exile on Elba, Napoleon landed in mainland France at the Golf Juan and made a triumphal progress through the French Alps to Gap, from where he pressed northwards through the Dauphiné. At Laffrey, just outside Grenoble, he found the garrison of royalist France waiting for him in a place now known as the Prairie de la Rencontre. Napoleon saw that the garrison, loyal to the newly-restored Bourbon monarchy, greatly outnumbered his own forces—but, undaunted, he walked forward and declaimed "Soldiers, I am your Emperor! If anyone among you wishes to kill his general, here I am." In spite of being ordered to fire by a young officer, the royalist troops rallied to him, shouting "Vive l'Empereur!" Napoleon then entered Laffrey in triumph and pressed on to Grenoble. "The eagle will fly from steeple to steeple until he reaches the towers of Notre Dame," he said, and nowadays the route he took from the Mediterranean coast to Grenoble is commemorated by the 325 kilometre-long Route Napoléon, whose symbol is a flying eagle (the route was designated as such in 1913 and was opened to motor traffic in 1932).

Besides this famous road, Napoleon also ordered the construction of a series of new roads over Alpine passes, to thank the people of this part of France for their warm welcome as he progressed through the country. The first of these was the Col de Manse; Napoleon also ordered the building of a road over the Mont Cenis pass, which is still in use. And there is a final, but very different, legacy of Napoleon in the spa town of Aix-les-Bains in the foothills of the French Alps: during the Emperor's brief sojourn in Egypt, where he fought the British at the Battle of the Nile, he became a fan of steam baths and shower massages, and these new devices were installed at Aix at his bequest, and quickly became the principal form of treatment on offer to patients.

After Napoleon's defeat at Waterloo and his exile to the remote British island of St. Helena, the French adventure in Europe began to unravel. In 1815 the Congress of Vienna was charged with the task of imposing some order on post-Napoleonic Europe. In terms of the Alpine region, the neutral status of Switzerland was once again confirmed, while Savoy was returned to the Kingdom of Sardinia and fortified itself against another French invasion (the impressive Esseillon Fortifications, impregnable military strongholds situated on the road up to the Mont Cenis pass, date from this time). Although Switzerland's borders remain to this day those fixed at the Congress, the arrangements made at Vienna regarding Savoy were not to last: the old kingdom Humbert the Whitehander had founded in the eleventh century finally broke up in 1860, when a popular plebiscite divided its territory between France and

Italy (which is why so much of the area around Aosta still has a French-speaking minority). But this came during an otherwise unmomentous time: the Congress of Vienna ushered in decades of peace in Europe, and apart from the Swiss civil wars in the 1840s, the Alps remained reasonably quiet for a century—until the Habsburg Empire once again stirred into life, and the mountains echoed with the sound of gunfire from the most bloody conflict the world had ever known.

The First World War

Swiss neutrality kept fighting away from the heart of the Alps during the First World War (and later during the Second World War too). The principal Alpine theatre of war during the 1914-18 conflict was in the south-east of the region, where Italy, anxious to gain favour with Britain and France and to settle some old scores with Austria, was determined to square up to the Habsburg Empire, despite its poorly trained and equipped army. When war broke out a large chunk of what is now Alpine Italy, including the cities of Trento and Bolzano, the northern fringe of Lake Garda, the mountain resort of Cortina, and the region of the south Tyrol, were part of Austria-Hungary (as was the whole of Slovenia). Italy joined the war in 1915, concluding a secret treaty (the London Pact) with the allies which stated that these areas, along with the port city of Trieste and numerous islands along the Adriatic, would be ceded to Italy in the event of victory. (A year later, in 1916, two Italian-speaking rebels, Cesare Battisti and Fabio Filzi, launched a campaign against Austrian rule in Trento, with Battisti forming a newspaper, *Il Popolo*, as a forum for protest; both men were shot as traitors outside the Castello del Buonconsiglio, the former palace of the Prince-Bishops of Trento, in the same year.)

The war initially went well for Italy, but in May 1916 the Austrians launched a massive counter-offensive on what was by then known as the Trentino Front. Italian forces resisted fiercely but were driven off the peaks they had captured the previous year; after a delay caused by heavy snowfalls the Austrians captured the vital strategic stronghold of Monte Pasubio and by the end of the month 30,000 Italian prisoners were in Austrian hands. The next month saw further fierce fighting, when the Austrians fired hydrocyanide gas shells at the Italians, only to have the gas blown back on their own troops by the wind. In May the Italians advanced and retook much of the ground the Austrians had captured, and were in control of the slopes of Monte Pasubio after another attack in October. In June 1917 fighting erupted yet again along this front, when the Italians took Mount Ortigaro only for it to be back in Austrian hands two weeks later; at the end of three weeks of slaughter virtually no new land was gained by either side, but 23,000 Italians and 9,000 Austrians were killed or wounded.

Troops on both sides endured terrible conditions along the Trentino Front throughout this period: ten thousand soldiers died in avalanches alone, despite the fortresses that had been dug deep into the mountainsides along the front line. The future historian G. M. Trevelyan was a commander of a British Red Cross Ambulance unit at Monte Pasubio during these years and wrote extensively about the battles that took place. He described one rock-cut fortress as consisting of "four storeys of galleries, one above the other, each brimming with cannon and machine guns. There were also medieval-looking machines for pouring volleys of rock down the gullies by which the enemy might attempt to ascend." The fortresses were reached by aerial cableways, down which "the sick and wounded came in cages, hundreds of feet in the air" to be met by Trevelyan's medical team.

The fighting around Monte Pasubio, which was some of the fiercest in the whole of the First World War, is commemorated nowadays in the nearby town of Rovereto, which lies in the main valley of the Adige river between Trento and Verona. On the valley side above the town is the Campana dei Caduti, a huge bell made from melted-down cannon that rings out a melancholy toll every evening in remembrance of the dead of both sides. The bell forms the centrepiece of a museum and educational complex dedicated to furthering peace between nations in the modern world. In the same town, the Sacario Militare di Castel Dante is a huge memorial to the Italian soldiers who died on the front during the terrible years of 1916 and 1917.

The second front in the south-eastern Alps was the Izonso (or Soča) front, which stretched ninety kilometres from the Adriatic coast into the high mountains around Monte Nero, roughly following the present-day border between Italy and Slovenia. The area around Mount Krn, close to the Slovenian town of Kobarid, saw some ferocious fighting in October 1917, when the Italians were routed by the combined armies of Austria and Germany; this was the so-called "twelfth offensive", which turned out to be one of the most decisive single breakthroughs of any side during the whole war. This lengthy, bloody campaign eventually resulted in over a million casualties on both sides. Some seven thousand Italian troops are buried in St. Anthony's Church in Kobarid, where there is also an excellent museum relating to the events of 1917 (today, though, Kobarid is better-known as the main town of the beautiful Soča valley, famed for its white water rafting). Elsewhere in this part of Slovenia there are many other reminders of the war, including the small chapel on the Vršič Pass that was built in memory of the three hundred Russian prisoners who died in an avalanche while constructing the road over the pass, and a church at Tolmin, south-east of Kobarid, whose panels list three thousand Austro-Hungarian soldiers who died during the campaigns here.

The map of the eastern region of the Alps was re-drawn following the victory of the Great Powers in 1918. The South Tyrol, including the southern approach to the Brenner Pass, and the towns of Blozano, Trento and Merano, became part of Italian territory and remain so to this day. During the 1920s the fascists made strenuous efforts to Italianize this area, renaming it the Alto Adige, forcing people and towns to adopt Italian names, and banning German from schools. Mussolini's personal architect, Marcello Piacentini, grafted an Italian quarter onto Bolzano, and placed a triumphal arch in the city's Piazza della Vittoria in 1928 to show that the Italians had arrived and were intending to stay. But over time, this area became peaceful, as did the rest of Europe.

In 1925 the main powers met in the Swiss lakeside resort of Locarno to sign an agreement imposing some sort of order on the battered continent; at around the same time many memorials to the Great War were constructed in those areas that had seen fighting during the previous decade. Memorials can today be found not only in Rovereto and Kobarid but also in the small town of Kufstein on the German-

Austrian border, where an enormous outdoor pipe organ was completed in 1931 to commemorate the dead of the war; the 4,307 pipes occupy one of the towers of the town's medieval fortress, and concerts on the instrument are still given daily. But even as the Kufstein organ was being unveiled and the Locarno Pact was being signed, the first stirrings of Nazism were becoming apparent in Weimar Germany, leading to Hitler's rise to power and war breaking out in Europe for a second time in 1939.

The Second World War

The Second World War saw less fighting in the Alps than in the First. Much of the military action involved insurgency groups who used the mountain regions of Alpine France and Slovenia, in particular, to launch attacks on the German occupation forces.

Many areas in the French Alps saw military action in the opening stages of the war, when Italy invaded in June 1940, pressing over passes such as the Col de la Seigne and the Col d'Enclave and meeting French garrisons stationed in the mountains. However, most of the military action in the French Alps during the years that followed involved clashes between the French Resistance and German or Italian occupying forces. One fierce battle took place on the high pastures of the Plâteau des Glières north of Annecy, where a Resistance camp was attacked unsuccessfully by German-backed Vichy French forces in February 1944; a second attempt also failed and the Germans then sent in twelve thousand troops who forced the 465 besieged men to retreat and scatter. These events are commemorated by a memorial chapel and cemetery at the summit of the Col des Glières, the 1,440-metre high pass that crosses the plateau.

Another area that was defended by the Resistance was the Vercors, the thickly forested and sparsely populated limestone massif that rises above Grenoble. By 1944 there were four thousand volunteers receiving military training on the Vercors, and on 15 June in that year (two weeks after D-Day) a German assault on the village of St.-Nizier was successfully beaten back. On 3 July the Resistance leaders were confident enough to proclaim the République du Vercors, independent of Nazi-occupied France, but fifteen thousand German troops were dispatched to the area and, after landing in gliders on an airfield at Vassieux-en-Vercors, they forced the army of the Resistance into a retreat. These events are now commemorated in Vassieux where there is a monument and a commemorative plaque on the town hall bearing the names of seventy-four civilian victims who died during these events; many are buried in the Cimetière National du Vercors, near the town.

In August 1944 the fortunes of the Resistance began to look up. In that month the allies made landings on the south coast of France, and the Département of Haute-Savoie was the first part of France to come fully under Resistance control. After British and American troops and supplies were parachuted into the region the German garrison at Chamonix found itself surrounded and quickly surrendered. The war in the Alps soon drew to a close, with one curious coda: in February 1945 a company of Austro-German mountain troops, based around the Torino hut on the Col du Géant on the slopes of Mont Blanc, staged a last-ditch counter-attack on liberated France, bombarding Chamonix from their positions established next to the cable car station on the Col du Midi. A dawn attack was met with fierce French resistance, which resulted in the Germans retreating with nine dead. This military action took place at an altitude of around 3,500 metres, and has been called the highest engagement of the entire war; the whole brief campaign was an act of supreme military folly, for which the Austrian commander, Captain Singel, who was one of the nine killed, must take most of the blame.

On the other side of the Alps, Slovenia was occupied by the Nazis between 1941 and 1945. Some of the worst atrocities of these years took place in Katzenstein Castle in Begunje, close to Radovljica on the fringes of the Julian Alps, where thousands of prisoners were detained and executed during the time the place was used as a Gestapo prison. Farewell messages can still be seen etched on to the walls of some of the cells, and there is a graveyard outside where many of those who were executed are buried. Deeper into the Julian Alps near Kranjska Gora, now the country's premier mountain resort, is a memorial to the partisans who fought in this region during the war; it takes the form of a karabiner and a piton, two pieces of equipment used in mountaineering, and is situated in the beautiful Vrata valley in the shadow of Triglav (2,864m), the highest peak in the Julian Alps.

The war had a very different impact on the Alpine areas of Austria and Italy. Ebensee, on the shores of the Traunsee east of Salzburg, was the site of a dreadful concentration camp in which eight thousand prisoners died between 1943 and 1945. A satellite of Austria's most notorious concentration camp, Mauthausen, near Linz, the prisoners here were engaged in blasting tunnels into a mountain, the 1,143-metre Seeberg, so that a missile testing centre could be hidden inside it, to replace the testing centre at Peenemünde on the Baltic, which was not safe from allied air raids. Little remains of the camp; the testing centre was never finished and the tunnels were eventually used for storage. The gate to the concentration camp can still be seen in Ebensee's Finkerleiten district, and there are mass graves and memorials too. Meanwhile, the Italian Alps were the scene of one of the oddest chapters of Second World War history, when the independent Republic of Saló was created by Mussolini on the shores of Lake Garda during the last months of the war. It was Mussolini's last-ditch attempt at creating a fascist state—which only lasted a few months: in April 1945 Mussolini was captured when a German motorcade in which he was travelling along the western shore of Lake Como was stopped by Italian partisans at Dongo; a search of the lorries turned up a number of Italy's deposed fascist leaders, including Mussolini and his mistress Clara Petacci. The former dictator was hanged in Milan shortly afterwards.

"Utterly careless of the fate of empires": Peasant Life

In all this description of the history of the Alps, little mention has been made of the people who have made their home in the mountains over the centuries, or of the sort of lives that they led in this beautiful but often inhospitable and isolated environment.

Until tourism began to make a big impact on the Alps in the early twentieth century most Alpine dwellers eked out a difficult existence based on farming, hunting or mining. Many visitors were shocked by the wretched conditions they saw in the region, and guidebooks warned visitors of the often pitiable scenes they would encounter. A nineteenth-century Baedeker guide to the Savoy Alps recounts that in the Aosta valley the "Peasantry appear a squalid and filthy race [and are] generally stunted and diseased." Another guide of the same era, this time a Murray *Handbook to Switzerland and the Savoy Alps* commented that "It is a remarkable fact that, amidst some of the most magnificent scenery of the globe... man appears, from a mysterious visitation of disease, in his most degraded and pitiable condition. It is in the grandest and most beautiful valleys of the Alps that the maladies of goitre and cretinism prevail." Goitre, a disease whose main symptom is a swelling of the thyroid gland, was common all over Europe but seems to have been particularly prevalent in the Alps: on his trip around Lake Geneva in 1816 with Lord Byron, the poet Shelley wrote of the "deformed and goitred children" he saw at Nernier, and later, in a letter to his correspondent Thomas Love Peacock, he described the "degradation of the human species" around Chamonix, where people "in these regions are half deformed or idiotic and all of whom are deprived of anything that can excite interest or imagination."

It was not only disease that was the problem; poverty, too, was endemic throughout the mountains. In 1865 the English traveller Thomas George Bonney commented on the conditions he witnessed in the High Alps of the Dauphiné, writing that "It is hardly possible to conceive the squalid misery in which the people live; their dark dismal huts swarming with flies, flees and other vermin... the bones and refuse of a meal are flung upon the floor to be gnawed by dogs." It seemed that even after the Second World War the situation had not improved very much. R. L. J. Irving was shocked by the conditions he saw in the Bernese Alps in Switzerland, which he described in *The Alps* (1947): "In such places... movement of population must have been very slight, and the resultant in-breeding may perhaps account for the special prevalence of cretinism... a cretin is just horrible, an idiotic and obscene creature, hardly human."

In former times, most mountain dwellers were farmers, and the hard conditions they faced accounted for the extreme poverty of the Alps. Nowadays, farming in high regions of the Alps is still very difficult, and yet many farmers still follow centuries-old traditions. One is the practice of transhumance, where animals are driven to upper pastures in the spring and brought down again in autumn. Famous for its traditional transhumance is the area around the Niederjoch Pass, which crosses from the Tyrol into Italy: in a practice that dates back to the thirteenth century, shepherds from the Schnaltal, on the Italian side of the border, drive thousands of sheep across this pass every summer, in search of fresh grazing land. Elsewhere in the Alps animals are transported to and fro in trucks rather than in a picturesque procession through villages and over the hillsides.

Although the practice of transhumance is in decline, as more and more hill farmers abandon their traditional practices for more modern methods, the movement of animals is still a pivotal part of the farming calendar and there are traditional festivals associated with it in many areas: the Almabtrieb festival is one of these, held in the Zillertal district of the Tyrol during the first weekend in October. The return of cows from Alpine pasture is marked by a colourful procession and by noisy, alcohol-fuelled merry-making, while its associated festival, the Gauderfest, held during the first weekend in May, still bears elements of the folk rituals that once marked the beginning of the summer cycle of the farming year. In Die in the western French Alps the start of the transhumance is celebrated somewhat differently, by the drinking of a sweet sparkling local wine called the Clairette de Die. Many villages in other areas of the French Alps, such as St. Bonnet in the Écrins National Park, celebrate the return of sheep from the high pastures in the autumn by holding vibrant local fairs.

Cheese production is still a vital part of Alpine agriculture. Many dairies are open to the public, such as the one at Gruyères in Switzerland, with its huge, churning metal vats and its blend of traditional and high-tech manufacturing methods. Cheese-making is one of the most parochial aspects of Alpine agriculture; in some areas each individual valley proudly produces its own unique cheese, such as the Vallée de Thônes in Savoy, where farmers have produced strong, creamy Reblochon cheese since the thirteenth century, and still sell it at markets in local towns. Many of the manufacturing methods are complex: another Savoy cheese, Beaufort, made near Albertville from the milk of the Abondance and Tarine cattle breeds, famously goes through ten different manufacturing stages, culminating in a maturing process that lasts six months: the rounds of cheese have to be kept in damp cellars at a constant temperature of ten degrees, and twice a week are turned over and rubbed with salt.

But although some traditional methods remain, other practices have long since died out; few farmers nowadays make their own cheese, and most belong to a co-operative, whose factory churns out the product using the milk supplied by all its members. In the nineteenth century the geologist James Forbes, who famously walked miles across high Alpine terrain in France conducting research into glaciers, witnessed a much older form of cheese production in operation. He described in detail the rough stone shacks high in the Dauphiné Alps where herders lived for weeks on end in summer, each herder preparing the cheese on his own using only basic equipment. The herders had two huts, a day hut where the cheese was made, and a night hut next door, which had to be accessed by crawling in through a three foot-high door; neither hut had a fire or windows, and at night the only warmth was provided by a covering of hay. "They count their wealth by cheeses," Forbes said of the hardy, individualistic farmers who owned these places. They "live on friendly terms with their dumb herds, so accustomed to privation as to dream of no luxury, and utterly careless of the fate of empires, or the change of dynasties."

In a couple of areas of the Alps farmers have traditionally practiced apiculture or beekeeping. The pine forests of north-western Slovenia provide a warm environment in which bees can flourish in the summer, and commercial apiculture in this region is at least four centuries old; by the nineteenth century Slovenian beekeepers were even exporting their honey and wax abroad. A unique form of folk art is associated with Slovenian beekeeping, namely the practice of painting the fronts of wooden hives with Biblical or historic scenes, or with depictions of peasant life. One popular figure to feature on these hive paintings is Job, the patron saint of beekeepers; humorous scenes are also depicted, including hunters being pursued by bears wielding guns. (There was a practical point to the paintings too: the bright colours were supposedly attractive to the bees.) Painted hives can still be seen in many parts of Alpine Slovenia, and in Radovljica there is even a museum exhibiting the panels. Another area with a history of apiculture is Valensole, in the very south of the French Alps, which buzzes to the sound of millions of bees every summer when thousands of beehives are set up on the plateau by beekeepers who rent the land from local farmers.

In a number of villages across the Alps traditional dwellings and farmhouses have been preserved as museums, in order to give an impression of life in bygone times. The Liznjek House in Kranjska Gora is one of these, a superbly preserved alpine homestead that was the property of a wealthy farmer in the late eighteenth century. The house is built of thick stone with small windows, making it dark and gloomy throughout (though cool on a warm day in summer); the floors, roof and stairs are all made from dark, creaking wood. The vast attic is still full of farmers' tools, while the kitchen walls have been blackened by soot through years of use. The capacious barn opposite the house was built in 1796 and was used for storing food and housing livestock. Another of these ancient village dwellings can be found St. Véran, high in the Alps of the Savoy, where a house dating back to 1641 has been similarly converted into a museum. The house was built with an outside yard for the household pig, an inner courtyard for cattle, and a shepherd's room for seasonal workers (who were usually migrants from Piedmont). In winter humans and cattle would have cohabited, as they did in one house in this remote village until as recently as 1976.

Mining and Industry

The other mainstay of the Alpine economy, besides farming, was mining. As long ago as the first millennium BC there was a flourishing salt trade in the Austrian Alps, much of it centred around mining towns such as Hallein, whose salt deposits were worked until as recently as 1989. Originally miners hacked the pure salt from off the gallery walls; later, techniques were developed for dissolving the salt in water and then pumping the resulting brine into pools in the valley floors, where the water would soon evaporate, leaving the salt behind in salt pans. The Habsburgs took the salt trade very seriously, exempting miners from military service, and towns such as Hallein are still full of burghers' houses from the seventeenth century, the homes of merchants who had grown wealthy administering the salt trade. Nowadays the salt mines at Bad Dürrnberg above Hallein are show-mines, with hundreds of visitors each day shuffling around subterranean galleries, and whizzing along tunnels in trucks that run on tracks built originally for the fast transport of salt and miners. (The highlight of a mine visit for many is a trip down the *arschleder*, a steep wooden slide used for getting down into the deepest galleries.)

Other salt-mining towns include Ebensee, where huge industrial vats of freshly-mined rock salt are still pulled across the main road through the town on an overhead cableway, and Altausee, where the Nazis used the old mining tunnels to store various works of art they had plundered from all over Europe during the war. Although most Alpine salt workings are around the city of Salzburg (whose name means "salt town" in German) there are also mines in other parts of the region, such at Bex in the Valais; the salt deposits here were discovered in the fifteenth century by a shepherd who noticed that his flock liked drinking from one particular spring, which was later discovered to be salty.

There is also a long history of metal ore mining in the Alps. Iron ore was mined in the Val Varrone close to Lake Como as long ago as the Bronze Age, while the powerful Celtic kingdom of Noricum grew rich because of the iron ore in the hills of Carinthia; the Romans later exploited the iron ore from hereabouts and used it to make javelins. The mines in this part of Austria, and the associated blast furnaces, finally ceased operations in 1978. Other centres of iron ore mining were around Železniki in the Slovenian Alps, where there were two blast furnaces in the seventeenth century, and around Kropa near Radovljica where some forges still remain, producing traditional pieces of decorative iron work. Lead was mined in Carinthia, at Bad Bleiberg near Fellach, until 1993, while gold was mined at Böckstein south of Salzburg, and silver was mined at Schwaz near Innsbruck, helping the Habsburgs fill their coffers during the reign of Maximilian I. (The church in Schwaz was deliberately built with two separate naves, one where the miners worshipped, the other reserved for merchants and burghers of the town.) Silver and lead were also mined in the French Alps at Cirque de la Gura, where Napoleon himself founded a mining academy. Yet another metal, copper, was mined from rich seams in Kitzbühel, in the days before the place became one of Austria's most fashionable ski resorts.

The mountainsides of the Alps yielded other valuable resources. Trees have been felled for timber and fuel since time immemorial. Slate was mined in the L'Oisans region of the department of Isère, while coal was mined at La Mure in the same region. The La Mure railway, one of the first mountain lines in the Alps, was built in 1888 to transport coal from the mines at La Mure to St.-George-de-Commiers, south of Grenoble; the line negotiates a difference in altitude of 560 metres by means of twelve curved viaducts and eighteen tunnels, and at the start of the twentieth century it became the first railway in the world to be powered by high-voltage direct electric current. Coal mining in La Mure ended in 1956 and the line—and the mines—are now a tourist attraction. A final, rather curious (though in the end perhaps not surprising) export from the Alps was ice: in 1866 a hundred thousand francs worth of ice was hacked from the Grindelwald glaciers and sent, wrapped in straw, to Paris and beyond; by 1900 a stone chute had been constructed above Grindelwald to facilitate export of this valuable commodity.

With the gradual expansion of mining, forestry and farming came industry and trade. Paper mills and wood-carving industries grew up in the forested department of Dauphiné. Small towns in the Swiss Alps began to manufacture textiles and chocolate. In the 1860s a factory owner in the Grésivaudan, north of Grenoble, learned how to harness *houille blanche*—white coal, or hydroelectric power—from fast-flowing rivers; now there are HEP plants all over the Alps, and in some areas of the mountains it can seem as if there are no valleys left without an arrangement of dams, lakes and turbines. These areas have in turn attracted electricity-hungry industries such as aluminium smelting or the manufacture of metal alloys. (When the Barrage de Serre-Ponçon on the Durance was built in 1955 the resultant lake, one of the largest in Europe, drowned an entire village, Savines-le-Lac, which remains consigned beneath the waters to this day.)

Other parts of the Alps offer a more unusual industrial heritage: watch-making is practiced in Cluses, near Chamonix, while glove-making and cement manufacture have long been traditional in Grenoble; Hergiswil on Lake Lucerne developed a glass-making tradition, while Swiss Army knives have been made at Ibach near Schwyz since a local entrepreneur named Carl Elsener founded his factory there in 1884; stonecutting in Samoëns in Haute-Savoie, and shoemaking in the Slovenian towns of Žiri and Tržič, are both much older industries, dating back to the Middle Ages. And of course once these products were made, they had to be sold and traded, often by risk-taking entrepreneurs who became rich in the process. Many Swiss and Austrian towns had a large and influential community of merchants, while the town of Brig in the Valais, which lies at the foot of the Simplon pass, is dominated by the Schloss Stockalper, a grandiose palace which was for a time the largest private residence in Switzerland; it was completed in 1678 to serve as the home of Kaspar Jodok von Stockalper, a merchant who controlled the trade in silk and other commodities over the Simplon Pass. Its peaceful, ornate courtyard, overlooked by graceful towers capped by onion domes, is testament to the wealth that Stockalper, like a number of other Alpine traders, was able to accrue for himself through shrewd control of trans-Alpine trade.

Minority Cultures

Although a network of trading routes has crisscrossed the mountains for thousands of years, many parts of the Alps remained isolated until well into the twentieth century. This remoteness meant that unique languages and cultures survived and flourished in some areas, particularly those untainted by too many outside influences. One of these areas was the central Dolomites where the Ladin language, once spoken across a wide area that stretched from Austria to the River Po, still survives in pockets, particularly around the town of Corvara, near Trento (the total number of speakers is reckoned to be around forty thousand). The Ladini themselves were a fiercely independent people; in early medieval times they were in almost continuous conflict with Germanic tribes, and later the Prince-Bishops of Brissone had to build a castle at St. Martino di Badia specifically to keep the Ladin-dominated Val Badia under some sort of control. Over time the Ladins adopted Christianity, but somehow managed to transform their own pagan (and exclusively female) deities into Christian saints: the figure of Santa Giuliana, often depicted wielding a sword, appears on paintings on the outside of many houses in and around Corvara to this day.

The most famous minority language in the Alps is however Romansch, which is still spoken by around seventy thousand inhabitants of the mountainous Graubünden canton of south-eastern Switzerland (Romansch speakers know the region as Grischun). Romansch is a hybrid of Latin, Italian and Swiss-German, and in many towns and villages in the remoter parts of the Graubünden people can be heard greeting each other with *allegro* ("hello") or *bun di* ("good morning") or *buna saira* ("good afternoon"). Romansch underwent a decline in the nineteenth century as the Graubünden opened up to the rest of Switzerland, and speakers of the language found that their native tongue was an impediment to gaining employment; but various cultural groups promoted Romansch and in 1938 an amendment to the Swiss constitution proclaimed Romansch a national language. (The fact that there are very different dialects spoken by different Romansch communities has not helped its preservation.) Nowadays there are two radio stations that broadcast in Romansch, in addition to a number of newspapers.

The heart of Romansch culture is the Lower Engadine valley (Engidina Bassa in Romansch), which occupies the very easternmost fringe of Swiss territory, and through which flows the upper stretches of the River Inn (En in Romansch). Many Romansch festivals and customs have survived here along with the language: on 2 January each year children swarm through the hamlet of Ramosch dragging a sledge behind them and collecting buckets of sweets, before the whole community indulges in a midnight feast of butter biscuits smothered in whipped cream, while in Scuol the first Saturday in February sees the ceremonial burning of the Hom d'Strom, the "man of straw", in front of the town's court building, in a ritual banishment of winter from the valley for another year.

Any study of the people of the Alps must include a mention of the Jenisch, a travelling community of gypsy descent that settled in the Graubünden canton in the seventeenth and eighteenth centuries. Here they lived a quiet, if separate, life for hundreds of years until the Swiss government supported a shameful attempt at wiping out their culture from the 1920s onwards. The *Kinder der Landstrasse* policy was formulated in 1926 by Alfred Siegfried, who openly stated his wish to eliminate this group of travellers by trying to prevent them from reproducing. According to the policy, Jenisch children were seized by police and placed in orphanages or passed on to foster parents—all without the knowledge of their birth parents. (Often the boys were sent to live on isolated farms while girls were placed in convents; some children were also placed in mental institutions, such as the notorious Waldhaus clinic in Chur.) Marriage between Jenisch was outlawed and some members of the community reported rough treatment at the hands of scientists who were "studying" them. In 1972 there was an outcry when this scandalous policy was exposed by a Swiss newspaper; in 1988 the government of Switzerland apologized to the Jenisch people for the affair and took full responsibility for it. The cruel treatment of the Jenisch, which has clear and uncomfortable Nazi overtones, remains a stain on the once admirable image of Switzerland (the other disaster to befall the country's reputation was the revelation that Swiss banks had offered a hiding place for Nazi gold during the 1930s and 1940s). Today there are thirty-five thousand Jenisch in Switzerland, most of whom have settled in cities, but five thousand of whom are still travellers, out on the roads each year just as their ancestors were.

Part Three

Imagination

It is nothing like a scene from real life. Instead, it is almost as if it is an illustration, lifted straight from the creamy-white pages of a child's book of fairy tales.

The scene shows a castle, perched on a high crag and surrounded by thick forest. The entrance to the castle takes the form of an arched gateway that might, in former times, have supported a portcullis. The gateway is set into a high wall of red bricks, rising to a regular line of battlements. On either side of the gateway are white, rounded towers, with narrow openings for windows in their walls and conical roofs fringed with crenellations at their summits. (You half expect a knight to ride up to the gateway on horseback, all billowing cloak and a mane of flowing hair, as the young maiden imprisoned in one of the towers leans out to catch a first glimpse of her rescuer—and instantly falls in love with him.) Beyond the grand entrance, narrow balconies jut out over steeply-sloping roofs, while curved turrets rise above shady courtyards to culminate in yet more sharply conical spires. The castle is neatly framed by its backdrop of snowy mountains and forested valleys. The whole thing is impossibly picturesque: a fussy, overwrought concoction that looks as if it has been painted rather than built, or made from marzipan and coloured icing rather than bricks and stones.

The Ultimate Fairy-Tale Castle

Even to those who have not been there, Neuschwanstein castle, in the Bavarian Alps, seems instantly recognizable. Its familiar forest of turrets and towers, often shrouded in swirling mountain mists, might have come straight out of a tourist brochure for the land of make-believe. This dreamy fantasy fortress, set in a beautiful landscape, is the prototype for every "fairy-tale" castle that ever appeared in a Walt Disney film. It was constructed in the 1870s by "mad" King Ludwig of Bavaria, a ruler celebrated for the construction of a number of grandiose flights of

architectural fancy that pepper the mountainous regions of his former kingdom.

Ludwig is one of the most bizarre figures to be associated with the Alps, and his story is worth telling. He grew up in a castle known as the Hohenschwangau built by his father, Maximilian II. Maximilian had chanced upon this fortress, then in ruins, while out hunting; he learned that it had originally been built by the Knights of Schwangau in the thirteenth century. The ruins stood on a forested bluff set above a jewel-like lake, right at the place where the final Alpine precipices plunge into the gently rolling meadowland that characterizes most of southern Bavaria. Maximilian soon understood that the history of the ruined castle matched its romantic location: the Schwangau knights had been the military servants of the powerful Staufen dynasty, the last of whom, the tragic boy prince Konradin, was beheaded in Naples in 1268. Konradin had grown up in the castle, in the care of the knights, and was just sixteen years old when he died. Later, the castle had sheltered Martin Luther after he had been condemned by the Diet of Augsburg, and had suffered destruction at the hands of the competing armies of France and Austria in the Napoleonic wars. Now, after re-discovering it, Maximilian had the place rebuilt as a hunting lodge and country residence: a series of box-like towers slowly emerged above the treetops, their walls of yellow ochre complementing the deep green of the surrounding forest. And it was here, in the rebuilt Hohenschwangau fortress, that the future King Ludwig spent his childhood.

Maximilian must have hoped that a better fate would await his son than that dealt out by history to the previous boy prince who grew up here, the unfortunate Konradin. But unlike Konradin, who had revelled in his courtly upbringing like the good medieval prince he was, Ludwig was a dreamer and an outsider, and this intelligent but reserved child spent much of his boyhood simply gazing out of the castle's windows at the forest and mountains. And on one particular steep craggy bluff across the valley, which overlooked a deep and romantic gorge where the River Pöllat plunged between high, narrow rocks, the boy dreamed he would one day build a castle of his own: a splendid edifice rising above the forest and the cliffs and the crashing waterfalls. And he resolved that it would be like nothing ever built in the Alps—or anywhere else, for that matter.

When Ludwig ascended the throne of Bavaria in 1864, at the age of eighteen, his vision for Neuschwanstein had already been imagined and dreamt for years. But it would be some time yet before it was expressed in bricks and stone. At the start of his reign, Ludwig was a reformist ruler, introducing public care for the poor and freeing up trade. In 1866, against his will but under pressure from his cabinet, he engaged Bavaria in the war between Austria and Prussia. Three weeks later the Austrian coalition, of which Bavaria was a part, was defeated at the battle of Königsgrätz in Bohemia. With his power deeply weekend, and the politics of this part of Europe shifting beyond his control, Ludwig followed the public mood and expressed support for the Prussian king to become the Kaiser of a newly-united Germany. This reduced Ludwig to the status of a powerless puppet with nothing but a meaningless title to his name. But Ludwig was born into the wrong age. He desperately wanted to be a ruler in his own right. As his own power was eroded by the creation of what we now know as Germany, he became disillusioned, and retreated to the Bavarian Alps to construct the castles and villas that would allow him to live out his fantasies.

One of Ludwig's obsessions was with pre-Revolutionary France, a political culture that had, to his mind, spawned *real* rulers (never mind that they had all eventually come to a bloody end at the hands of the operators of *Madame Guillotine*). Many of his palaces bear witness to his adulation of the absolutist monarch Louis XIV, and none more so than the elegant rococo palace known as the Schloss Linderhof, situated in remote and mountainous countryside close to the passion-play town of Oberammergau. In fact, this absurd *Schloss* seems almost like a shrine, constructed both in honour of the "sun king" and as a memorial to Ludwig's own failed dreams. The place is surrounded by French gardens boasting fountains, pools, statuary and follies—a mini-Versailles, incongruously hemmed into a deep, narrow, forested valley that so obviously lacks the opulent acres of space of the admired original. Inside, the ceiling of the entrance hall features an enormous sunburst with two cherubs holding aloft the Bourbon family motto; the sun bursts right above a bronze statue depicting Ludwig on a horse. Beyond the entrance halls, the rooms of the palace are overblown and overwrought, stuffed with mirrors and murals and decoration to the point of being lurid. And in the hillside above the palace is the final piece of empty-headed ostentation: an opening set into a shallow cliffs marks the entrance to the Venus grotto, an artificial cave crammed with stalactites and stalagmites and watery caverns—the whole thing nothing but artifice, creating an impression, one might cruelly be tempted to think, as hollow and as meaningless as the life of the prince himself.

For Ludwig lived in a fantasy world of princes and castles, of courageous knights battling mythical beasts and coming to the rescue of lusty maidens. He craved power, opulence and heroism; and his palaces were where he withdrew from the world, and indulged himself. He was a friend and patron of Richard Wagner (the Venus grotto at Linderhof was in fact intended as a stage set for Wagner's opera *Tannhäuser*); the stories depicted in paintings and tapestries throughout his palaces reveal an obsession with the same Teutonic myths and legends that inspired Germany's greatest composer of operas. But it was not just Teutonic legends that inspired Ludwig: he was clearly influenced by the exoticism of the Orient, too. Another castle, the Jagdschloss Schachen, situated in a remote location high above Garmisch-Partenkirchen, looks like a Swiss chalet from the outside and something out of the Arabian Nights inside.

Here the king would instruct his servants to wear turbans and burn incense while he smoked water pipes and dreamed his lofty dreams. And as he did so, he withdrew from the world around him. There is no sadder reflection of this in all his castles than the amazing gadget in the Schloss Linderhof which allowed the king to eat off an ornate table that rose up through the floor with his meal already set out for him—so he would not have to have any contact with the servants who had prepared it.

While Ludwig certainly craved solitude and isolation, he could not decide whether his ideal retreat was amongst mountains or beside lakes. The castle at Schachen provided a refuge in the Alps, but another palace, the Schloss Herrenchiemsee, home to a Great Hall of Mirrors that rivalled that in Versailles, was built on an island in the middle of a lake near Munich. And his name is associated with another Alpine lake, too. In 1865 he famously floated away from the resort of Brunnen, on the Urnersee (part of Lake Lucerne), to the accompaniment of teams of alpenhorn blowers, who serenaded him while he bobbed around on the water at midnight, gazing up at the stars.

But Ludwig's principal legacy is Neuschwanstein, the ultimate fantasy castle that he dreamed of building when he was a boy. The castle was modelled loosely on Wartburg, a medieval knight's castle in the Thuringian forest in central Germany, but was designed by a theatre set designer rather than an architect. In the royal bedroom, the bed is topped by a forest of wooden turrets and spires, emulating a Gothic church, while the throne room takes the form of a Byzantine church. Murals on the walls of this room depict canonized kings from all corners of Europe looking down from on high at any empty space in the centre of the floor: this was where the throne should have been, but Ludwig never lived to see it installed. Another mural in the throne room shows St. George fighting a dragon in the shadow of a castle that looks just like Neuschwanstein. But the opulence in the castle is skin-deep: the tapestries are not really tapestries, as weaving them all would have been too expensive. They are actually designs painted straight onto canvas. And, to cap it all, many of the rooms in Neuschwanstein and other castles were unfinished at the time of Ludwig's death, and were simply left bare or partially decorated after he was gone.

The tragic, remarkable and controversial circumstances surrounding Ludwig's death in some ways reflected the grandiose folly of his life. In

1886 he was declared medically unfit to rule after undergoing a psychological examination, and was taken to live on Schloss Berg on the shores of Lake Starnberg, south of Munich. He drowned in the waters of the lake a few days later. Reports and documents about his death were later found to have been tampered with, leading to theories of foul play. To this day nothing has been proved. But every year, on 13 June, a wreath is laid on the shores of Lake Starnberg in a small ceremony designed to commemorate his death. And to this day the fascination with Ludwig continues. In 2000 a melodramatic musical, *Ludwig II*, opened in a custom-built theatre on the Forggensee lake close to Neuschwanstein. Subtitled *Longing for Paradise*, it combines fantasy, monumental spectacle and history to celebrate the life and achievements of one of the oddest figures in European history.

Immortal Ghosts and High-Flying Giants

Perhaps the real point about Ludwig—or, more specifically, Neuschwanstein—was that up until his time, the Alps had been seen as a strange, frightening place. The medieval knights who built the first fortress of Hohenschwangau could never have conceived that, centuries later, this remote location could fire the imagination of a prince and become the ideal location for a highly desirable royal residence. What to Ludwig was a dreamily romantic setting was to the medieval imagination a place where demons lived and wolves lurked; to the knights of Hohenschwangau, the forest was fit only for hunting or hiding, but seven centuries later, when Ludwig conceived Neuschwanstein, a series of artistic and scientific revolutions had ensured that mountains were celebrated for their idyllic beauty rather than feared as the abode of devils. It was thanks largely to these monumental shifts in sentiment that Ludwig was able to see the Alpine landscape of Bavaria as an appropriate setting for his outlandish but picturesque folly.

The story of how the Alps have been re-imagined over the centuries starts in the Middle Ages. By that time, as we have seen, the fields in the valleys had been cultivated for millennia, and the passes over the mountains had been used for trade since at least the time of the Romans. The rich mineral seams deep within the mountains had long been plundered for gold, silver, copper and iron ore. Castles, like the one at Hohenschwangau, were built on defensive positions above valleys and beside lake shores. But very few ventured onto the peaks themselves. For above the highest meadowland was the realm of beasts and devils, who occasionally unleashed terrific storms or cascades of rocks on those unfortunate enough to dwell beneath their gaze. Their fearsome territory was uncharted and unexplored. No-one ever climbed mountains; why should they? To do so would undoubtedly antagonize the malevolent creatures and unquiet spirits that dwelled amidst the rocky crags and inhospitable ice fields.

Stories and legends concerning witches, devils, giants, and wild beasts abound in the Alps. In the Middle Ages every valley, in fact practically every village, seemed to revel in its own particular set of superstitions, handed down from generation to generation. As late as the nineteenth century, the Catinaccio range in the western Dolomites, a remote region of sheer rock walls and deep valleys, was described by a local judge and writer, Theodor Christomannos, as being "the gate into the kingdom of immortal ghosts, of high-flying giants." One of many mountains in the Alps with a terrible story attached to it is Watzmann, close to Berchtesgaden in Bavaria. The toothy peaks of this formidable mountain (two big, seven small) were said to represent a sadistic king, his queen and their children, who were changed into stone as punishment for their cruelty after terrorizing the surrounding area. In another part of the mountains, the inhabitants of the tiny farming community of Chamonix knew the mountain that glared down over them not as Mont Blanc but as Mont Maudit, the "Accursed Mountain". And a day's journey away from Chamonix along the Trient valley was a village, Les Diablerets, which seemed to have accrued more than its fair share of fantastic tales. Today, this tiny, family-oriented mountain resort is best known for hosting the International Alpine Film Festival; but its name (in French, "the abode of devils") hints at the stories that the locals must have told and retold around the communal fires centuries ago, as they shivered through the harsh Alpine winters.

The most terrifying tale told in Les Diablerets concerned the freezing and formidable glacier, the Tsanfleuron, whose name strangely translates as the "Field of Flowers" in local dialect. The story goes that this ice field above the village was once a sunny meadow, which is how it got its name. Then one day some mischievous devils came to these mountains to play at throwing stones at the Quille du Diable (Devil's

Skittle), a huge lump of upstanding rock high on the valley sides. The devils were never seen; but the rocks they threw (actually, boulders prized off the valley sides by the growth of ice crystals) would often hit the few shepherds brave enough to venture up here. Eventually the shepherds grew tired of the rolling boulders and the area's pastures were abandoned. Gradually, with the help of the devils, the Tsanfleuron was transformed from meadowland into the icy wasteland of today.

Other stories linked with this tiny Valaisian settlement feature the mournful groaning of lost souls, whose moans heralded catastrophic landslides in 1714 and 1740, and the presence amidst the deserted slopes of elves and goblins—not to mention a *servan*, a type of imp, who one night turned himself into a fox and then sat up in a hayloft through the hours of darkness, knitting with the hair of his own tail.

Elsewhere in the mountains, the stuff of popular legend was fuelled by the presence of giants. They feature prominently on the panels of the medieval Kapellbrücke in Lucerne, while outside Wilten Abbey in Innsbruck are statues of two more of them, Haymon and Thyrsus—the latter killed in a dispute by the former (the was abbey subsequently founded by the victor as an act of penance). And if there were not giants to scare the locals, then there were all kinds of wild and terrifying beasts. In the Swiss canton of Uri, which occupies a wild area of lakes and high mountains south of Lucerne, a bull was bred specifically to frighten away a local monster, known as the Griess—and to this day, the same bull is depicted proudly on Uri's cantonal flag.

Religion, Magic and the Medieval Imagination

Perhaps the most potent of all the local legends in the Alps are those associated with the steep, towering presence of Pilatus, the formidable mountain that rises above the serene shores of Lake Lucerne. The peak is supposedly named after Pontius Pilate, who according to legend rises every Good Friday out of the lake just below the summit, clad in the blood-red robes of his terrible judgment—causing death within a year to anyone unfortunate enough to see him. Here is Mark Twain's account of the story:

> The legend goes that after the crucifixion [Pilate's] conscience troubled him and he fled from Jerusalem and wandered around the earth, weary

of life and a prey to tortures of the mind. Eventually he hid himself away, on the heights of Mount Pilatus, and dwelt alone among the clouds and crags for years; but rest and peace were still denied him, so he finally put an end to his misery by drowning himself.

There are several different versions of the legend: one is that Pilate in fact committed suicide in Rome, whereupon his body was thrown into the Tiber, and then the Rhône at Vienne, both times causing evil spirits to rise from the water; so eventually the lake on Pilatus was chosen as a place where his spirit could rest, disturbed and anguished but with no-one close by to terrify. (In reality, the name of the mountain probably comes from the Latin *pileatus*, meaning capped—by clouds, of course, as anyone who has walked the shores of Lake Lucerne, wondering where the perpetually obscured peak actually is, will testify.)

For many centuries an attempted ascent of Pilatus was expressly forbidden by edict. In 1387, when six clerics tried it, they were imprisoned. Nearly two centuries later, in 1518, Joachim von Watt, the Burgomeister of St. Gallen, obtained permission from the authorities to climb the peak, and reported nothing untoward at the top. In August 1555 the naturalist Conrad Gesner climbed Pilatus and marked his conquest by giving a triumphant blast on his alpenhorn. Then in 1585 Pastor Johann Müller of Lucerne went up the mountain and defied the evil spirits by throwing stones into the grey waters of the lake at the top. But nothing happened. Gesner later wrote that the belief in evil spirits at the top of the mountain had "no raison d'être in the laws of nature, [and] commands no credence from me... For my own part I am inclined to believe that Pilate has never been here at all, and that even had he been here he would not have been accorded the power of either benefiting or injuring human kind."

The legend of Pontius Pilate and Pilatus is just one instance of how Christianity and pagan superstition became confused in the medieval imagination. There are dozens of other examples throughout the Alps of Catholic monks and priests getting mixed up in local stories of beasts and devils. In 1690 the community of Chamonix paid the Bishop of Annecy to exorcise the glaciers above them that threatened to advance and overwhelm their houses and farms (it worked; the glaciers retreated by an eighth of a mile, and the bishop presented the villagers with a huge bill for his services). In the twelfth century, during the heyday of new monastic foundations in the Alps, a band of Augustinian monks was sent to Berchtesgaden to establish a monastery. They said that dragons caused an apocalyptic thunderstorm to tear the roofs off their cottages, and ran away—but their archbishop soon sent them back to the original spot, and their monastery was finally completed in 1122. (Their behaviour stands in marked contrast to those of other monks. There are records of members of other Alpine monasteries crawling up onto high peaks to sleep under a cowl, so as to be closer to God; they must have been some of the very few people who actually ventured above the tree-line and into the rocky peaks, braving the attention of the evil beings that supposedly lived there.) Later, during the era of Europe-wide witch-hunts in the early seventeenth century, the mountains were supposed to be the hiding places of cowled and cackling women, who defied their pursuers and inflicted storms and blizzards on the villages below their rocky lairs.

The final stories involving religion and magic come from the French Alps. In one, a native of the Savoy village of Bessans was supposed to have sold his soul to the devil in exchange for supernatural powers. But the man grew old and regretful, and went to the Pope to ask forgiveness. The Pope forgave him on condition that the man would hear mass in Bessans, Milan and Rome on the same day. The man used his supernatural powers to accomplish this seemingly impossible task—and so had the last laugh, outwitting the Pope and claiming forgiveness at the same time. To celebrate the legend, carvings of devils are still popular in Bessans, forming the last of a tradition of woodcarving present since the Middle Ages. Meanwhile, the "seven wonders of Dauphiné" are sites or monuments that are steeped in myth and legend in that particular department of Alpine France. They include Mont Aiguille, dominating the Vercors, which was once believed to be occupied by angels; the Grottes des Sassenages near Grenoble, supposedly the abode of fairies; and the *fontaine ardente* near the Col de l'Arzelier, apparently haunted by the devil himself.

Here Be Dragons

All such tales of witches, fairies, wild beasts, giants and devils in the mountains are overshadowed by those involving the most awe-inspiring creature of Alpine legend: the feared and fabulous dragon.

By the Middle Ages dragons were seemingly everywhere in the Alps. They had become enshrined in popular imagination like no other beast—and their mythology was pervasive. As late as 1723 the Swiss scientist Johann Jacob Scheuchzer, a professor of physics and mathematics at Zurich University, a Fellow of the Royal Society of London and a correspondent of scientists including

Isaac Newton and Gottfried Leibniz, drew up a compendium of all the species of dragon known to exist in the Swiss Alps, canton by canton. There were cat-faced ones, serpentine ones, inflammable ones, and non-combustible ones; some were fork-tailed and others fork-tongued, some smelt bad and some were loud, some flew and others slithered. (The most biologically bizarre has to be the one with a ginger tom cat's head, a snake's tongue, scaly legs, sparkly eyes and a hairy tail with two prongs.) Some dragons sported crests, and Scheuchzer wondered whether these were the male of the species; he also recorded the specific stories attached to many of the beasts. For instance, the dragon in the Val Ferret was friendlier than most, and sported a diamond-encrusted tail, while the *ouibra* of the Valais did a useful job in guarding all the liquid gold hidden in the depths of the mountains. According to Scheuchzer, a peasant who had fallen into the lair of this particular dragon had managed to live there for seven years (although he never retrieved the gold).

Another story about the deeds of an individual dragon comes from the French Alps, where the village of St. Véran, celebrated as being the highest in Europe (2,040 metres), is named after a sixth-century archbishop who fought off and wounded a dragon that was terrorizing the local area. As this particular beast flew away to Provence, twelve drops of blood dripped from its wounds; the places where they hit the ground later became the traditional locations where shepherds halted as they moved their livestock during the transhumance, from the valleys of the Luberon to the high summer pastures in Queyras.

At around the same time, in a different part of the Alps, a monk called Beatus (who like many missionaries in the region at this time probably hailed from Britain or Ireland) was travelling on a mission from the Pope to convert the heathen Swiss. He was told by locals around Interlaken of a fearsome dragon that lived in a cave above Lake Thun. Beatus headed up to the cave, invoked the name of the Holy Trinity and stood in the mouth of the cave with his crucifix raised high—whereupon the creature was sent tumbling down the mountainside and into the lake. The monk then set up residence in the damp cave, and lived there until the age of ninety, consigning himself to legend as yet another miracle-performing Alpine hermit. Today, his cave is known as St.-Beatus-Höhlen. It is a popular excursion from Interlaken, and tourists can get there by crossing Lake Thun on the Draschenschiff, the dragon boat, whose prow is fashioned in the shape of a fire-breathing bestial face, while a forked tail curls away over the water to form the vessel's stern.

Dragons also feature prominently in the medieval mythology—and now the tourist lore—of Lucerne. One of the pictures on the city's famed Kapellbrücke, the fourteenth-century wooden bridge crossing the River Reuss, depicts the local hero Arnold von Winkelried slaying a dragon. Winkelried was a real person, a native of Stans, near Lucerne, and was honoured for diverting the attentions of the Austrians in the Battle of Sempach in 1386, leading to his own death but resulting in victory for the Swiss confederates. In 1614, when the artist Heinrich Wägmann painted the designs on the bridge, he chose to portray Winkelried as a near-legendary figure, fighting the most feared of mythical Alpine beasts. Some years later, in 1649, the Sheriff of Lucerne went some way to confirming Wägmann's fabulous vision when he apparently climbed Pilatus and saw a dragon there: "when flying," the sheriff recounted, "it threw out sparks like a red-hot horse-shoe hammered by the blacksmith." Back in Lucerne, and right next to the Kapellbrücke, the city's historical museum keeps as one of its most prized exhibits a smooth and highly polished round stone, a little smaller than a tennis ball, which would appear to confirm the sheriff's sighting. For this brown and cream coloured ball is the famous "dragon stone", apparently dropped by a passing dragon as it flew between Rigi and Pilatus, the great peaks by the shores of Lake Lucerne. According to legend, the stone was picked up by a local peasant in 1421. It instantly became a local curiosity and was believed to cure all manner of maladies. Nowadays, the ancient preoccupation with dragons is nicely mocked by one of the tourist maps of Pilatus, which is covered in cheery red flying lizards—one skiing at the summit, one waving from the windows of the train that winds its way perilously up the mountainside, and one lying on its back wearing sunglasses, sunbathing on the terrace of the Pilatus Kulm hotel where the railway terminates. In twenty-first-century Lucerne, the dragons of Pilatus seem at last to have been subdued, or at least domesticated.

Lucerne is not the only place in the Alps with an apparent dragon fixation. They are also seemingly everywhere in Innsbruck. In one square in that city, Boznerplatz, a fountain built in 1863 to commemorate five centuries of Habsburg rule over the Tyrol is surrounded by dragons proudly bearing shields depicting the Austrian Imperial eagle; behind them, some of their winged cousins spit jets of water, perhaps poking fun at the days when people genuinely believed that surrounding mountains were populated by fire-breathing beasts. Elsewhere in the town, sculptural representations of St. George and a vanquished dragon feature prominently on both the Annasäule monument, built to commemorate the defeat of the Bavarians in 1703, and the funerary monument in the Domkirche to Archduke Maximilian III. In another church, the Hofkirche, a representation of King Arthur, one of a dozen mythical and actual European monarchs who gaze over the empty mausoleum of the Emperor Maximilian, is literally crawling with dragons; depicted as lizards the length of a man's hand, they cling to Arthur's breast plate and shoulders as if they have just landed there.

Dragons are not unique to the Alps—or even to Europe. Ancient Chinese tradition venerated these creatures as lords of the sky and guardians of celestial wisdom; the Christian interpretation was exactly the opposite, that they were winged servants and the embodiment of Satanic evil. That Christianity associated evil beasts with high places has been linked with Christ's temptation, when the devil took Jesus to a high mountain and showed him all the kingdoms of the world (Matthew 4:8). In fact, this might be a clue as to why mountains were seen in the pre-Romantic imagination as inherently bad places, not only in popular mythology but also in high culture; for almost all writers, painters and thinkers before the eighteenth century regarded mountains with near universal loathing and suspicion, and for centuries the pervasive current of European thought assumed that no good could be expected to come out of rocky peaks and deep valleys.

Low Culture, High Art

The medieval and Renaissance imagination venerated neatness and harmony in the countryside. Well-ordered gardens and neatly ploughed fields bounded by hedges were the order of the day. By contrast, mountainous terrain was seen as being terrifying and untameable, belonging to wolves and to unquiet spirits. This attitude was orthodox through the centuries, and lasted well beyond the dark days of the Middle Ages. "There are few who do not prefer the busy scenes of cultivation to the greatest of nature's rough productions," wrote the philosopher William Gilpin in 1791, at the tail-end of what became known as the Age of the Enlightenment. Agriculturally barren and aesthetically repellent—not to mention cold and dangerous—mountains were seen as being an unfortunate blemish on the face of the earth. No wonder that in *Utopia* Thomas More created a race of mountain-dwellers, the Zapoletes, whom he described as a "hideous, savage and fierce race". Two centuries later Samuel Johnson dismissed mountains as "considerable protuberances"—things that got in the way of civilization.

Intrepid travellers crossed the passes of the Alps, for sure, but they entrusted their safety to the communities of monks who manned the hospices at their summits. Some travellers even paid to be carried over passes blindfolded, such was the presumed awfulness of the scenery around them. A Canterbury monk, John de Bremble, passing through the Alps in 1188, was so horrified by what he saw around the Great St. Bernard Pass that he was impelled to mutter a prayer: "Lord, Restore me to my brethren, that I may tell them not to come to this place of torment" (he also discovered that, when he came to write his journal, his ink had frozen solid and his beard was stiff with frost).

Not much had changed by the seventeenth century, when the diarist John Evelyn crossed the Alps on his way to Italy and wrote of being disturbed by the "strange, horrid and fearful" appearance of the mountains. The following century, Bishop Berkely claimed in 1714 that "Every object that here presents itself is excessively miserable." Dozens of similar accounts exist. And the same opinions were expressed in art. Pieter Bruegel the Elder crossed the St. Gotthard to Italy in the 1550s, and used the impressions of fearful precipices and abysmal chasms in his works *The Suicide of Saul* and *The Conversion of St. Paul.* In 1618, the biggest natural disaster in Alpine history occurred, when 2,430 people were killed by an avalanche in Pleurs, near Chiavenne in the Savoy Alps. No wonder that there was no hint, as yet, that mountains could ever be venerated for their beauty in mainstream European culture.

Certainly, no-one ever willingly climbed them—or at least, hardly anyone. Occasionally peaks were climbed by chamois hunters, smugglers or those collecting mountain crystals. One of the earliest instances of a mountain being climbed simply because it was there was the ascent of Mont Inaccessible (2,086m), an isolated table mountain twenty-five miles south of Grenoble, overlooking the village of La Trieves. In 1492 it was climbed at the request of Charles VIII who was travelling to Notre Dame d'Embrun on pilgrimage and heard tales of supernatural manifestations at the top of the mountain. He ordered his chamberlain Antoine de Ville to lead an expedition of ten men up to the summit, to see what was there. (Arguably, the expedition was also an exercise in vertical colonialism. This was the great era of Spanish and Portuguese conquests, and the French were feeling rather left out. To an absolute monarch such as Charles, the very name of the mountain presented a challenge: nothing should be "inaccessible" and beyond the reach of *his* sovereignty.) The expedition used ladders, ropes and hammers in the climb. When the men reached the top they found a mountain meadow picked over by gently grazing chamois—not the dancing angels foretold by local legend. The party stayed on the summit for six days, constructing a primitive chapel, setting up three enormous crosses (as on Calvary), and re-naming the peak Mont Aiguille (Needle Mountain). Oddly, although Ville and his party wrote of living in an "earthly paradise" at the top of the mountain, a party that followed in their footsteps in 1834 found just bare rock at the summit, a far cry from the verdant scene that Ville had described.

Apart from isolated instances such as Ville's 1492 expedition, mountains remained resolutely feared, untamed and unclimbed. But things were slowly changing. With hindsight, Conrad Gesner's ascent of Pilatus in 1555 to tempt the dragon that supposedly slumbered in the lake at the summit marks the beginning of the end of the superstitions surrounding mountains. After his ascent Gesner wrote of the wonder of the peaks, hinting even that they could be beautiful: "Of a truth the highest parts of the loftiest peaks seem to be above the laws that rule our world below," he exclaimed, "as if they belonged to another sphere." He went on to describe the clarity of mountain water, the fragrance of wild flowers, the verdant brilliance of mountain pastures, and the richness of the milk produced by the Alpine cattle; he even sat amidst the peaks and played on his Alpine horn, whose sound he sent booming over the desolate slopes. "[Human] consciousness is in some vague way impressed by the stupendous heights and is drawn to the contemplation of the Great Architect," he wrote, calling the Alps "the theatre of the Lord [where] one might observe... on a single day... the four seasons of the year, spring, summer, autumn and winter... as well as the whole firmament of heaven open to your gaze."

Gesner's was a lone voice, to be sure; but one that was increasingly heard. Although mountains had gone unmentioned in the Creation account in Genesis, some Renaissance thinkers were coming to see them as attesting to the creativity of God. How could mountains, the Biblical scholars wondered, be considered an unfortunate oversight in creation? In *De Venustate Mundi et de Pulchritudine Dei* (*Of the Magic of the World and the Beauty of God*) the Dutch Carthusian Monk Dionysus van Rijkel expressly included mountains among naturally beautiful forms, and declared them to be an indication of divine benevolence (an idea that was contradicted in the 1680s by the Anglican churchman Thomas Burnet, who, as we saw in Part One, considered mountains, along with the Flood, to be part of God's punishment of mankind). By the end of the sixteenth century people were increasingly following the radical leads of Gesner and van Rijkel, losing their fear of the mountains and beginning, for the first time, to appreciate their beauty up close. In 1578 the first detailed maps of the High Alps were prepared by Bern physician and geographer, Johannes Stumpf, while Josias Simler, Professor of Theology at Zurich University, advised walkers on which snowshoes and ropes they should take on expeditions.

The shift in the way of thinking was gradual, but steady and irreversible. The pioneering mountaineer, writer and biographer of the Victorian age, Leslie Stephen, was later to identify the eighteenth century as being a "turning point... [before which] a civilized being might, if he pleased, regard the Alps with unmitigated horror." He was, of course, writing with the benefit of hindsight, but he was right: it was during this century that the view that mountains were places of evil and terror became increasingly, and then decisively, unfashionable. Some of the shift in fashion was undoubtedly the result of the growth in popularity of "natural theology", a doctrine whose premise was that God's grandeur could be appreciated in landscape and that the veneration of nature was a form of worship. According to the champions of the new philosophy, mountains were both spiritually as well as physically elevated. For the first time, the benevolent hand of God was seen to be at work in the mountains.

It must be remembered, however, that this change in how mountains were seen was evolutionary rather than revolutionary. One eighteenth-century writer who did not follow the new creed was Horace Walpole (1717-97), Earl of Oxford and son of the formidable Whig Prime Minister Sir Robert Walpole. He crossed the Alps in 1739 with his old friend from Eton, the future poet Thomas Gray. At that time Walpole was an undergraduate at King's College, Cambridge; he decided to go travelling after enduring yet another damp East Anglian winter. But he did not have a very happy time in the mountains. He described the monks of the Grande Chartreuse, near Grenoble, as "lonely lords of glorious desolate prospects", and later wrote of the mountains: "Such uncouth rocks, and such uncomely inhabitants... I hope I shall never see them again!" In one incident described by Walpole, his King Charles spaniel, the "prettiest, dearest creature" called Tory, was taken by a wolf which darted out from the forest, just as his master was giving the poor creature some air.

Interestingly, Walpole's impressions of the mountains stand in stark contrast with those of Gray. At that time, Gray was training to be a lawyer, but later became one of the most widely-read poets of the eighteenth century. He found majesty and spiritual excitement in the scenery of the Alps, and thought that it represented God's work in its most dramatic form: "Not a precipice, not a torrent, not a cliff, but is pregnant with religion and piety," he wrote. (In his best work Gray was to wax lyrical about the English Lake District and become a well-known chronicler of the sublimity of mountain scenery of his home country.)

As the eighteenth century progressed, it was the response of writers like Gray—and later on, the Romantic poets—that was to inform the way mountains were imagined in intellectual circles, while the views of writers like Walpole were gradually consigned to an earlier, less enlightened age. As for the feared beasts of the mountains, Henry Gotch was able in 1877 to inform the Alpine Club in London that "Goblins and Devils have long vanished from the Alps, and so many years have passed without any well-authenticated account of the discovery of a dragon that dragons too might have assumed to have migrated." By then, as we will shortly see, the Alps had been discovered by tourists, the words of eighteenth-century Romantics such as Byron and Shelley ringing in their ears as they ascended the peaks on newly-built mountain railways. The superstitions of the past seemed to have finally been laid to rest.

Some visitors in the Alps are lucky enough to observe the magnificent effects of the Alpenglow, where the sky seems lit from below by vibrant pink or red light, at dawn or dusk, while the mountains themselves turn a deep mauve. Once it was thought that the brilliant illumination of the heavens and the peaks was caused by the reflection of sunlight off the troves of buried treasure watched over by dragons. Nowadays it is known that the cause of the extraordinary effect has a rational explanation: the reflection of the rays of the rising or setting sun on white snowfields. How wrong the ancient mountain dwellers were, with their fantastic stories and primitive fears. How enlightened we are now, with our appreciation of the beauty of mountains and our scientific understanding of their formation. But of course it is not the mountains that have changed over all that time—it is us.

New Ways of Seeing Mountains: Jean-Jacques Rousseau and Albrecht von Haller

If the cause of the great eighteenth-century transformation in how mountains were seen has to be ascribed to one figure, it would be Jean-Jacques Rousseau (1712-78); in fact Leslie Stephen was later to identify Rousseau's pivotal role in changing our ideas about mountains by declaring that "if Rousseau were tried for the crime of setting up mountains as objects of human worship, he would be convicted by an impartial jury." Rousseau was, of course, a leading intellectual figure of his day—a philosopher, a novelist, a political and social theorist, a composer of operas (and, as he notoriously revealed in his posthumously published autobiography *Confessions*, an obsessive flagellant). Scholars count him as one of the earliest figures in the development of what came to be known as the "Romantic" movement in literature, art and music, which was to bring such figures as Byron and Shelley to the Alps within fifty years of Rousseau's death.

Rousseau was born in Geneva but at the age of sixteen rejected his stultifying Calvinist upbringing and fled to Annecy in the Savoy Alps. There he met the exotic Madame de Warens, who employed him as her steward and converted him to Catholicism—an easy task, Rousseau later wrote, as he was "sure that a religion preached by such a missionary could not fail to lead him to paradise." Her country house was located in the village of Les Charmettes, close to Chambéry, where Rousseau stayed between 1736 and 1742—"a time of innocence", according to his *Confessions*. The house is now preserved, still decorated in eighteenth-century style—and it is not difficult to see what Rousseau found so beguiling about the place, with its music room and its terrace affording a commanding view over the mountains. It was here that Rousseau fell in love with wild scenery; here, perhaps, that some of the first seeds of the Romantic movement and its celebration of Alpine landscapes were sown.

Nearly two decades later, in 1759, after several years spent in the decadent salons of fashionable Paris, Rousseau was staying at another country hideaway. This time it was the home of Madame d'Epinay at Montmorency, north of the French capital. It was here that Rousseau wrote his only novel, *La Nouvelle Héloïse*. This epistolary romance, which gained a large readership in Europe, Britain and America during the last part of the eighteenth century, is set mainly in the villages of Vevey and Clarens, beside Lake Geneva; in fact the work's full English title is *Julie, or the New Eloise: Letters of Two Lovers, Inhabitants of a Small Town at the Foot of the Alps*. The lovers in question are Julie d'Etange, the daughter of an aristocrat, and the middle-class Saint-Preux, the latter clearly based on Rousseau himself.

The novel's crucial importance in the story of how the Alps were re-imagined over the centuries is that it portrays mountains, for perhaps the very first time, as alluring. On one occasion, tortured by the implications of beginning an affair with Julie, who not only belongs to a higher social class than he does but is also his pupil, Saint-Preux seeks calm and solace by going for long walks in the mountains. In a letter to Julie he describes the scenery that engulfs him, the

> immense rocks [which] hung ruinous over my head. Sometimes high and clamorous waterfalls deluged me with their heavy mist. Sometimes a perpetual torrent at my side would open an abyss which my eyes dared not fathom. Sometimes I was lost in the obscurity of a luxurious forest. Sometimes as I emerged from a gorge a pleasant meadow suddenly gladdened my eyes.

The mountains are described as "serene", and in the "purity of that air" Saint-Preux rediscovers his "interior peace". "It seems," he goes on, "that in being lifted above human society, one leaves below all base and terrestrial sentiments, and that as [a man] approaches the ethereal regions, his soul acquires something of their eternal purity. One is serious there but not melancholy, peaceful but not indolent, content to exist and to think." No wonder, with lyrical descriptions like this, that the book is credited with creating a kind of secular mountain worship which went hand-in-hand with the religiously-inspired doctrine of natural theology that had made its mark in the first part of the century. Rousseau went on to write in *Confessions* that "There is a kind of supernatural beauty in these mountainous prospects which charms both the senses and the minds into a forgetfulness of oneself and everything in the world," and maintained that heading into the mountains meant that "the soul imbibes something of their eternal purity... all hardships vanish where liberty reigns and the very rocks are carpeted with flowers."

Rousseau's view of mountains could not be more at odds with those of previous writers. Instead of torment and evil among the high peaks, Rousseau saw tranquility and beauty—the appropriate setting for his intense and passionate love story. But there is a direct link between him and Conrad Gesner, the sixteenth-century dragon-worrier of Lucerne who was one of the earliest writers to dare to suggest that mountains could be beautiful. The link is a Swiss poet named Albrecht von Haller, who like Rousseau was something of a polymath: he was a scientist, mathematician and poet, but also a botanist, geologist and a businessman, the director of the salt works at Bex. In 1732, when Rousseau was twenty, Haller published his poem *Die Alpen*. The work took time to be accepted, particularly in Haller's native Switzerland, but it gained a very secure following abroad, and eventually went through many editions and translations when it finally caught on. The poem's sentimental descriptions of mountain mists and "scenes from another world" include many verses such as these:

When Titan's first rays turn the snowy peak to gold
And his transfigured gaze contains the fog,
Nature's spleandor is seen with renewed vigour
From high above, on a mountaintop...

Not far from the ice, a fertile mountain stretches
its broad back, with meadows rich with fodder;
its gentle slope glistening with ripening grain,
its hills heavy with a hundred herds.

Haller's poem is also credited with creating the mythical ideal of the Alpine peasant—protected from lowland greed and fashion, breathing pure Alpine air, drinking pure Alpine spring water and, as the above verses show, living amidst hills bountiful with grazing herds and ripening crops. The idealized peasant in *Die Alpen* wore the skins of mountain animals and lived happily in a rustic chalet: "Blessed is he who with self-raised oxen can plough the soils of his own fields; who is clothed in pure wool, adorned with wreaths of leaves... who can sleep carefree on soft grass, refreshed by Zephyr's breeze and cool waterfalls... who is satisfied with his lot and never wants to improve it!" The poem also celebrated the mountain dwellers for their attachment to local democracy (which of course was confirmed by the William Tell legend) and their rejection of rule by a centralized bureaucratic government.

Just as Gesner had influenced Haller, the latter's poem was read by Rousseau, leading to the portrayal in *La Nouvelle Héloïse* of the lives of stubborn virtue led by those who lived in the mountains. But Rousseau went further than Haller: in his political writings he championed Switzerland itself as a beacon of democracy and liberty—a sentiment widely expressed elsewhere by writers such as William Coxe, who in

Sketches of the Natural, Civil and Political History of Switzerland (1776) maintained that "Nature designed Switzerland for the seat of freedom." (It is ironic that Rousseau was banished from a number of Swiss cantons following the controversy surrounding his major work of political philosophy, *The Social Contract*; the fuss forced him to seek sanctuary in England and he later had to return to France incognito.)

The work of Haller and particularly Rousseau was ground-breaking. For the first time, the popular imagination was beginning to appreciate mountains—and specifically, the Alps—as places whose wildness could set emotions free rather than hinder the progress of rational thought. It is Rousseau's rejection of the decorum and restraint of the previous era that has given him his scholarly reputation as the spiritual father of Romanticism. But this great change in European thought needed a broader intellectual base than the writings of just one man: and this came in the form of the doctrine of the "sublime", which was to form the predominant current of European thought in the middle of the eighteenth century, and which went out of its way to celebrate wildness and irregularity in landscape.

The Sublime and the Romantic

The Age of the Enlightenment in Europe (which reached its apogee in the early eighteenth century) had celebrated order, regularity and a sense of proportion in the natural world. In keeping with these ideals, by the middle part of the century, all the great houses of England were surrounded by carefully laid-out gardens, complete with fountains and neat lawns (and even the occasional obelisk) that seemed defiantly to reject the apparent randomness of the real countryside. But by the later decades of the century, something strange was happening in the refined world of English country houses: manicured estates were being transformed into symbolic wildernesses, while fountains became grottoes and rocky waterfalls. Suddenly the unkempt became fashionable. One case is that of Richard Hill, who succeeded to the Hawkstone estate in Shropshire in 1783. He developed a cave complex in the grounds of his estate, in which a hermit was paid to live, and also constructed a hundred-metre high hill, named Grotto Hill, from which the views were breathtaking. Dr. Johnson climbed it and remarked that the "ideas which it forces upon the mind are the sublime, the dreadful, and the vast."

Dr Johnson's use of that particular word—"sublime"—was wholly deliberate. The new doctrine of the sublime delighted in chaos, irregularity, cataclysm and fear. Its adherents celebrated wild landscapes for—well—their sheer wildness. Empty deserts, impenetrable forests, frozen ice wastes and, in particular, rugged mountains were newly experienced through fascinated, awe-struck eyes. The chronicler of this way of thinking was the Dublin-born writer and MP Edmund Burke (1729-97), whose 1757 work *A Philosophical Enquiry into the Origin of Our Ideas of the Sublime and the Beautiful* considered the passions evoked in the human mind by terrible scenes. He suggested that things that terrified us also pleased us, through their size, and their complexity, and their hectic uncontrollability, and in particular their sense of danger. According to Burke, mountains inspired in the observer feelings of awe, pleasure and terror—the latter a passion which "always produces delight when it does not press too close." He wrote of the "dark, confused, uncertain images" which took on the imagination through "grander passions than those which are more clear and determinate."

This was why all those neat gardens in English country houses suddenly seemed so unfashionable. Orderliness and regularity were out; untamed wildness was in. One of the best celebrations of the sublime is Rousseau's description in *La Nouvelle Héloïse* of what his heroine Julie calls her "Elysium", the garden close to her house near Clarens on the shores of Lake Geneva: it is "the wildest, the most solitary place in nature… without order and without symmetry"—the very antithesis of lawns and hedges. In fact, Rousseau imagines how a "rich man of Paris or London" would see Julie's Elysium—"with what disdain he would enter this simple and rude place!"—indicating that such a visitor would want to tame it, to cut manicured paths through the foliage and create "fine hedges [that are] well designed, well squared, well contoured! Beautiful plots of fine English grass—round, square, crescent-shaped, oval"—to form a garden replete with trimmed yew trees and bronze vases. The result, Rousseau wrote, would be a "dismal place", a far cry from the wild and untamed "Elysium" that Julie had so assiduously created.

By the end of the eighteenth century the doctrine of the sublime had taken hold, eclipsing the taste for clarity and precision that had characterized the Enlightenment. The brilliance of that *siècle des lumières*—literally, the "century of lights"—was decisively and irredeemably dimmed on the streets of revolutionary Paris. After 1789, reason and order were dead; the Romantics were to embrace the sublime, spurning the rationalism and confidence of the Enlightenment as complacent and spiritually moribund. Above all, the Romantic imagination was to emphasize feelings and sentiment as being the true pathways that writers, artists and musicians would have to follow in the search for spiritual truth. In his *Dictionary* of 1755 Dr. Johnson had described "Romantic" as meaning "full of wild scenery"; this was prescient, because although the word is actually derived from medieval "Romances" (that is, epic stories), many poets, writers and artists of the Romantic era (roughly 1780-1840) came to be known for their celebration of the beauty of mountain landscapes.

Artists whose eyes were caught by the beauty of the Alps included John Robert Cozens (1752-99), whose painting *Between Martigny and Chamonix* (1778) depicts tiny figures on the rocky pass dwarfed by high crags and bold snowfields. The scenery is both magnificent and terrible, very much in keeping with the tradition of the sublime. And what Cozens expressed on canvas, writers were increasingly expressing with words. "I must have torrents, rocks, pines, dead forests, mountains, rugged paths to go up and down, precipices beside me to frighten me, for the odd thing about my liking for precipitous places is that they make me giddy, and I enjoy this giddiness greatly, provided that I am safely placed," Rousseau wrote in *Confessions*, recalling his love for walking in the remoter parts of the Alps. And in *La Nouvelle Héloïse* his heroine Julie justifies her wild and untamed garden by commenting that "it is on the summits of mountains, in the depths of forests, on desert islands that [nature] displays its most affecting charms." The doctrine of the sublime clearly had no better champion than Rousseau, and as we have seen, the Romantic movement was to look no further for an appropriate spiritual father.

There was a further element in the Romantic tradition that was articulated in *La Nouvelle Héloïse* and other works. Not only did the novel describe intense emotions and spontaneous sentiment, but its countryside setting also gave it a new and radical edge. The Age of the Enlightenment, with its love of logic, reason and rationalism, had celebrated the urban cultures of the great classical cities of Athens and Rome. But now

Romanticism looked towards the countryside as the place where man could understand and fulfill himself: as Saint-Preux finds during his mountain walks in *La Nouvelle Heloise*, wild scenery had the power to heal emotional wounds and reveal the truth about sentiment.

Some forty years after the publication of *La Nouvelle Héloïse*, another work of Romantic literature also celebrated the liberating quality of mountains. This, of course, was Schiller's play *William Tell*, whose hunting hero lives the life of one of Haller's idealized peasants, wedded to his bow, his wife, his son and his land. In one of the opening scenes of the play, Tell's son Walter plays with a miniature crossbow while his wife goes about her domestic duties and his father chops wood; "With the cross-bow and his quiver the huntsman speed his way," young Walter sings happily as he sits in the sunshine, "over mountain, dale and river at the dawning of the day." And much of the rest of the play is full of the glories of the mountains, expressed in a similar vein: "When the cuckoo is calling, and wood-notes are gay, when flowers are blooming in dingle and plain, and the brooks sparkle up in the sunshine of May," sings a herdsman on the mountains, while later a chamois hunter on a dizzying ridge is undaunted by the "ice-covered wild, where leaf never budded, nor spring ever smiled". Like Haller's peasants, the hunters, horsemen, and tough farmers who populate the play seem wedded to their mountain environment, which gives them an identity and lends their characters strength and purpose. None of it could have happened before the dawning of Romanticism.

Taking their lead from new literary fashion, whether it was Rousseau or Schiller, tourists in Europe began to want to see mountains, rather than cities, or classical remains by the Mediterranean. One of them was the poet Byron, who called Switzerland "the most Romantic region of the world", and wrote in *Childe Harold's Pilgrimage* that "to me/High mountains are a feeling, but the hum/Of human cities torture." His writing, along with that of Wordsworth, Shelley and other Romantic poets, came to define the way we perceive mountains today, and formed the decisive shift away from the "terrible" towards the "beautiful".

English Romantics in the Alps: Wordsworth, Byron and Shelley

With the emphasis of Romanticism on meditation and solitude, it is no wonder that poets and writers were in love with high places; after all, where better to think lofty thoughts than at the top of a mountain? Spiritual enlightenment and a fine view came to be a standard part of the Romantic package. Charles Darwin recognized this in 1836 when he wrote that "Everyone must know the feeling of triumph and pride which a grand view from a height communicates to the mind." So did Ralph Waldo Emerson, who in 1860 remarked in *The Conduct of Life* that "The influence of fine scenery, the presence of mountains, appeases our irritations and elevates our friendships." An even greater champion of the elation of being high up was the French academic and Alpinist Horace-Bénédict de Saussure, one of the earliest climbers of Mont Blanc. His experience of mountains seems to have been almost transcendental. "What language can reproduce the sensations... which these great spectacles [mountains] fill the soul of a philosopher who is on top of a peak?" he wrote, adding that one could "dominate our globe... [and] recognize the principal agents that affect its revolutions."

Many poets all over the Alps began to celebrate the beauty of the mountains in their own languages. Of particular note was the Slovene poet France Prešeren (1800-1849), who became a major figure in the development of his country's national identity, writing about Lake Bohinj and other places around the idyllic Lake Bled, where he was born. His image is still on 1,000-*tolar* notes and his words form the Slovene National Anthem. Another similarly lyrical poet was Lamartine, whose famous poem *Le Lac* celebrates the Lac du Bourget, with its rugged shoreline and the changing colour of its surface through the seasons.

The beauty of the Alps was also described in English, by poets who travelled there from England, including Wordsworth, Byron and Shelley. Wordsworth was the earliest of the three, and his work embraces the tenets of the sublime as well as the traits of the Romantics. In fact, he pays tribute to Edmund Burke, the chronicler of the sublime, in his posthumously published verse autobiography *The Prelude*. Part of this poem describes a walking tour of the Alps that Wordsworth undertook in 1790, when he was an undergraduate at Cambridge. This tour of Europe was monumentally ambitious: he journeyed three thousand miles, two thousand of which were on foot—and this in the days when only the poor undertook pedestrian travel. His companion Robert Jones recalled that the two were "early risers... [we] generally walked twelve or fifteen miles before breakfast, and after feasting on the morning landscape afterwards feasted on our dejeuner whatever the house might afford." After following the valley of the Rhône, and visiting the "wondrous vale of Chamounix", the pair crossed the Simplon Pass, where Wordsworth wrote in *The Prelude* of being awe-struck by "Nature's... Alpine throne"; when he descended the Simplon Pass he described entering "a narrow chasm" where

> Winds thwarting winds, bewildered and forlorn,
> The torrents shooting out from the clear blue sky,
> The rocks that muttered close upon our ears,
> Black drizzling crags that spake by the wayside
> As if a voice were in them...

And later, he summed up the scene as being "like the workings of one mind, the features"

> Of the same face, blossoms upon one tree;
> Characters of the Great Apocalypse,
> The types and symbols of Eternity
> Of first, and last, and midst, and without end.

When he left the Alps, Wordsworth wrote that "the idea of parting from them oppresses me with a similar sadness to what I have always felt in quitting a beloved friend... I feel a high enjoyment in reflecting that perhaps scarcely a day of my life will pass in which I shall not derive happiness from these images." Of course, Wordsworth was most famously celebrated for wandering lonely as a cloud among the hills and valleys of another mountainous region—the Lake District of his native England. For this reason, his writing about the Alps has been overshadowed by the work of two English poets who followed him to the mountains and whose names often seem inseparable from one another, and from the scenery they described: Percy Bysshe Shelley (1792-1822) and George Gordon, Lord Byron (1788-1824).

Byron and Shelley first met on the jetty of the Hotel d'Angleterre at Sechéron outside Geneva in 1816. Byron had been at Harrow and Cambridge, where he had gained a reputation for high-spirited behaviour. In 1812 he published the first part of *Childe Harold's*

Pilgrimage after which he remarked "I awoke one morning and found myself famous." Four years later, and still very famous, Byron travelled to Switzerland in a huge copy of Napoleon's coach with his valet, his footman, his Swiss guide and his Italian physician. It was the break-up of his year-long marriage to Annabella Millbanke that had forced him to flee London; the gossip surrounding a possible relationship with his own half-sister, as well as the visit of the bailiffs to his house in Piccadilly Terrace to collect unpaid debts, ensured that Byron would spend the rest of his life in Europe.

Shelley, like his new friend, was a minor aristocrat whose education was wholly in keeping with that of an English gentleman of the day. But after Eton he was thrown out of Oxford for writing a pamphlet entitled *The Necessity of Atheism,* and by the time he met Byron, at the age of twenty-four, he had already fathered two children through a failed marriage to Harriet Westbrook. She drowned herself in the same year that Shelley came to the Alps with his new mistress, Mary Wollstonecraft Godwin. Both men had been inspired to travel to the mountains through their reading of early works of Romantic literature such as *La Nouvelle Héloïse*; more practically, their travels were made easier by the ending of the Napoleonic wars in Europe, which we will see in the chapter brought unprecedented numbers of visitors to the continent in the early part of the nineteenth century.

At the time of their meeting Byron was the subject of intense gossip and curiosity; if the early nineteenth century had anything approaching a celebrity-fixated culture similar to today's, he was at the heart of it. In particular, Byron was watched constantly (even through telescopes) by onlookers interested in his romance with Claire Claremont. Weary of all this attention, Byron asked Shelley to dine with him alone on the evening of their fateful meeting; Shelley accepted and a remarkable literary partnership was born. Soon they were staying in neighbouring villas at Cologny with their respective partners: Byron in the Villa Diodati, and Shelley in the Maison Chapuis. After a spell of bad weather kept them confined to their villas, the two men took to the waters of the lake for a week, taking with them not much more than Shelley's Swiss boatman, Maurice, and a copy of *La Nouvelle Héloïse,* which Shelley worshipped.

With Rousseau's novel as their guide, the poets visited Meillerie, where Julie and Saint-Preux had walked hand-in-hand and inscribed their names on stones. They also walked in the Elysian Garden in Clarens, but were disappointed that Julie's wild garden had been turned into a monastery vineyard. At one point on their travels, a storm on the lake reminded them that Rousseau's lovers had escaped a watery end during similarly bad weather. But their itinerary also took in many of the conventional tourist sights of Lake Geneva too. When in tourist rather than literary mode, the two men often behaved like arrogant dandies, such as when they landed at Évian, on the Savoy side of the lake, and found they had forgotten their passports. Rather than going back to fetch them, Shelley promptly announced in a loud voice that his travelling companion was none other than "George Gordon, the sixth Lord Byron, an Englishman—like myself"; Byron, who had once met the King of Sardinia (the ruler of Savoy at the time) at the opera in London, threatened to speak to the monarch personally if they were not let through.

Their visit to the Château de Chillon must have been rather more fulfilling, and has certainly gained a prominent place in literary history. Byron and Shelley were drawn to this enigmatic castle on the lake shore by the story of François Bonivard, who as we have seen earlier, was imprisoned there in the sixteenth century. With the Romantic imagination celebrating the theme of freedom, it was not surprising that the two poets ended up here. They were simply following in the footsteps of recent literary tradition. Burke had championed the rights of slaves, the Irish, and the American colonists, and Rousseau had written extensively on the theme of social injustice; Byron, moreover, was to meet his end at the age of thirty-five, helping the Greeks in their fight for independence from the Turks. Both poets wrote extensively of their own love of liberty and hatred of tyranny and oppression; the place where Bonivard had been imprisoned would have been an unmissable draw. (On their trip around the lake, Byron and Shelley also visited St. Martin's Church in Vevey, where there are memorials to Bishop Ludlow and General Broughton, who had been signatories to Charles I's death warrant; the pair had fled to Vevey at the time of the Restoration.) According to Rousseau, Bonivard was "a Savoyard who loved liberty and toleration", and the two poets from England were anxious to see the exact place where he was chained. During their visit, Byron famously carved his name on one of the pillars of Bonivard's dungeon; it is the

third along from the entrance, and the inscription is now reverentially protected by a sheet of glass which has been rounded to fit the shape of the pillar. (The letters, which simply spell "Byron", are formed in bold block capitals that slope towards the final letter "N".)

The graffiti is almost as famous as the poem that Byron wrote about Bonivard, *The Prisoner of Chillon*. In the poem, Bonivard is imprisoned with his two brothers (chained to the dungeon's first and second pillars) who die, leaving Bonivard to contemplate his captivity alone. After their deaths he looks out of the "barr'd windows" of his dungeon and sees the "mountains high" and longs for the freedom of the world outside:

> I saw their thousand years of snow
> On high—the wide long lake below,
> And the blue Rhone in fullest flow;
> I heard the torrents leap and gush
> O'er channell'd rock and broken bush;
> I saw the white-walled distant town,
> And whiter sails go skimming down.

But when he is finally released there is the tiniest tinge of regret. Bonivard had grown to enjoy the company of the spiders and mice with whom he shared his cell. He had been imprisoned so long that

> My chains and I grew friends
> So much a long communion tends
> To make us what we are:—even I
> Regain'd my freedom with a sigh.

Byron wrote his poem at the Hotel de l'Ancre, now the Hotel d'Angleterre, at Ouchy, near Montreux. He was so immersed in his work that Shelley was often left to dine alone before he got on with his own writing—he was at that time working on the *Hymn to Intellectual Beauty*, a personal homage to Rousseau and *La Nouvelle Héloïse*. But soon after their trip around the lake and their stay at Ouchy, the two men went their separate ways, all the while indulging in yet more literary creativity. Shelley took his wife Mary, and Byron's lover Claire (who was Mary's half-sister) to Savoy, while Byron stayed in Switzerland, residing for a time at Montbovan, a tiny village situated between Montreux and Gruyères on the western fringes of the Bernese Oberland. There he wrote in his *Alpine Journal* of "the music of cowbells in the pastures... and the shepherds shouting from crag to crag and playing on their reeds... I realized all that I ever heard of or imagined of a pastoral existence... I have lately re-peopled my mind with Nature." He described the cottages and cows in the surrounding countryside as being "like a dream; something too brilliant and wild for reality" and wrote that, through his works composed in the Alps, he tried to "lose my own wretched identity in the majesty, and the power, and the glory, around, above and beneath me."

Shelley, meanwhile, was in Chamonix. When Samuel Taylor Coleridge (1772-1834) had passed this way, he had written "Who would be, who could be an atheist in this valley of wonders?" in his *Hymn before Sunrise in the Vale of Chaumoni.* Shelley provided an answer to Coleridge's question by signing himself into a Chamonix guest house in Greek as "Democrat, great lover of mankind and atheist". Aside from making witty remarks in hotel registers, Shelley was overawed by the scenery around the town. He wrote in one of his letters that "I never imagined what mountains were before... the immensity of these aerial summits excited, when they suddenly burst upon the sight, a sentiment of ecstatic wonder not unallied to madness." The experiences moved him to write one of his most famous poems, the *Ode to Mont Blanc.*

> Where power in likeness of the Arve comes down
> From the ice-gulfs that gird his secret throne,
> Bursting through these dark mountains like the flame
> Of lightning through the tempest; - thou dost lie,
> Thy giant brood of pines around thee clinging,
> Children of elder time, in whose devotion
> The chainless winds still come and ever came
> To drink their odours, and their mighty swinging
> To hear—an old and solemn harmony...

Shelley later wrote of his poem that it was "an undisciplined overflowing of the soul... composed under the immediate impression of the close and powerful feelings excited by the objects which it attempts to describe." But unlike Wordsworth, the atheistic Shelley did not see the manifestation of the hand of God in the beauty of the mountains; nor, like Wordsworth (and before him Haller) did he idealize the seemingly robust and healthy life of the Alpine peasant. In fact, the writings of all the Romantics approached the mountains in different ways: if Wordsworth saw the mountains as being spiritually uplifting, then Shelley and Byron saw them as being sources of inspiration and enlightenment, while Rousseau looked towards the moral benefits of contact with high, beautiful and inspiring countryside. Hand-in-hand with such poetic and moral concerns were scientific advances which led to new understanding of the geology, glaciology, and botany of the Alpine environment. This combination of the aesthetic and scientific caused the great shift in the way that mountains were perceived and represented during the early decades of the eighteenth century.

Romanticism was the culmination of a trend which, through Haller and Rousseau, finally killed off the dragons and demons that had plagued the Alps since time immemorial. Yet, surprisingly, the Romantic tradition—or rather its literary offshoot, the Gothic novel—was to spawn one final creature that spent time lurking among the glaciers and rocky peaks. The creature was the hideous "child" of a fictional scientist, Victor Frankenstein, and the creator of this dark fantasy was none other than Percy Shelley's wife, Mary.

Mary Shelley and *Frankenstein*

Mary was born in 1797, the daughter of the philosopher William Godwin and the radical feminist writer Mary Wollstonecraft. Shelley was an admirer of Godwin's work and often came to his house; he met Mary when she was just seventeen. Two years later they married, following the death of Shelley's first wife, and they travelled together to Switzerland in 1816.

Mary Shelley's most famous work was conceived on the shores of Lake Geneva. Shortly after Byron and Shelley's trip on the lake, a period of bad weather set in which confined the poets and their respective partners to their villas. Mary described the thunderstorms that boomed overhead as being "grander and more terrific than I have ever seen before." During one appropriately stormy night, Byron came up with the idea that each of them should think up a ghost story and recount it to the rest of the party. Mary writes in her introduction to *Frankenstein* that she wanted to create a story "which would speak to the mysterious fears of our nature and awaken thrilling horror [which would] make the reader dread to look round, to curdle the blood, and quicken the beatings of the heart." Her story, which was eventually published in 1818, concerned a native of Geneva, a scientist named Victor Frankenstein, who builds a creature that takes on a life of its own. Mary Shelley describes the monster as being "the hideous phantasm of a man stretched out and then... shows signs of life, and stirs with an uneasy, half-vital motion."

The novel is set in many parts of Europe, including Ingolstadt in Bavaria, where Frankenstein builds his creature, and London, St. Petersburg and Archangel, the frozen city in Arctic Russia where Victor pursues and finally kills his creation. But the opening is set in Belrive, on the eastern shores of Lake Geneva. Here the fifteen-year-old Victor observes one of the region's famed thunderstorms crashing over the water, which sets his scientific mind racing. "I stood at the door, [and] on a sudden I beheld a stream of fire issue from an old and beautiful oak which stood about twenty yards from our house; and so soon as the dazzling light vanished, the oak had disappeared, and nothing remained but a blasted stump... reduced to thin ribbons of wood." Seeing this noble tree destroyed by lightning introduces Victor to the potential of electricity—the method by which he eventually breathes life into his monster.

The Gothic novel was a literary genre that grew out of the Romantic fascination with the bizarre, the supernatural and the exotic. But there are also elements in Mary Shelley's descriptive writing that are straight out of the pre-Romantic tradition of the sublime, where terror mixed with awestruck fascination seizes anyone who confronts nature in its rawest, most spectacular form. Another thunderstorm on Lake Geneva is described as making the lake "appear like a vast sheet of fire... so beautiful yet terrific". Later, the scientist follows his creature into the Arve valley near Chamonix, described in ways very familiar to those familiar with the work of Edmund Burke.

> The abrupt sides of vast mountains were before me; the icy wall of the glacier overhung me... these sublime and magnificent scenes afforded me the greatest consolation that I was capable of receiving. They elevated me from all littleness of feeling... the unstained snowy mountaintop, the glittering pinnacle, the pine woods and the ragged bare ravine, the eagle, soaring amidst the clouds—they all gathered round me and bade me be at peace.

The Mer de Glace, which Mary visited with her husband, is described as being "awful and majestic... a terrifically desolate spot... [which] filled me with a sublime ecstasy." In the novel, Frankenstein follows his creation across the ice to a remote mountain hut, where for the first time the creature begins to tell his creator the extraordinary story of his life—and Mary Shelley's dark and terrifying fantasy begins slowly to unfold.

John Ruskin: the Alps in Art

Nearly twenty years after Byron and Shelley forged their remarkable literary partnership on the shores of Lake Geneva, a thirteen-year-old boy from England named John Ruskin (1819-1900) was getting his first glimpse of the Alps from the city of Schaffhausen in northern Switzerland. He was there with his parents, who were taking him on a journey around Europe prior to his training for the priesthood. "The Alps," Ruskin later remembered, "were as clear as crystal, sharp on the pure horizon sky, and already tinged with rose by the sinking sun. [The scene was] infinitely beyond all that we had ever thought or dreamed... it is not possible to imagine a more blessed entrance into life." And he goes on to make a claim that acknowledges just how much the Romantics had changed everything about how people looked at mountains. "True," he wrote, "the temperament belonged to the age: a very few years before, no child could have been born to care for mountains, or for the men that lived among them, in that way."

Ruskin never fulfilled his parents' wishes of following a career in the church. Instead, he became one of the leading intellectual figures of the nineteenth century, a well-known painter, writer, architectural

historian and social theorist who in 1869 was appointed the first Slade Professor of Fine Art at Oxford. He travelled extensively and his 1856 book *Of Mountain Beauty*, the fourth volume of his seminal five-volume work *Modern Painters* (published 1843-60), defined how mountains were seen in the immediate post-Romantic period. In it he declared that "Mountains are the beginning and end of all natural scenery," and said more about how our way of looking at mountain scenery had changed forever: "Those desolate and threatening ranges of dark mountain, which in nearly all ages of the world men have looked upon with aversion or terror and shrunk back from as if they were haunted by perpetual images of death are, in reality, sources of life and happiness far fuller and more beneficent than all the bright fruitfulness of the plains."

Ruskin famously fell in love with the Matterhorn, writing that "the effect of this strange Matterhorn upon the imagination is so great that even the greatest philosophers cannot resist it." But, perhaps surprisingly, he came to the conclusion that the mountains were not jagged at all—they were curved, if you looked at them carefully enough, and mountain ranges were arranged in waves; moreover, they were not static but were in a constant state of change and motion. That initial view from Schaffhausen was to define his whole outlook: unlike the Romantics, who saw jagged rocks almost everywhere they looked, Ruskin viewed mountains from afar and saw grace and roundedness in the peaks. He was enthralled at the "endless perspicuity of space, the unfatigued veracity of eternal light" which characterized the Alps. His feeling for mountains was almost spiritual: in his own mind, Mont Blanc was really "Mount Beloved"—a far cry from the name given to it by the residents of Chamonix, who once called it "The Accursed". (Throughout his life, he always preferred looking at mountains from a distance, and rarely climbed them. "All the best views of hills are at the bottom of them," he wrote; during a visit to Stresa, on Lake Maggiore, he ascended Monte Mottarone, which towers above the town, and called it "the stupidest of mountains", while the top of the St. Gotthard was likewise "very dull and stupid.")

According to his obituarist Douglas Freshfield, a fellow Alpinist, Ruskin "saw and understood mountains, and taught our generation to understand them in a way no-one had ever understood them before...

no writer has added so much to our appreciation of Alpine scenery." But Ruskin did much more than wax lyrical about spectacular scenery; he played an important role in determining how the Alps were conceptualized by artists. As an art critic he championed the work of the English landscape artist J. M. W. Turner, bringing to public attention many of Turner's works such as *Hannibal Crossing the Alps* and *The Passage of Mount St. Gotthard,* in addition to Turner's various views of well-known spots such as the Rigi and the Château de Chillon. Turner's handling of colour and the expressive dynamism of his work was new and radical and upset and confused many of his contemporaries. But through *Modern Painters* Ruskin introduced Turner's works into the public arena—and he later painted many fine Alpine scenes himself. Gradually, and partly through Ruskin's encouragement, artists like Turner began to capture in paint and oils the drama of mountain scenery that had been described so well in words by the Romantic poets in the previous decades.

But Ruskin was writing in a very different era to that of Shelley and Byron. By the mid-nineteenth century scientists, artists, writers, tourists and climbers were seemingly jostling for position on virtually every peak. Knowledge and understanding of the Alpine environment was improving all the time, and, as we have seen in Part One, it was realized that mountains were not permanent and fixed, but were dynamic places, subject to immense and ongoing change. In 1805 the English scientist Humphry Davy wrote that "to the geological enquirer, every mountain chain offers striking monuments of the great alterations that the globe has undergone. The most sublime speculations are awakened, the present is disregarded, past ages crowd upon the fancy..." Leslie Stephen also recognized this when he wrote in 1871 that "Our imaginations may be awed when we look at the mountains as monuments of the slow working of stupendous forces of nature through countless millenniums."

Perhaps this sense of scientific awe went some way to underpinning Ruskin's ethereal love of the mountains: he saw their ridges and peaks as the crests of waves blown by some scarcely understandable geological tempest. And like Wordsworth, he also saw mountains as being blessed with spiritual and religious significance. In *Of Mountain Beauty* he observed:

... in the hills the purposes of their Maker have indeed been accomplished... the best image the world can give us of paradise is in the stage of the meadows, orchards and cornfields of the sides of a great Alp with its purple rocks and eternal snows above... mountains are the great cathedrals of the earth, with their gates of rock, pavements of clouds, choirs of stream and stone, altars of snow... they seem to have been built for the human race.

Yet Ruskin deplored the interest in the mountains that was sparked at least in part by his own writing; tourists and other visitors drew steely contempt from his pen, and he condemned the "convulsive hiccoughs of self-satisfaction" shown by mountaineers who had reached a summit, writing that this new breed of mountain visitor had none of the reverential respect towards the Alps shown by poets of earlier generations. Instead, mountaineers were accused by Ruskin of turning the Alps into "racecourses", and of regarding mountains "as soaped poles in a bear garden, which you set yourselves to climb, and slide down again, with shrieks of delight." But Ruskin was fighting a rearguard action. By the time of his death, in the first year of the twentieth century, the Alps had seeped firmly into contemporary consciousness, and the tide of mountaineers and visitors was by then unstoppable. Ruskin ended his life watching Canute-like as his own works became submerged beneath an encroaching sea of true-life adventure stories and popular fiction set amidst the peaks.

Heidi and Kekec

As the Alps came to feature in more and more writers' works, and were celebrated both for the beauty of their scenery and for the honest, hard-working qualities of the people who lived in them, the mountains were soon grabbing the imagination of children's authors as an ideal setting for their stories. One was Johanna Spyri (1827-1901), who grew up in the village of Hirzel above Lake Zurich, tending goats and (one imagines) spending her childhood days skipping around the wild meadows, picking the pretty flowers and watching the sunlight glimmer on the shimmering water below—an ideal upbringing for the author of the most famous Alpine story for children, *Heidi*, which was published in 1880. Set in the hills above the small town of Maienfeld, just north of

Chur, *Heidi* is the story of a recently orphaned young girl who is sent to live in the mountains with her grumpy old grandfather (known as "Uncle Alp"). To most children the tragic loss of their parents, combined with the fate of being marched up a mountainside to live with an unlovable elderly relative, would be the recipe for a fairly miserable existence; but Spyri's plot has more holes in it than the proverbial Swiss cheese, and instead of feeling sorry for herself Heidi has the time of her life in her new home. She makes friends with a young goatherd, Peter, and with his goats too (who are given names like Dusky, Daisy and Snowflake). She delights in watching the changing seasons in the mountains, in the winter snow and the summer flowers and the wind in the trees, and spends a lot of her time with Peter as he takes his goats off to their various different pastures. But then Heidi is suddenly whisked off to Frankfurt to be a companion to a wheel-chair-bound invalid, Clara. When she returns to Maienfeld, and Clara follows soon after, Peter is jealous of all the attention Heidi pays to Clara, so he pushes the girl's wheelchair off the mountain: "with wicked glee he watched it, far below, bouncing off the rocks and leaping on until it crashed to its final destruction... he told himself that now that horrid girl would go away and everything would be as before." Peter is found out, of course, but instead of a receiving dire punishment from Uncle Alp as he fears, he is praised for his deeds, as the disappearance of the chair has meant that Clara is encouraged to learn to walk. After which, everything is right again.

Johanna Spyri's self-righteous parable of goodness and faith has proved attractive to film-makers over the years. In 1937 the title role was played by Shirley Temple, the ubiquitous child star of pre-war Hollywood; her characteristically bright eyes and winning smile go some way towards masking the fact that the mountain scenery behind her was really painted backdrops in a California movie studio. In 1977 German television managed to spin the story out into twenty-seven half-hour episodes. The latest screen adaptation, an English-language film released in Britain in 2005, stars the veteran Swedish actor Max von Sydow as Uncle Alp, and was filmed in Slovenia and Wales.

In fact, very few of the screen adaptations of the book have actually been filmed on location in the Alps, and really the story could have been set in any mountainous context—but this has not stopped Maienfeld from cashing in on its Heidi connections. The little town sits on the banks of the River Rhine as it flows north from Chur towards Liechtenstein and Lake Constance. Its centre, with tall shuttered houses and sloping cobbled square, is undeniably pretty, but a twenty-minute walk from here is the execrable Heidiland, which is centred on the hamlet of Oberrofels (now renamed Heididorf). Here there is an attractive old chalet, built in the traditional manner using stone and wood, which has been converted into a museum to show how Heidi would have lived—complete with heavy ancient furniture, an authentically soot-blackened kitchen, logs piled high under the eaves and dingy rooms with small windows, in one of which a mannequin Heidi sits at a table teaching a mannequin Peter the Goatherd how to read. This is called "the original Heidi House" but there is no evidence that Spyri was thinking of this (or any other) chalet when she wrote the book.

A good hour's walk up the hill from Heididorf, through thick woodland that opens out into a beautiful summer meadow whose sweeping views along the Rhine valley stretch all the way to Chur, is another piece of Heidiland whimsy, the Heidi-Alp, a remote cottage where Uncle Alp supposedly lived. Of course, it is nothing of the sort, but when I was there, the white-haired man who owned the place was enjoying posing for photographs for visiting tourists, who possibly thought they had stumbled on the real Uncle Alp, living in a remote cottage on a sunny mountain meadow.

Over two hundred miles east of Maienfeld, another part of the Alps is indelibly linked with another fictional child. But there are significant differences between Heidi and Kekec, the "clever shepherd boy" of the Julian Alps in Slovenia. For a start, and most obviously, Kekec is a boy and a child who has grown up in the mountains, rather than one sent to live there from the big city. In addition, Heidi seems to have seeped into the consciousness of the entire western world, whereas Kekec seems little known outside his native Slovenia. His creator, Josip Vandot (1883-1940), was born in the remote Alpine village of Kranjska Gora, situated where Slovenia comes face to face with both Italy and Austria. Vandot's stories of the relentlessly cheerful, cunning and brave shepherd boy, who gets out of the most fiendish scrapes and always ends up saving the day, are based on popular oral tradition of this part of the Alps. Only one book, *Kekec From Our Mountains* (1936), was published while the author was alive; others, published posthumously, had titles such as *Kekec above the Solitary Precipice* (1952) and *Kekec on the Wolf's Track* (1957).

As with *Heidi*, the combination of charming children and magnificent scenery has meant that the Kekec stories had strong appeal to film-makers; three Kekec films were made, in 1951, 1963 and 1969, with different boy actors taking the role of the clever shepherd each time. In the 1951 film, which won the best children's film award at the Venice Film Festival, the young hero frees a herb-picker who has been tied to a tree by the evil poacher Bedanc. He then makes Bedanc promise he will leave the area while the poacher is dangling over a precipitous abyss; the man keeps his promise, and Kekec, the only person in the district who has stood up to him, is the hero of the day. By the time of the 1963 film *Good Luck Kekec* (*Srečno Kekec*), the magnificent scenery of the Trenta Valley immediately south of Kranjska Gora was in full colour, showing off its pale rocky crags and green meadows and carpets of wild flowers; so, too, was Kekec himself, in his jaunty yellow hat, orange jacket and brown lederhosen. On this occasion our young hero (aged around twelve in the films) helps a blind girl, Mojca, miraculously recover her sight after leading her across a raging torrent at the bottom of a gorge.

According to the films, the Trenta Valley was a fairy-tale mountain area filled with grazing cows, obedient herds of sheep, occasional (and benign) brown bears, merry peasants, quaint houses with smoke billowing from chimney stacks, and inhabited by the irrepressible Kekec himself, marching along with his shepherd's crook, playing his mouth organ and even bursting into occasional song or a screech-like yodel that echoes around the hills. Little hint is given that the main features of the area in the time the books were set were grinding poverty, harsh winters, remoteness and isolation; but then, like Heidi, the Kekec books take their leads from earlier writers such as Haller, Rousseau and Schiller, who ignored the poverty of the Alps and saw only hard-working peasants living an honest and life-enhancing existence among the magnificent scenery.

Although Kekec is much-loved in Kranjska Gora—a company there even shows the films in an outdoor cinema in summer—the books have never been translated into English, and the films have had only minimal showings outside Slovenia. Kranjska Gora, meanwhile, has been transformed from simple peasant village into the biggest winter sports centre in that country: modern hotels, sports shops and ski lifts jostle for space with the barns and traditional wooden houses that Josip Vandot would have recognized. And in summer, the village is the starting point for walkers visiting the Trenta Valley, whose corkscrew-twisting road runs over the Vršič Pass (1,611m) under the shadow of high, near-vertical limestone cliffs that rise like teeth above this wonderful corner of the Alps.

The Alps in Nazi Ideology

By the 1920s and 1930s, the Alps had become a prettily-packaged stereotype, defined by chocolate, Heidi, cowbells, cuckoo clocks, glistening lakes and that most familiar of mountains, the almost pyramid-perfect Matterhorn. "Mad" King Ludwig had built his cod-medieval castle at Neuschwanstein, a Romantic vision in both the artistic and popular sense of that word. The nineteenth century had witnessed huge growth in mountain tourism, and the Alps were busy with skiers in winter and walkers in summer, who were all part of an urbanized western culture that venerated the mountains as somewhere offering an easily accessible wilderness (which by then was not actually terribly wild any more).

As we have seen, mountain scenery has always been interpreted in the way different cultures want it to be; responses to it are devised according to collective memory and experience. Mountains, like any environment, may stay largely the same, but the way of imagining them has undergone radical shifts. And in the third decade of the twentieth century came the final twist in the story of how the Alps are interpreted through the prism of a particular culture.

The adulation of mountains espoused so strongly in Nazi ideology has its beginnings in the popular series of *Bergfilme* (mountain films) made by the German film director Arnold Fanck (1889-1974) at the same time as Hitler was rising to power. Fanck's first encounter with mountains had come at the age of eleven, when he spent some weeks in the spa of Davos, high in the Swiss Alps, having his chronic childhood asthma cured in the crystal-clear air. His first film, made in 1919, was a documentary entitled *The Wonders of Skiing*, which depicted the ascent and descent of the Jungfrau; five years later came *Mountain of Destiny*, the first feature film made on location in the Alps. This film was seen in a cinema in Berlin by a young actress and dancer named Leni Riefenstahl, who later wrote that "on screen, the mountains were alive and more entrancingly beautiful than I had ever dreamed they could be... I dreamed of wild mountains crags, I saw myself running across the rocky slopes, and always, the leading performer in the film, the symbol of all the feelings aroused in me." She sought out Fanck and persuaded him she should be in his next film; Fanck duly obliged, and in 1926 *The Holy Mountain* was written specifically for her. This strange film, lasting an hour and three quarters, with no spoken dialogue (the era of "talkies" was yet to dawn), is a surreal mix of dance and dream sequences, interspersed with scenes depicting fast downhill skiing and intrepid, ledge-dangling mountaineering; "a heroic song from the towering world of heights" is how the film introduces itself: "a drama poem with scenes from nature".

The film was made entirely on location in Interlaken, Zermatt (the Matterhorn features prominently) and the Austrian ski resort of St. Anton, glorifying the mountains as arenas for bravery, endurance and the display of physical strength. Riefenstahl, who plays a dancer named Diotima, swirls and pirouettes across the slopes, gazes adoringly at the brave climbers (one of whom she falls in love with), and encounters the hardy peasantfolk of the mountains (including a young boy who in one early scene sits on a rock playing a harmonica while tending his sheep—Peter the Goatherd incarnate). Riefenstahl later claimed Fanck was in love with her—a claim that is easy to accept, given how much his camera seems to dwell on her classically beautiful but often icily unexpressive face—but that she was not interested in reciprocating. Nevertheless, *The Holy Mountain* was the first of six mountain films the pair made between 1926 and 1933. Fanck became notorious for his perfectionist approach, often filming in terrible conditions and on one occasion covering his star with an avalanche that nearly killed her. But as the series progressed Riefenstahl became a nimble mountain-climber as well as dancer, and she started to move behind the camera to direct scenes too; in 1932 she split from Fanck to write, direct, produce and star in *The Blue Light,* filming the slow, pretentious story of a mysterious crystal-hunting mountain-maiden entirely on location in the South Tyrol. All these films introduced a popular Alpine consciousness to Nazi Germany, sparking off an interest in skiing and climbing; to this day the St. Anton Film Festival, held every September, shows the Fanck/Riefenstahl collaborations alongside more recent films about the Alps and winter sports.

Adolf Hitler was not born in the Alps. But his birthplace, the little Austrian town of Braunau-am-Inn, is close to the foothills of the mountains. He loved mountain scenery and in time the Alps came to play an important role in Nazi mythology: for in the mountains lived communities of hard-working white-skinned peasants, toiling in the fields alongside their buxom wives and healthy children, all of which seemed to embody to perfection the "Aryan" ideal. Hitler was a big fan of the *Bergfilme* and of Leni Riefenstahl in particular (after finishing with the mountain films she chronicled the Nazi rise to power on celluloid, and in 1935 made the notorious *Triumph of Will*, which many consider to be the greatest example of propaganda film-making in the history of cinema). Capitalizing on the popularity of Fanck's work, and embracing the films' celebration of the mystical power of mountains, Hitler began to encourage an idolization of mountaineers, who were courageous, physically strong and clearly lived up to fascist ideals of maleness and muscularity.

Mountains themselves presented a challenge to the Nazis in the way that opposing ideologies such as communism did. The unconquered presence of mountains was an affront to the Nazi desire for domination; to climb them was to fight them, to reach the summit was to defeat them. In the 1930s the Reich sponsored teams of young German climbers, known as the Nazi Tigers, to climb various Alpine peaks for the greater glory of Germany and Aryanism. In 1931 two brothers called Schmid cycled from Munich to Zermatt and then climbed the notoriously difficult north face of the Matterhorn. Despite crossing gulleys streaming with water, spending the night hanging on to the narrowest of rock shelves, and facing a ferocious storm just below the summit, the climbers made it and were ecstatically lauded by the German press (although one of the brothers, Toni, was to fall to his death from the Weissbachhorn a few years later). Soon enthusiastic teams of young men known as *Bergkameraden* were cycling to the Alps each summer to embark on ever more daring and dangerous climbs; the successful ones came back to an Aryan hero's welcome and received a personal handshake from Hitler. (Mussolini got in on the act too, giving

Pro Valore medals to successful Italian climbers.)

After the Matterhorn, attention inevitably focused on the challenging north face of the Eiger, also in the Swiss Alps; Hitler believed that only German climbers could succeed on the Eigerwand and promised medals to the first conquerors. When the north face was finally climbed in July 1938, it was by a team of two Germans and two Austrians; appropriately, the face was conquered just a few months after the *Anschluss* had united the two countries politically. The four victorious climbers were later presented to Hitler at a rally in Poland. One of them, Heinrich Harrer, who died in 2006 and whose book about the Eiger, *White Spider*, has become a classic mountaineering text, told Hitler he had dedicated the climb to him (although after the war he made strenuous efforts to deny that he had tried to plant a swastika flag on the summit).

Events inspired by the Nazis were taking place, too, in the thin sliver of the Alps that actually lies within German territory. Although they may be lacking in aerial extent, the Bavarian Alps more than make up for this in height: all along the south-eastern fringe of Germany the peaks are mightily steep and the scenery is some of the most ruggedly spectacular anywhere in the Alps. The crowning peak is the Zugspitze, which soars to a height of 2,964 metres. In its shadow is the pretty town of Garmisch-Partenkirchen, which in the 1930s emerged as German's most prestigious winter resort (a position it still holds to this day). Everyone seems to know the story of the 1936 Summer Olympics, staged by Hitler in Berlin to glorify the presumed athletic prowess of Nazi Germany; but the events of the same year's winter games, staged in Garmish-Partenkirchen, seem less well known. A great stadium, with a capacity of sixty thousand, was built in the town for the games; during the events themselves trains left Munich every two minutes crammed with spectators and participants heading for the Alpine resort. (It was suggested by the Germans in the run-up to the games that mountain-climbing should be introduced as a sport, but this was turned down by British and Swiss Olympic delegations.) At the opening ceremony there was disagreement over what form of salute the competing teams should give Hitler: arm raised in front, Nazi-style, or to the side, Olympic style? The British team was led by Peter Lunn, son of the Alpinist and travel agent Arnold Lunn, of whom we shall hear more later; he instructed his team to give the Olympic salute, while the Swiss and American teams gave no salute at all. The look on the Führer's face as these delegations passed must have been a picture: along the same lines, perhaps, as his expression a few months later, when he saw the black American Jesse Owens beat a German runner in the summer games at Berlin.

Hitler's love of the Alps was to change the landscape. Around one hundred and fifty kilometers east of Garmish-Partenkirchen, the border between Austria and Germany takes a distinctive southward plunge, and a small but significant wedge of German territory pushes hard into Austria. It was here, around the resort of Berchtesgaden, that Hitler's love of mountain scenery was expressed in bricks and mortar. He made Berchtesgaden the southern headquarters of the Nazi party, covering an area above the town called the Obersalzburg with party buildings and villas, while on a high mountain ridge above the Obersalzburg was built one of his most notorious legacies, the famed retreat known as the "Eagle's Nest".

Hitler at Berchtesgaden

Berchtesgaden today is a pretty collection of Alpine-style hotels and villas set around a churning mountain river whose waters drain a beautiful, crystal-clear lake, the Königsee. The resort stands at the head of a winding wooded valley, along which run a road and railway line from Munich. (The railway station in the town, the line's terminus, was built by the famed Nazi architect Albert Speer in 1937.) Hitler had first come to Berchtesgaden in the 1920s with his friend Dietrich Eckhardt, a leading member of the German Workers Party. He grew to like the place, with its clear mountain air and possibilities for walking, and made many subsequent visits; his favourite place to stay became the Pension Moritz, whose owners, the Buchners, were early supporters of the Nazi movement. (Hitler wrote the second volume of *Mein Kampf* while he was staying with them, and on one occasion he was given a heavy dog-whip made from hippopotamus hide by Frau Buchner as a gift.)

Later, Hitler bought a villa situated on the sunny stretch of Alpine meadow immediately above Berchtesgaden. It was called the Haus Wachenfeld; the previous owner had been a businessman and keen party member. In 1933 Hitler enlarged the villa and fortified it, and it became known as the Berghof. Over the next ten years this place was to act as

both a home for Hitler—he spent up to six months of each year here—and also the most important focal point of Nazi government outside Berlin. The Führer made sure that everything about the Berghof was appropriately monumental in scale: the view from its Great Hall encompassed a magnificent Alpine panorama, seen from a window that consisted of the biggest single sheet of glass in the world and which could be raised and lowered hydraulically. Other Nazi top brass also had houses and villas nearby, all built in opulent Alpine style, with prettily-decorated wooden balconies and roofs edged with wide gables. The creation of this entire government complex, known as the "Obersalzburg", resulted in the confiscation of thirty-two square kilometres of land and the tearing down of a number of ancient farmhouses. Surrounding the complex were guardhouses and a two-metre-high fence, and underneath it all the government buildings and villas were linked by miles of underground bunkers for use during an attack or siege.

Hitler loved to show off his mountain home to visiting dignitaries. To an extent, the political shape of 1930s Europe was forged in meeting conducted in the villas of the Obersalzburg. One of the first came in 1934 when Kurt Schuschnigg, the weakened and beleaguered Austrian premier, met with Hitler at the Berghof at the suggestion of Franz von Papen, the German ambassador to Austria. When Schuschnigg remarked on the wonderful view from the villa's picture window, Hitler snapped back, "Yes, here my ideas mature. But we haven't come here to talk about the beautiful view and the weather." (During the stormy Berghof meeting, Hitler went on to force to Schuschnigg to appoint more Nazis to the Austrian cabinet: independent Austria was by then in its final death throes, and Schuschnigg's successor, Seyss-Inquart, was to invite the German army into the country, paving the way for the *Anschluss*.)

Two years later, in September 1936, David Lloyd George came for a meeting at the Berghof, exchanging memories of the Great War with Hitler and coming away convinced that the German leader was "a great man". Then in 1938 Hitler hosted Chamberlain at the Berghof during the infamous negotiations that paved the way for the Nazi takeover of Czechoslovakia. (Chamberlain and his entourage stayed in a hotel in Berchtesgaden during the negotiations and travelled to and from Munich in Hitler's personal train.) Another British party that met Hitler here was that of the Duke and Duchess of Windsor (the ex-King Edward VII and former Mrs. Wallis Simpson) who were thought to hold Nazi sympathies. Hitler also had meetings at the Berghof with his senior military staff immediately before the invasions of Poland and Russia; apparently these meetings largely took the form of him shouting loudly and at great length at his terrified underlings, brooking no opposition and telling them to get on with implementing his often wildly over-ambitious orders.

When not busy shaping the course of world events, Hitler liked to relax at the Berghof. (The "fake" musical show *Springtime for Hitler*—the staging of which forms the storyline of the Mel Brooks film *The Producers*—is actually subtitled, *A Gay Romp with Adolf and Eva at Berchtesgaden*.) The Führer had a fixed routine while he was staying here. He would get up late, after watching films the previous evening into the early hours in his personal cinema, and spend the afternoons indulging in lengthy meals with favoured Nazi lackeys. During these occasions he often compared himself with Bismarck, Napoleon and other great figures of European history, or simply droned on for hours about topics ranging from military strategy to why there were no tenors who could sing Wagner well. "He can be Führer as much as he likes, but he always repeats himself and bores his guests," Magda Goebbels once remarked of these dinner parties. During fine days, when the weather was known as *Hitlerwetter* by the locals, he went for long walks, often accompanied by his Alsatian bitch, Blondi. On these occasions thousands of devoted fans and curious onlookers would see if they could catch a glimpse of their leader through binoculars from the surrounding mountainsides. (If they were very lucky, and he passed by, they would gather up the stones from the path where he had walked, and keep them as souvenirs.)

The role of the Obersalzburg changed as the war began to go badly for the Nazis. . On two occasions in 1944, in March and July, assassination attempts were made on Hitler's life at the Berghof. The second attempt was by a lieutenant colonel, Claus von Stauffenberg, who took a briefcase bomb into a conference but decided not to set it off as Himmler and Goering were not present at the time. (Nine days later von Stauffenberg orchestrated the most famous assassination attempt on Hitler, when he detonated a bomb in the Führer's East Prussia military headquarters.) Hitler was by then very wary of his personal safety and spent less and less time at the Berghof. One of his last visitors was Leni Riefenstahl, who came here in March 1944 shortly after her marriage to a prominent Nazi officer; by that time she had fallen somewhat from the political scene, and was living in a remote farmhouse near Kitzbühel in the Tyrol, directing and editing a pet project entitled *Tiefland* and barely registering the allied bombers that flew overhead almost daily. (*Tiefland*, based on an opera by Dalbert and not released until 1954, is full of artfully-shot monochrome images of Tyrolean scenery; Riefenstahl was later fiercely condemned for her use of gypsies from an Austrian concentration camp as extras in the film.) Of her meeting with Hitler, she recalls in the remarkable three-hour documentary film. *The Wonderful, Horrible Life of Leni Riefenstahl*, that when she visited the Berghof the Führer was, by that late stage of the war, "distracted... he no longer seemed like a man in touch with reality... he was more like a ghost."

The following year, as the allies advanced on Berlin, Hitler abandoned the Berghof for good and commanded what remained of his troops from his beloved capital city. On 25 April 1945, right at the end of the war in Europe, the whole of the Obersalzburg complex was bombed to rubble by the RAF, whose planes dropped over twelve hundred bombs in the space of just ninety minutes; by then, Hitler was holed up in his bunker in Berlin, watching the city collapse around him as the allies moved in.

Nowadays the Obersalzburg is given over to tourism, and to the memory of the pivotal role it played during the Nazi era. There is a fine new museum, the Dokumentation Obersalzburg, built on the site of Hitler's former guesthouse. The exhibits and audio-visual displays vividly recall the time when this area was an Alpine playground for the Nazi elite; the museum also gives access to the cold, grey tunnels that formed the Obersalzburg's network of underground stores and bunkers, their crude fixtures and fittings, including rudimentary air-cleaning systems, still in place. Although the museum has been highly praised, controversy came to the Obersalzburg in March 2005 when with "an international hotels group opened a new $120-million hotel a few hundred metres away from the museum, on a site where Bormann and Goering's villas had once stood. The opening of the hotel raised objections from many quarters. Michel Friedman, former deputy head of Germany's Central Council of Jews, commented that "The use of the site as a hotel masks the historical reality. Such places should be preserved and used for a totally different purpose." Lord Janner, chairman of the Holocaust Educational Trust in Britain, said that "They are turning a centre of murder into a tourist attraction... I find it offensive, objectionable and totally unacceptable." The hotel group argued that a book on the history of the region, entitled *Die Tödliche Utopie* (The Deadly Utopia), had been placed in each room, and that the staff were all thoroughly screened for potential Nazi connections. On the hotel's opening day the region around Berchtesgaden experienced temperatures of minus 43 degrees centigrade, one of the coldest ever recorded in Germany.

Between the museum and the new hotel much of the Obersalzburg is covered by an unsightly area of car and coach parks. This is the place from where, in summer, dozens of buses each day transport visitors up the mountainside to Hitler's retreat, the Kehlsteinhaus or "Eagle's Nest" (there is no access for private cars, which accounts for all the car parks at the bottom of the hill). Unlike the Obersalzburg, the Kehlsteinhaus escaped the allied bombs, and visitors today who make it all the way up come face-to-face with one of the most remarkable buildings of the Nazi era, much of which is still exactly as Hitler knew it.

The road the buses take from the Obersalzburg up to the Eagle's Nest is the one built on the instructions of Martin Bormann, who ordered the construction of both the road and the Kehlsteinhaus as a fiftieth birthday present for the Führer. Bormann, a Nazi so vile that even Göring called him "the dirty pig", had noticed how while he was staying in the Berghof Hitler was in the habit of taking after-dinner walks to a small tea pavilion on the Mooslahnerkopf. This gave him the idea of building the Führer a tea-house of his own. Bormann also wanted a place where he could meet Hitler undisturbed so that he could wield influence over him away from other schemers. He chose the site in 1936: a steep, precipitous promontory overlooking the Obersalzburg from a height of 1,834 metres, with commanding views over Berchtesgaden and the surrounding Alpine area stretching all the way to the city of Salzburg, whose towers and spires are visible in the far distance. Opposite Bormann's chosen site was a mountain called the Untersberg, where according to legend Charlemagne and an army of five thousand sleep, waiting to restore the fame and glory of the German Empire. To Bormann it all sounded ideal. In the spring of the following year he climbed up to the site with Dr Fritz Todt, a road engineer, and the Munich architect Roderich Fick, who was to be the designer of the teahouse. Then on August 23 1937 Bormann personally put the pegs for the Kehlstein road into the ground; three thousand workers then got to work constructing it.

Thirteen months and thirty million *Reichsmark* later, the teahouse and road were ready. Bormann was especially proud of the road. Undeniably well engineered, it rises 750 metres in six and a half kilometres, with only one hairpin turn. At its highest point the road enters a 124-metre tunnel drilled into the rock. The tunnel terminates at the base of a lift shaft, from where a brass-clad lift rises to the Eagle's Nest itself. (Today's visitors use the same lift and tunnel to reach the house as Hitler once did; the lift is still operated by the original machinery and has a chunky 1940s emergency telephone still affixed to the wall.)

The tea house's nickname, the Eagle's Nest, comes from a report that the French ambassador, François Poncet, wrote on the house for the

French Foreign Minister of the time. "Hitler's house," he remarked in the report, "gave me the impression of being in a building which was floating in space." Ironically, though, Hitler did not much like the sensation of floating in space, as he was supposed to suffer from vertigo and rarely enjoyed Bormann's expensive present. (The Kehlsteinhaus is very bad news for vertigo sufferers: perched on a narrow finger of land, near-vertical slopes drop precipitously from three of its four sides, echoing the dramatic but precarious setting of the gaunt, grey medieval castles that cling to rocky bluffs in many parts of the Swiss and Italian Alps.) Hitler also complained that the air was too thin, which was bad for his blood pressure, and that he was worried about an accident on the road, or in the lift. For a time, however, many assumed that the Führer was overjoyed with the place, and intended it to be his mausoleum.

In the end, only people whom he needed to impress were brought all the way up. They met Hitler in the centrepiece of the house, the large conference room, whose five picture windows revealed a magnificent panoramic view; the fireplace, made from red marble and bronze tiles, was a present from Mussolini, while the floor was covered by a magnificent Oriental carpet, a gift of Emperor Hirohito of Japan. And, while Hitler was uneasy about going to the teahouse, Eva Braun loved it, often coming here to walk her dogs Susi and Negus (her sister Gretl had her wedding reception in the Kehlsteinhaus in June 1944 when she married a Waffen SS General). In fact, it was rumoured that Eva Braun liked it so much that she wanted to install a heating system under the road so that the snow would melt in the winter, making the house accessible through the year and not just in the summer.

The road-heating system was never installed. But the Kehlsteinhaus survived the war as an emblem of the empty-headed ostentatiousness of the Nazi era. After the war the Americans, whose zone of occupation included Bavaria, were persuaded not to dynamite the house by Berchtesgaden's mayor, and in the 1950s it was opened up to visitors. The road is not cleared of snow in the winter, and access to the teahouse is only possible between May and October; but on many days during this time it attracts hundreds of visitors who come to admire the views and eat in the reasonably smart restaurant that now occupies the building (the restaurant's profits are donated to charity). People also walk the terraces that Hitler walked, and gawp at the view that he once admired. And, although the Kehlsteinhaus is nowhere near as high as somewhere like the Jungfraujoch (or even Germany's own Zugspitze), the view is in many ways just as stunning: it stretches round from the jewel-like Königsee in the west, whose near-vertical slopes rise straight from the water's edge, across the green bowl of Berchtesgaden and the Obersalzburg immediately below the Kehlsteinhaus, to the flatter countryside around Salzburg to the north (the Austrian city is a full hour by train from Berchtesgaden); to the south the forbidding grey wall of Mount Kehlstein looms ominously behind the promontory of land on which the house is situated.

Bavaria was always the homeland of Nazism. Munich was the early focal point of the movement but the mountains were its spiritual heart. And still in today's Europe there are echoes of the attachment of far-right ideology to high places. For nowhere in the continent does far-right sentiment linger on most tenaciously than in the mountain regions of Austria. The leader of Austria's notorious Freedom Party, Jörg Haider, sees the Alpine region of Carinthia as his own party's heartland; he was elected governor of that region in 1990 and in 1995 drew worldwide criticism when he addressed an annual reunion of former Austrian SS members on the slopes of the Ulrichsberg peak, close to Carinthia's main city of Klagenfurt (he called the assembled veterans "men of character"). And over the border in Switzerland, the place where far-right stirrings have been felt most keenly is in the city of Lucerne. It seems that some Alpine regions, with their parochial concerns and their distrust of outsiders and rapid change, have for decades maintained something of a tradition of fomenting extremist political opinion.

The Nazi shadow still hangs darkly over the Alpine regions of Austria and Bavaria. But in the 1960s, when memories of the *Anschluss* were still very fresh, the Nazi era in the Alps was brought into the consciousness of the entire western world, through the popularity of a Hollywood film. Ironically, although the film is set during the bleak days of the late 1930s, it is covered in such cheerfully sentimental gloss that it seems even kitschier than *Heidi*.

The Sound of Music
The 1965 film about the exploits of the von Trapp family during the Second World War, and their escape from Nazi Austria, must be the

most instantly familiar Alpine story committed to celluloid. Too bad, then, that the beautiful mountains form the backdrop to a Hollywood feel-good spectacular, full of cardboard characters, simplistic emotional entanglements and cartoon-like representation of one of the most evil regimes in history. But it is all based on a true story: the source of the Broadway musical, and subsequent film, is Maria von Trapp's 1949 memoir *The Story of the Trapp Family Singers*.

In 1938, Georg von Trapp, a former commander in the Austrian Imperial navy, had appointed Maria as tutor to one of his seven children, his wife having recently died. By that time the von Trapp family were internationally famous and were invited to sing at Hitler's birthday party (the invitation was refused). Maria fell in love with her employer and married him, and when Captain von Trapp received his call-up papers, he decided his family was in danger and determined to take them to the comparative safety of Italy. Later, travelling via Sweden, the family sailed to the United States, and eventually settled in Stowe, Vermont. The Captain died in 1947, but the rest of the family went on singing, setting up a music camp and lodge in Stowe, under the slogan "a little of Austria, a lot of Vermont". Maria eventually died in 1987, but her children (and their children) carry on the tradition of singing and of serving *Apfelstrüdel* to the thousands of visitors who still descend each year on the Trapp family lodge at Stowe.

The musical, however, plays fast and loose with history. The names of the family (in reality, Rupert, Maria, Agathe, Johanna, Martina, Werner and Hedwig) were all changed to make the lyrics flow more easily (and what rhymes with Hedwig, after all?) and to avoid the confusion of having two Marias. In reality, Maria was appointed as a tutor to one of the children rather than a governess to all of them. (She did, however, have a guitar, and Captain von Trapp really did summon his children with a whistle.) Although, as in the film, Captain von Trapp shunned his fiancée, Elsa Schrader, for Maria, the events of the film are squeezed into one summer whereas in fact they took place over several years. The family escaped initially to Switzerland, rather than Italy, and never hid in a nunnery. Still, there is no denying that the musical's lyrics, by Oscar Hammerstein, are clever and witty, a perfect match for Richard Rogers' rousing and memorable show-tunes. The pair began writing the piece in the spring of 1959 and by September the musical received its first staging in New Haven, Connecticut. Then came the film and the rest, as they say, is history.

Its appeal never seems to dim: in Christmas 2004 the BBC put together an hour-long celebration of the film, hosted by comedian Graham Norton, with groups of celebrities wearing wimples singing *How Do You Solve a Problem Like Maria?* Christopher Plummer, who played Captain von Trapp, once dubbed the piece "The Sound of Mucous". Maybe, but over four decades the film has amassed a dedicated band of followers, who seem to be as keen to affectionately mock the film as they are to wrap themselves up in its sugar-coated sentimentality.

The film, too, has created a virtual pilgrimage centre out of Salzburg and the surrounding mountains. Every day bus tours head out from the city into the nearby Lake District, full of people humming the songs and wanting to see where the musical was filmed. Disappointing news: many of the interiors were actually built on sound stages in Hollywood, and other locations, such as the grand houses, are private property and off-limits to visitors (or should one say pilgrims). But the famous "sixteen going on seventeen" gazebo is still there, in a public park in Salzburg, and the wedding church located in the beautifully situated lakeside town of Mondsee, with its distinctive red marble altar steps, is just as it is in the movie.

Whatever one makes of all this, the whole *Sound of Music* experience is at least a refreshing antidote to the high culture that Salzburg otherwise oozes, with its music festivals and smug cult of Mozart. In the end, the film is a delicious piece of Alpine kitsch, as shallow and attractive as the cuckoo clocks sold in the souvenir emporia alongside the Austrian lakes. And a final piece of *SOM* trivia: the film was shown for the first time on Austrian television only in January 2001, and despite having an Austrian setting and characters, there was no stage production in the country until March 2005, when it was the highlight of the season in Vienna's Volksoper. But it is perhaps not surprising that the Austrians do not take to it: this is a part of the country's history which most would prefer not to think about. With far-right politics seemingly so popular in places such as the Tyrol and Carinthia, cartoon Nazis are the last thing that the more liberal, urban intelligentsia wants to put on the country's TV screens or theatre stages.

More Alpine Films

The Alps have provided a spectacular setting for films ever since the days of Arnold Fanck and his *Bergfilme*. Besides *The Sound of Music*, the Kekec films and (some of) the *Heidi* adaptations, a number of star-studded action movies have been made on location in the mountains, including at least two outings for James Bond. The Piz Gloria restaurant, which revolves at the top of the Schilthorn (2,970m) to give fantastic views stretching from the Eiger to Mont Blanc, famously featured in *On Her Majesty's Secret Service* (1969) as the remote mountain-top lair of evil Bond nemesis Blofeld. Even though this is reckoned to be one of the lamest Bond films (George Lazenby takes the lead role, trying to stop Blofeld from destroying the world with a new scientific gizmo), the chases by ski and bobsleigh, and the helicopter assault on the Piz Gloria itself, are fantastic set-pieces, and to this day the restaurant has an audio-visual display relating to the film. In fact, the construction of the restaurant was part paid-for by the film's producers; its revolve mechanism and helipad were installed by the production company, and when the restaurant opened, just after filming finished, it was given the name Piz Gloria because that was the name of Blofeld's remote mountain-top lair in the film (the cable-car ride up to the restaurant from Mürren, in the Lauterbrunnen valley, is still one of the most spectacular in Switzerland).

The opening of another Bond film, *Goldeneye* (1995), involves a spectacular bungee-jump off the immensely high Verzasca Dam near Locarno. In 1975 Clint Eastwood starred in and directed another Alpine adventure saga, *The Eiger Sanction*, in which our hero is a cold-blooded assassin hired to kill his victim while climbing the notorious north face of the Eiger. The film was made on location on the mountain, with cameras and sound equipment hung from booms and ropes, and Eastwood doing all his own stunts; it is spectacularly shot, but on the second day of filming a British-born climbing expert assisting on the production, David Knowles, was killed by a falling boulder, and in the following weeks the cast and crew also had to contend with the blizzards and freezing temperatures familiar to climbers on the north face of this treacherous mountain.

Aside from these dramatic action-adventure films there are dozens of more low-key offerings that also make good use of Alpine scenery. Here are four of them. In 1949, hot on the heels of his success with the London-based Dickensian melodrama *Oliver Twist*, the acclaimed British director David Lean took a film crew to the wide open spaces of the French Alps to shoot part of *The Passionate Friends* in Annecy and Chamonix; the story, based on a novel by H. G. Wells, features a three-way love triangle between a married woman (played by Ann Todd), her husband (Claude Rains) and her former lover (Trevor Howard) whom she meets while on holiday in the Alps.

Heart of a Child is an odd, rather sentimental English film from 1958 based on a novel by the unlikely-sounding Phyllis Bottome. The film tells the story of a young boy who lives in a picture-postcard village high in the Austrian Tyrol with his constant companion, a Great St. Bernard dog called Rudi. One day young Karl's cruel father decides to sell Rudi, but our plucky hero embarks on a perilous journey across the mountains to be reunited with his beloved four-legged friend. There are echoes here of Kekec, but in this case the film's good intentions are undermined by the scenery around Innsbruck being shot in a not-so-glorious and very flat black-and-white, while the unmistakably Tyrolean setting does not work well in such an unmistakably British production.

More successful is the 1991 film *American Friends*, written by and starring Michael Palin, which features a love-affair that starts when a young American woman, on a walking holiday in the Swiss Alps, spies a tweedy middle-aged Oxford don through her telescope striding across the mountains in his plus-fours. The pair are ill-matched but, predictably, love still blossoms among the meadows; the film is set in the nineteenth century and was based on the diaries of Palin's own great-grandfather. *Careful* (1992) is very different, a Canadian film made by the avant-garde director Guy Madden, and shot entirely in a studio rather than on location. Set in a fictional Alpine village called Tolzbad, whose inhabitants are forced to talk only in whispers for fear of setting off an avalanche, the film is strikingly photographed, with its sepia-tinting and silent-film style inter-titles deliberately harking back to the Fanck/Riefenstahl *Bergfilme* collaborations.

Perhaps more bizarrely, the Swiss Alps have been used by Indian movie makers in recent years as a location for all-singing, all-dancing 'Bollywood' productions. This is partly because the Kashmir region of the Indian Himalayas has been rendered off-limits to Indian film-makers owing to that region's political troubles. It is hence easier and cheaper for film crews and actors to fly to Switzerland than to go through the difficult process of getting permits to film in the Indian Himalaya. The main area for location shoots is around Engelberg, which is only two hours travelling time from Zurich airport but which has guaranteed background snowy mountains year round (specifically Mount Titlis which rises to 3,239 metres above the resort). The Hotel Terrace in Engelberg has played host to many Bollywood directors and stars over the years, and was actually used as a specific location in the very first Indian film shot in Switzerland, *Sangam (Union)*, where an Indian couple take their honeymoon in Europe.

The best-known Indian director associated with Switzerland is Yash Chopra, whose *Vijay* (1988) included a song-and-dance number filmed on a cable car. Hindi movies are essentially escapist, and because much of their audience is urban-based, mountains and lakes are often seen as a suitable backdrop to love stories. Moreover, Switzerland is also a consumer dream for India's burgeoning middle classes: wealth, consumption and scenery combine to create an easily-packaged escapist fantasy for movie-goers in Delhi or Bangalore. In recent years these Bollywood epics have been partly responsible for encouraging huge numbers of Asian tourists to come to Switzerland on holiday, particularly to the area around Interlaken: these days, on any trip up the Jungfrau railway in summer, as many as a third of the passengers will be from south or east Asia. This new trend in tourism has been acknowledged by the opening of an Indian restaurant (the "Bollywood") at the top station of the Jungfrau railway, which permeates the whole complex of summit buildings with a slightly surprising, though certainly not unwelcome, aroma of curry. And yet this influx of foreign visitors, and the positive and pragmatic encouragement of them, is not a particularly new phenomenon: it is just the most recent chapter in the long history of Alpine tourism, whose beginnings date back over two hundred years.

Part Four

Visitors

"The Playground of Europe"

Four times a day, a bright red narrow-gauge electric train pulls away from the railway station in Zermatt, in the shadow of the Matterhorn, with the words "Glacier Express" emblazoned on its destination board. Eight hours later, after passing over 291 bridges and through ninety-one tunnels, the train finally draws up in another world-famous ski resort, St. Moritz. To take the Glacier Express is to travel one of the great train journeys of the world: a twisting, climbing, plunging voyage through the spectacular scenery of south-eastern Switzerland. The highest part of the line is where it climbs up from Andermatt over the Oberalppass (2,033m). Here the train rises above the tree-line into rocky scenery covered in rough, patchy grass and strewn with fallen boulders. This part of the Alps is deserted, save for the ancient stone barns scattering the bleak hillside. There are no cows, nor mountain pasture; this is the mountains in their rawest form. Then, with wheels screaming around the tight curves and the rack and pinion mechanism bumping and grinding under the locomotive, the train drops down to the more verdant valley of the River Rhine, here little more than a gurgling mountain stream, but getting wider and more confident as it flows towards Chur. Beyond that city, the train leaves the river behind and heads up into the mountains again, towards St. Moritz, the viaducts and tunnels following each other in even more dazzling and breathless succession.

Amazingly, all this scenery can be viewed from the panoramic windows of the train's dining car: beef stroganoff, rice and Vichy carrots is a popular choice from the menu, washed down perhaps with a selection of white wines from Aigle, or reds from Sion or Maienfeld. The dining car of the Glacier Express must provide the most wonderful view of any restaurant window in the world. And all the while the train continues to rise and fall and spiral back on itself through tunnels and

over curving viaducts, at a stately speed of thirty kilometres per hour: this has to be the slowest "express" train in the world.

The construction of the Glacier Express line was not as troublesome as that of the railway up to the Jungfraujoch, which involved tunnelling through ten kilometres of rock over the course of sixteen gruelling years. During the opening ceremony of that railway in 1912, the British Ambassador to Switzerland, Sir Frederick St. John, lamented the "vulgarization" of the "playground of Europe", which stemmed, he implied, from the construction of the Jungfrau and other mountain railways. But he was fighting a rearguard action: the conquest of the Alps by tourists was by then very much underway.

As early as 1816 Mary Shelley, visiting the Mer de Glace, had commented that she "met, I lament to say, some English people here... the melancholy exhibitions of tourism which... corrupt the manners of the people and make this place another Keswick." Her feelings are echoed by Mark Twain in *A Tramp Abroad.* "What a change has come over Switzerland this century," he wrote in 1880. "Now everybody goes everywhere, and Switzerland, and many other regions which were unvisited and unknown remotenesses a hundred years ago, are in our days a buzzing hive of restless strangers every summer." By the time Twain wrote those words the Alps were well on the way to becoming the tourist paradise that they remain to this day.

The Coming of Mass Tourism

The transformation of the Alps from rural backwater to tourist playground was partly the result of revolutions in politics and technology that took place during the nineteenth century. To deal with the politics first: in 1815 the Congress of Vienna signalled the end of the Napoleonic wars and heralded an era of prolonged peace in Europe. Suddenly the continent was safe to visit; and it was fashionable, too, following the poetic outpourings of celebrity travellers such as Shelley and Byron. Travellers from England began to flock to the Alps, inspirational volumes of poetry stuffed into their mountains of luggage.

They quickly discovered that travelling conditions could often be uncomfortable: in 1830, the thrice-weekly diligence from Geneva to Chamonix took a bone-grinding eighteen hours to cover the distance between the towns, and the journey included stretches undertaken by horse, mule and portered chairs; but sixty years later, at the turn of the century, the journey time had been reduced to eleven hours, and the arrival of the diligence outside the post office in Chamonix would be the major event of the day in the French resort. Then, in 1901, this trip was consigned at a stroke to the dustbin of transport history: for in that year Chamonix felt the impact of the technological—or specifically transport—revolution which also played a huge role in bringing tourists to the Alps. For in that year, the railways came to Chamonix, linking the French resort with a system that had been covering Europe since the 1850s with an ever-expanding network of tracks. By then, in fact, trains had already been travelling across, under and up the highest peaks in the Alps for over three decades, carrying tourists along lines that were true marvels of civil engineering (and often tourist attractions in their own right). As the new century dawned, the old century's greatest technological revolution was well on the way to changing the Alps forever.

With better ease of transport came more people—and, in particular, the *wrong sort* of people. It was not just Mary Shelley who complained about the vulgar new breed of tourist. In 1833, the artist William Brockedon heard cockney voices in a Swiss restaurant and in his book *Journals of Excursions in the Alps* expressed the "disbelief that such vulgarity could have reached the Great St Bernard... I had no idea that the gentilities of Wapping had ever extended so far from the Thames." An article that appeared in *Blackwood's Magazine* in 1848 similarly bemoaned the modern phenomenon of mass tourism, which "spoils all rational travel; it disgusts all intelligent curiosity; it repels the student, the philosopher, and the manly investigator from subjects which have been thus trampled into the mire by the hoofs of a whole tribe of travelling bipeds, who might rejoice to exchange brains with the animals which they ride."

Yet every year the hordes descended on the Alps in ever increasing numbers, trampling underfoot places that a breed of earlier, more loftily-minded travellers considered rightfully theirs to enjoy alone. The new railways, and regular steamship services across the Atlantic, just made things worse: in *Putnam's Magazine* of May 1868, it was remarked that "If the social history of the world is ever written, the era in which we live will be called the nomadic period. With the advent of ocean steam navigation and the railway system began a travelling mania which has gradually increased until half of the earth's inhabitants, or at least of its civilized portion, are on the move." In particular, middle-class Americans flocked to Europe to bathe in the old culture that had spawned their new and increasingly powerful nation. The novelist Henry James, an American who towards the end of his life settled in England, was, for one, not impressed. In *Americans Abroad* he scorned the "very large proportion of Americans who annually scatter themselves over Europe and are by no means flattering to the national vanity... they are ill-made, ill-mannered, and ill-dressed."

One key individual who was instrumental in introducing these "travelling bipeds" to the delights of the Alps was a remarkable entrepreneur whose name is still indelibly linked with organized tourism. Thomas Cook left school at the age of ten to become a gardener's boy near his home in Leicester. In his adult life, his Baptist faith and missionary zeal led him to organize trips and holidays that would induce those who had wandered from the path of righteousness back towards temperance and moral restraint. A trip "provides food for the mind," Cook wrote; "it helps pull men out of the mire and pollution of old corrupt customs... it accelerates the march of peace and virtue and love." In 1845 the first group of what Cook called his "excursionists" left Leicester for a holiday in the English Lake District; in the following year another group went to Scotland. The year 1855 saw the first group of excursionists venture across the Channel, and in summer 1863 came the first trips to the Alps, with the Mont Blanc and Jungfrau regions on the itinerary of this new breed of package tourists. Over the next decade, encouraged by the proliferation of new railways, the list of destinations available to Cook's tourists mushroomed to include Oberammergau (for the 1871 passion play) and St. Moritz. Of course, there were more grumbles from the "old guard": in 1872 the Egyptologist Amelia Edwards was travelling alone and off the beaten track in the Dolomites, deliberately enduring hardships so that she did not have to put up with "hackneyed sights, overcrowded hotels... and the flood of Cook's tourists". The Alpinist and critic Leslie Stephen also wrote contemptuously of package holidaymakers. In *Playground of Europe* he described Cook's tourist as having "a total incapacity to live without *The Times*... [and] a deep-seated conviction that foreigners generally are members of a secret society intended to extort money on false pretences. The cause of his traveling is wrapped in mystery…" But Thomas Cook, undaunted, was well on the way to transforming the whole shape of European, and later world, tourism. In 1897, by which time Cook's tourists were visiting places as far away as Egypt and the Holy Land, the *Excursionist* magazine remarked that "Since Thomas Cook's first excursion train it is as if a magician's wand had been passed over the face of the globe."

Lucerne: "out come the backward sons"

Lucerne is one of the most attractive towns in the Alps. Its curving medieval streets, lined with frescoed buildings and stone arcades, curl away from the main, cobbled square towards the town's famous wooden bridges that for centuries have taken pedestrians over the churning River Reuss. On its eastern edge the town centre opens out onto the shore of the Vierwaldstättersee, the body of water known to generations of English-speaking tourists as Lake Lucerne, along whose thickly wooded and frequently misty shores Switzerland's earliest history was forged. Rising above Lucerne are two distinctive peaks: to the south slumbers the mountain giant Pilatus (2,120m), a former haunt, supposedly, of dragons and the ghost of Pontius Pilate, while to the east is the Rigi (1,798m), its lower, flatter and less forbidding summit dominated by a bluntly austere communications tower.

Not surprisingly, the town has been a favourite with visitors for nearly two hundred years, ever since the earliest days of mass Alpine tourism. In fact, in the nineteenth century Lucerne was so famous among English travellers that Queen Victoria herself came here for an extended holiday, checking into a hotel incognito. The highlight of her visit in August 1868 was a trip up Pilatus on the back of a mule, during which her Scottish adjutant, John Brown, put the local porters to shame by outpacing them with his Highland strides. The queen wrote in her diary: "What am I to say of the glorious scenery of Switzerland… I can hardly believe my eyes… [the view of Pilatus and the Rigi] seems like a painting or decoration… a dream!"

It was not only the British who came here: in the nineteenth century the town was also full of American visitors. The great chronicler of the American experience as a tourist in Europe was Mark Twain, who passed through Switzerland in the late 1870s to collect material for his comic travelogue *A Tramp Abroad*. The book, written during Twain's most fertile period as a writer, came hot on the heels of *The Adventures of Tom Sawyer* (1876) and was followed by *The Prince and the Pauper* (1882); like this whimsical tale set in Tudor England, *A Tramp Abroad* catered to the mushrooming interest among middle-class Americans in the "old world" their ancestors had left behind when their country was founded. Twain describes his work as an "autobiographical fantasy" and crams it full of stories, anecdotes and outrageous flights of fancy that seek both to celebrate and to lampoon the habits of American tourists. He mercilessly mocks the ignorance of his fellow countrymen, who in his eyes are weighed down by an idleness borne of overblown and frequently dashed expectations; but he also satirizes popular travel literature of the day, casting himself as the antithesis of the fearlessly heroic American adventurer. For Twain prefers leisure and comfort to excitement and danger: the book's central conceit—that its author sets out to walk across Europe but in fact never actually ends up going anywhere on foot—sets the tone for its humour and deliciously-observed irony. Heading up the Rigi, Twain observes that "the mountains were bigger and grander than ever, as they stood there thinking their solemn thoughts with their heads in the drifting clouds," and decides to watch the sunrise from the summit: "The great cloud-barred disk of the sun stood just above a limitless expanse of tossing white-caps," begins his wonderfully purple description:

> ... a billowy chaos of mountain domes and peaks draped in imperishable snow, and flooded with an opaline glory of changing and dissolving splendors... the cloven valleys of the lower world swam in a tinted mist which veiled the ruggedness of their crags and ribs and ragged forests, and turned all the forbidding region into a soft and rich and sensuous paradise.

But after all this hyperbole, the joke is on Twain—and also on his readers; for the writer and his companion, Harris, have slept for a whole day, and gradually realize that the sun is not rising at all—it is *setting*. So they turn round and go back to bed in the summit hotel, determined to watch the sun rise the following morning; but they miss that too,

because their eyes are focused on the part of the sky where the sun had set the previous evening, and they waste their time arguing while the sun rises gloriously, and out of view, behind them.

Throughout *A Tramp Abroad* Twain expresses withering contempt for tourists and for those who cater to their needs. "The commerce of Lucerne consists mainly in gimcrackery of the souvenir sort... The shops are packed with Alpine crystals, photographs of scenery, and wooden and ivory carvings," he writes, before going on to pour scorn on the most iconic piece of Swiss tourist kitsch—the infamous cuckoo clock. "For years my pet aversion has been to the cuckoo clock; now here I was, at last, right in the creature's home; so wherever I went that distressing *hoo*'hoo! *hoo*'hoo! *hoo*'hoo! was always in my ears... no sound is quite so inane, and silly, and aggravating as the *hoo*'hoo! of a cuckoo clock." Twain wonders about buying one, if only to offer it as a gift to a literary critic back home who had given one of his books a rotten review.

Up on the mountain itself, in the Rigi-Kulm hotel at the summit, things did not get much better. "The tourists were eagerly buying all sorts and styles of paper-cutters, marked 'souvenir of the Rigi', with handles made of little curved horn of the chamois," he observes. "I was going to buy a paper-cutter, but I believed I could remember the cold comfort of the Rigi-Kulm without it, so I smothered the impulse." Yet Twain's writing also rises above his trademark brand of often self-deprecating humour to achieve a mellowness of tone that allows for a more thoughtful perspective on the profound changes that the tourist flood has wrought on nineteenth-century Switzerland. "Seventy or eighty years ago Napoleon was the only man in Europe who could really be called a traveller," he comments:

But now everyone goes everywhere... I have met dozens of people, imaginative and unimaginative, cultivated and uncultivated, who had come from far countries and roamed through the Swiss Alps year after years... they said they could find perfect rest and peace nowhere else when they were troubled; all frets and worries and chafings sank to sleep in the presence of the benign serenity of the Alps; the Great Spirit of the Mountain breathed his own peace upon their hurt minds and sore hearts, and healed them.

What would Mark Twain or Queen Victoria make of Lucerne, Pilatus and the Rigi now? In many ways the town by the lake has been a victim of its own success. Just over eighty years after Victoria's visit, the English love affair with Lucerne brought a jaded response from the author John Russell, who lamented the passing of an older style of elegant, sophisticated tourism. "There is nothing really wrong with Lucerne, except the people who go there," he wrote in *Switzerland* (1950); "the general defects of life in Lucerne must be ascribed, I am afraid, to a century of English patronage." The time when he missed the old days most was on a wet Sunday afternoon in August, when "out come the backward sons; silently and six abreast, chewing their unlit pipes and tucking loose strands of hair into mackintosh hoods, the family parties come out for a tramp." Lucerne's present annual crop of tourists numbers five million, and its ancient streets are crammed with nothing but hotels, restaurants, and bland and expensive fashion and jewellery boutiques. It is one of a small number of towns in the Alps (Chamonix and Interlaken are two of the others) which seem to exist solely for tourists, their presence drowning any remaining vestiges of local culture in a gaudy, multi-lingual tide of aimlessly shifting crowds and boredom-induced conspicuous consumption (the latter of the same tat that Mark Twain saw on sale nearly a century and a half ago).

"It is difficult to procure beds, food or even attention"
Publishers in Britain and America quickly realized that the new tourists in Europe needed a helping hand in deciding where to go and where to stay on their travels. The nineteenth century saw a proliferation of guidebooks to the Alpine regions, brought out by the likes of Baedeker

and John Murray, whose descriptions and advice now provide a valuable record of the formative days of mass European tourism.

The writers of these books did not necessarily hit the nail on the head when describing the places their readers would visit: in *A Tramp Abroad* Mark Twain constantly moans about his Baedeker and grumbles that he will write to the book's editors to put them right on certain matters: while Twain found the conditions in the Rigi-Kulm hotel to be mostly acceptable (although his room was rather cold), the author of Murray's *Handbook to Switzerland* had quite the opposite impression. According to the unappealing description in Murray, the hotel on the Rigi's summit was

> crammed to overflowing every evening; numbers are turned away from the doors, and it is difficult to procure beds, food or even attention. The house presents a scene of utmost confusion, servant maids hurrying in one direction, couriers and guides in another, while gentlemen with poles and knapsacks block up the passages. Most of the languages of Europe [can be heard], muttered usually in terms of abuse or complaint, and the all-pervading fumes of tobacco enter largely as ingredients into this babel of sounds and smells, and add to the discomfort of the fatigued traveller. In the evening... it takes some time before the hubbub of voices and the trampling of feet subside... a few roistering German students [might well] prolong their potations and noise far into the night.

Twain did not seem to have any trouble sleeping in the hotel—in fact, it was his prolonged doze through the hours of daylight that caused him and his companion to confuse the sunrise and sunset—although his extreme fatigue from the climb up to the summit might well have allowed him to dream through the noise kicked up by any pickled German students whose stay at the hotel coincided with his. As to the sunrise he unfortunately missed out on, Baedeker gives a ray-by-ray description of the event, as observed by crowds of early rising hotel guests who "prostrate themselves before the great source of light and life... [turning their gaze] in silent adoration towards that mighty hand which created 'the great light which rules the day.'"

Guidebooks exist to warn travellers of potential problems in an area, as well as give them advice about what to see. Murray commended the cleanliness of Swiss inns but warned that conditions deteriorated once travellers crossed into France or Italy. One inn near Brissone, close to Aosta, was described as having "filth... and disgust in every direction... and the [nearby] Cheval Blanc with its dirty hostess cannot be forgotten." But problems of poor accommodation were nothing compared to the constant aggravation from hustlers, con-men and spivs that seems to elicit the greatest concern from authors writing for Baedeker or Murray. Baedeker advised readers that they should always keep small coins to hand, to pacify the inevitable alpenhorn players or lustily melodic Swiss maidens ("ruthless songsters") who were, apparently, lurking around every corner. (The nineteenth-century mountaineer Edward Whymper memorably dismissed a visit to Lauterbrunnen on account of having to put up with the "echoes which are exhibited by idiots blowing on horns.") The writer of the Baedeker guide goes on to comment ruefully that the admiration of the tourist "must not be engrossed by a cascade, be it ever so beautiful, or by a glacier, be it ever so imposing and magnificent; the urchin who persists in standing on his head, or turning somersaults for the tourist's amusement, must have his share of attention." On the popular road between Geneva and Chamonix, tourists are "beset by all sorts of vagabonds, who plant themselves in the way openly as beggars, or covertly as dealers in mineral specimens, or guides to things which do not require their aid." And this time, Mark Twain's experience of travel in Switzerland seems to match that of the guidebook writers.

> At short distances all along the road [between Lucerne and Interlaken] were groups of neat and comely children," Twain writes "with their wares nicely and temptingly set forth in the grass under the shade trees, and as soon as we approached they swarmed into the road, holding out their baskets and milk bottles, and ran beside the carriage, barefoot and bareheaded, and importuned us to buy. They seldom desisted early, but continued to run and insist—beside the wagon while they could, and behind it until they lost breath.

At other times, however, the constant clamouring of urchins could be put to good use: on mountain walks, according to Baedeker, "the traveller may engage the first urchin he meets to carry his bag or knapsack for a trifling gratuity."

Edward Whymper, crossing the Col de Forclaz on his way to Zermatt in 1864, had a similar experience; he wrote that the road over the pass "is not creditable to Switzerland... children swarm there like maggots in a rotten cheese. They carry baskets of fruit with which to plague the weary tourist. They flit around him like flies...'give me something' is the alpha and omega of all their addresses. They learn the phrase, it is said, before they are taught the alphabet." It all sounds very different to the experiences of today's travellers in Switzerland, who ride on some of the most nuisance-free public transport in the world, and who are more likely to encounter a Martian than a bevy of begging children or pushy guides.

"The luxury of tea may always be had in perfection"

Although Alpine inns saw plenty of guests from America and continental Europe, the principal visitors to the mountains in the nineteenth century were the English. The Romantic poets had blazed the first trail of Alpine tourism; in their wake came writers, railway engineers and Queen Victoria, and plenty of more lowly tourists besides. English-speaking clubs sprung up in lakeside resorts all over the Alps, while some hotels became favourites among English travellers. One was the Hôtel de Londres et d'Angleterre in Chamonix, which, according to Murray, "never forfeited the reputation of being one of the best appointed inns to be found in the Alps... where Victor Tairrez and his excellent wife are so practiced in their acquaintance with, and their provision for, the wants of travellers, especially English, that more *confort* will be found there than in almost any other inn out of England." In the mid-nineteenth century Queen Victoria's physician John Forbes, who published a popular account of an Alpine tour, remarked that the hotel "was a splendid establishment... [where he] partook of an excellent dinner in the company of thirteen other persons—all English."

Tourists did not have to go specifically to Chamonix for a taste of England among the peaks. Murray's *Handbook* of 1838 indicated that English travellers could be assured of a warm welcome in hotels throughout Switzerland. "It may be laid down as a general rule that the wants, tastes and habits of the English are more carefully and successfully studied at Swiss inns… Thus at most of the large inns there is a late table d'hôte dinner at 4 or 5 o'clock, expressly for the English; and the luxury of tea may always be had in perfection." (The same book, however, also commented that English hotel guests were charged more than Germans, on the basis that the English have "more numerous wants, and are more difficult to serve.")

As well as afternoon tea and a bed for the night, English travellers were also deemed to be in need of spiritual sustenance, and by 1914 there were fifty-two English churches spread throughout Switzerland, while over a hundred of the country's hotels held English church services. One of Murray's nineteenth-century *Handbooks* maintained that Swiss hoteliers actually built chapels as an inducement to travellers to stay in their establishments: "in many mountain inns an English clergyman is offered free lodgings with the same object, and the guests are ejected from public sitting-rooms while the English service is performed." (Leslie Stephen echoed this comment while sneering at Cook's tourists: "…never does he shine with such obvious complacency as when, armed with an assortment of hymn-books and Bibles, he evicts all the inferior races from the dining-room of a hotel.")

The first resort in the Alps to provide regular Anglican services was Meiringen, a small town located in a narrow, picturesque valley just east of Interlaken, where in 1851 the Revd C. T. May, formerly Principal of the Collegial School of Nottingham, officiated at a service in the Hotel du Sauvage. The services were well-attended and May persuaded the authorities to let him hold services in a deconsecrated medieval church rather than the hotel dining room. In 1868 an entirely new church was built in the hotel's grounds, its architect a certain Mr. Billing of Tooley Street, London. The church was rebuilt in 1891 after a fire, and it is this building that still stands today, fronting a fairly ordinary square which opens up from Meiringen's main street. It is a plain, unadorned affair, with a steeply sloping tiled roof and walls punctured on each side by thin, narrow, pointed windows. This former church now serves as an art gallery; but a better fate has befallen other English churches in Switzerland, such as those in Zermatt and Davos. The former is situated on a ridge above the centre of the popular resort and is surrounded by a tiny graveyard, the burial place of many climbers who met their end on the Matterhorn; a plaque on the wall inside the building indicates that its roof was paid for by the Friends of the Alpine Club in 1925, while a notice outside introduces the present English vicar and his wife and provides details of times of services.

The church across the mountains in Davos seems, if anything, to be even more iconically English: wall plaques faithfully record that its foundation stone was laid by the Hon. Evelyn Ashley MP in January 1882, while the stone steps leading up to the front door were a gift of Mary Broadbent, widow of Percival Broadbent of Colwall near Malvern in Worcestershire. The organ builders were Henry Willis and Sons of London. Now that high tea is a thing of the past in most Alpine hotels, and the custom and patronage of East Asian tourists seems to be chased more than that of Europeans or Americans, it is churches like the ones in Zermatt or Davos that provide the most tangible reminder of what is often referred to as the English "colonization" of the Alps during the nineteenth century.

"The strange shifting of the compass"

None of the tremendous growth in tourism could have happened without the construction of the railways, and later on, the building of brilliantly-engineered roads and aerial cableways high in the mountains, which brought tourists to previously inaccessible ridges and peaks with ease. By 1900 it was no longer necessary to resort to mules or ice-axes to reach the most scenic locations. The move away from a system of getting around that relied mainly on horse and carriage (and people's own two feet) started in the 1850s when Robert Stephenson, son of George Stephenson and at that time Britain's leading railway engineer, visited Switzerland at the invitation of the federal government. With their encouragement he drew up plans for an integrated railway system, which consisted of one main west-east line (from Lake Geneva to Lake Constance), and another north-south line (from Basel to Lucerne), both of which then joined up with various branch lines feeding the valleys. (At that time there were no plans to drive railways through tunnels into the heart of the Alps.)

In the end the federal government abandoned this plan and let individual cantons sanction the building of the lines they wanted. Although Stephenson's plans had been jettisoned, a number of British engineers worked on the first Swiss railways, and in the 1860s one of them, John Barraclough Fell, decided to tackle the pressing problem of how to build railways over steep terrain. He came up with the idea of a rack-and-pinion system, where a cog wheel under the locomotive would grip the teeth of a rail laid between the two running tracks. The first line operated by this system crossed the Fréjus pass on the slopes of Mont Cenis in the French Alps. Built with a maximum gradient of 1 in 12, this was soon superseded by the first of the great Alpine rail tunnels, the Mont Cenis, whose engineer was another Englishman, Thomas Brassy. The tunnel opened in 1871 after fourteen years of construction, and was the first to make use of new ventilation technology that distributed air by means of water-powered fans, and sent "used" air out through a duct in the ceiling of the tunnel that led up through the rock to the open air.

Other tunnels soon followed, opening up the Alps to transport and tourism as never before, but often at the expanse of tragedy and disaster during their construction. The building of the 15-kilometre Gotthard Rail Tunnel in the 1870s led to the deaths of 307 people, who are commemorated by a memorial at the tunnel's southern portal at Airolo. The tunnel opened for traffic in 1882, its approach routes along steep river valleys built at gradients of one in forty. To gain height, as they climb or descend these valleys, the tracks constantly spiral and double-back on themselves by means of tunnels bored into the valley sides. The surveying required for these lines was staggering, but the resultant journeys are breathtaking: "The traveller may amuse himself by watching the strange shifting of the compass," remarked a Murray handbook on the twisting journey up to the Gotthard, which remains a spectacular route to this day.

After the Gotthard came the Arlberg Tunnel, which provided a link from the west Tyrol to the rest of Austria and was built between 1880 and 1884 by three thousand workers; its eastern portal opens at the famed Austrian ski resort of St. Anton. In 1905 the Simplon Tunnel was opened, engineered by yet another Englishman, Francis Fox. The tunnel meant that there was now a new route from Lausanne to Milan, providing the impetus (and the name) for the Venice-Simplon Orient Express that linked Paris and Constantinople. To the north of the Simplon, the Lötschberg tunnel linked Interlaken and northern Switzerland with Brig and the Simplon route, but tragedy also struck here on two occasions during its construction, firstly, when twenty-five tunnel workers were killed when water broke through the walls, and then in a separate incident when an avalanche killed thirty more.

As this book is going to press, a new generation of Alpine tunnels is being made ready: in recent years, after a break in tunnel boring of more than a century, engineers have once again been peppering the mountainsides with holes and smothering the valley approach routes in concrete and bridges. The new Gotthard and Lötschberg "base tunnels" will provide fast routes through the Alps at a lower altitude than their forebears and will have none of the slow, winding approach routes of the older tunnels; the new routes plunge into the hillside where the slopes rise rather than snake and spiral up the valley sides, and when these tunnels eventually open they will cut drastically the time required to travel from central Switzerland into Italy, just as their predecessors did in an earlier era of Alpine engineering.

Travel by train through the Alps remains alluring and exotic: by far the best way to see the mountains. It is not only the Glacier Express that offers fine views: a myriad of lines throughout Switzerland cater to those who just want to sit back in a railway carriage and drink in the constantly changing scene. There are dozens of routes to choose from: main lines run along the shores of Lake Geneva, Lake Lucerne and Lake Lugano, so close to the bank that the water seems almost to lap against the rails, while other lines run along the broad, narrowing valleys of the Rhône and the Rhine, linking with twisting narrow gauge lines whose low-slung trains grind and squeal around tight curves on their journeys up to St. Moritz, Davos, Klosters, Gstaad or Zermatt.

The writer Paul Theroux took the Orient Express through the Alps in 1975, the first leg of a journey from London to Tokyo which he recounted in *The Great Railway Bazaar*. Theroux found the scenery in Switzerland uninvolving: from the window he watches the "fruit farms and clean villages and Swiss cycling in kerchiefs… calendar scenes that you admire for a moment before feeling an urge to move on to a new month." He then endured the Simplon tunnel in complete darkness because the lights failed: "Minutes had passed and we were still in the tunnel," he muses; "we might be dropping down a well, a great sink-hole in the Alps that would land us in the clockwork interior of Switzerland, glacial cogs and ratchets and frostbitten cuckoos." (A fellow passenger comments wryly, "they say if the Swiss had designed these mountains, they'd be rather flatter.") Another travel writer, Bill Bryson, also had a disappointing time in the Alps: travelling the same route as Theroux along the Rhône valley, he recalls in his book *Neither Here Nor There* passing through a "succession of charmless industrial towns... places that seem to consist almost entirely of small factories and industrial workshops filled with oil drums, stacks of wooden pallets and other semi-abandoned clutter. I had forgotten that quite a lot of Switzerland is really rather ugly." (The words of Theroux and Bryson are strikingly similar to those of a much earlier tourist in the Alps, Lord Brougham, who travelled through Switzerland in 1815 and wrote that "it is a country to be in for two hours, or two and a half, if the weather is fine, and no longer. Ennui comes on the third hour, and suicide attacks you before night.") But the busy year-round tourist scene in Switzerland, together with its ever-popular trains, suggests that the experience of these writers is not shared by many.

Perhaps Theroux and Bryson should have abandoned the sleek main lines, laid along flat valley floors, and headed into the hills along one of Switzerland's famed mountain railways. Most of these date from the turn of the twentieth century, when it was realized that there was a market for lines whose tracks went nowhere but up, allowing tourists to ascend to look at a view and come down again, in perfect safety and with no physical effort. The oldest tourist railways in the Alps was a rack-and-pinion line that rose from a station beside the church at Vitznau, a short boat ride across the lake from Lucerne, to the summit of the Rigi. It was inaugurated in 1871, beating a rival line that approached the summit from the other direction, with its lower terminus at Arth-Goldau on the main line running up to the Gotthard. (The Rigi had been a very popular excursion before the tracks were laid; the hotel on the summit predates both lines, and when Twain ascended the mountain he walked up, barely acknowledging the railway's existence.) The rack and pinion system used for both routes was that devised by John Blenkinsop, who managed a Leeds colliery, and it was adapted for use on the Rigi by the local engineer Nikolaus Riggenbach. The locomotives that worked the Rigi routes were built at Winterthur in north-eastern Switzerland, in a major new engineering works founded by yet another English engineer, Charles Brown. They can be seen in the fine transport museum at Lucerne, distinguished by their characteristic but odd-looking upright boilers that meant their steam tubes were always surrounded by cooling water, even on a gradient.

After the success of the two Rigi lines mountain railways began snaking up slopes all over the Alps. Soon tourists in Lucerne could opt for a trip up Pilatus, which was more spectacular and higher than the Rigi, while from 1908 another famous mountain line, the Montenvers, hauled visitors from Chamonix up to a spectacular lookout point over the Mer de Glace. Soon plans (which never came to fruition) were being drawn up for railways to the summits of Mont Blanc and the Matterhorn. Not surprisingly, Alpinists viewed all this with disdain: Charles Pilkington, President of the Alpine Club, remarked that the slopes of the Alps were being "disfigured with unnecessary railways, their cliffs degraded with iron lifts," and said that Englishmen had a responsibility to protect the mountains from future schemes. But his words fell on deaf ears. In 1912 the king of all mountain lines, linking Kleine Scheidegg above Grindelwald with the snowy Jungfraujoch ridge, began operating after a construction period dogged by accidents and financial problems; the Alpinist Claud Schuster wrote of the Jungfrau railway that "the entrance into the internal regions of the Eiger, the galleries and restaurants scooped from the rock, are like nothing but a scene from Jules Verne." Dozens of trains a day still grind through these tunnels, which are built largely into the north wall of the Eiger; the famous Eigerwand mid-point station, with its window lookout built into the mountain's formidable vertical slope, has played its part in many climbing attempts (and rescues) on the treacherous north face.

In places where the terrain meant railway construction was impossible, wires supporting cable cars began to sprout in every direction. The first Alpine lift to open ran from the foot of the Upper Grindelwald Glacier to the Wetterhorn and began operating in 1908; soon afterwards Kitzbühel, Davos and St. Anton had strung up lines and pylons as their reputation for skiing grew. The most famous cable car route in the Alps, which runs from Chamonix up to the Aiguille du Midi on the slopes of Mont Blanc, opened in 1955; the top station, at 3,842 metres, is the highest place in the Alps reachable by mountain transport of any kind (although it is still a full thousand metres lower than the summit of Mont Blanc); another cable car also reaches this location from Courmayeur on the Italian side of the same ridge.

In terms of the excitement and thrill of a ride into the mountains, roads come a poor second to railways and aerial cableways. But road engineering in the mountains nevertheless has an illustrious history. In 1937 the President of France opened one of the first mountain roads, the Route des Grandes Alpes, which ran from Évian to Nice over passes opened up by mountain troops. And as early as 1910, a guide had been produced (by C. L. Freeston) to motoring in the Alps, entitled *The High Roads of the Alps—a Motoring Guide to One Hundred Alpine Passes*. Yet with many high road passes beset by problems with snow for much of the year, trans-Alpine road travel did not enter the big time until the construction of major road tunnels from the 1950s onwards. Some of these, such as the Gotthard and the Arlberg, were built adjacent to existing rail tunnels, but others, most famously the Mont Blanc tunnel, opened up entirely new transport routes through the mountains. In 1787 the Alpinist Horace-Bénédict de Saussure had written, "a day will come when we build a safe road through Mont Blanc and unite the valleys of Aosta and Chamonix"; nearly two centuries later his vision was finally realized when the road linking Courmayeur and Chamonix was finally opened after seven years of tunnelling. In previous centuries it had taken three days to travel between these two Alpine centres, over the high and permanently snow-bound Col du Géant (3,365m), whose ascent was almost as difficult as that of Mont Blanc; now the twelve-kilometre tunnel, which burrows a mile beneath the Aiguille du Midi at its deepest point, allows the journey to be done in a mere forty-five minutes.

The tunnel suffered a disastrous fire in 1999 that killed 41 people and kept it closed it for two years—a reminder of the potential dangers which travellers in a mountain environment still face. Nevertheless, the Alpine tunnels indicate how different travel over the mountains is today compared with centuries ago: one section of the Col du Lautaret near Briançon was once known as the Rampe des Commères, which translates as "gossips' rise". This was so-named because that section was too steep for horse-drawn carriages to cope with when fully laden, so their passengers had to get out and walk, presumably making the best of the situation by having a good gossip. Things have moved on considerably since then.

Out into the Fresh Air

Although by the late nineteenth century tourists could easily reach the major peaks and viewpoints by train, walking (as opposed to climbing) in the Alps remained a resolutely popular pastime. (As early as 1843 the geologist James Forbes had written caustically of the "beaten tracks, along which tourists follow one another, like a flock of sheep, in interminable succession.") Even so, early editions of Murray and Baedeker contained little information about walking, and to fill this gap in the market a Dubliner by the name of John Ball wrote *The Alpine Guide* (1863), whose intention was "not to conduct his readers along certain beaten tracks, but to put them in a position to choose for themselves such routes as may best suit their individual tastes and powers... to show what is open to the prudently adventurous." Soon the lower, safer slopes of the Alps were dotted with walkers brandishing alpenstocks and packed lunches.

There was, of course, a dress code to be adhered to: men wore dark tweed, while women were dressed in voluminous black dresses with thin gauzes of muslin over the brims of their hats to protect their complexion from the Alpine sun. And all carried a four or five foot-long alpenstock. Mark Twain observed that some tourists even came down to breakfast with their alpenstocks, and that "when his touring in Switzerland is finished, [the tourist] does not throw that broomstick away, but lugs it home with him, to the far corners of the earth...You see, the alpenstock is his trophy; his name is burned upon it... it is his regimental flag, and bears the record of his achievement."

When the going got tough, some resorted to being carried. A good description of how the weak or tired were ferried around in the mountains is provided, not surprisingly, by Twain, who can never resist recounting the more eccentric habits of tourists, particularly the weary ones:

> The Alpine litter is sometimes like a cushioned box made fast between the middles of two long poles, and sometimes it is a chair with a back to it and a support for the feet. It is carried by relays of strong porters. We met a few men and a great many ladies in litters; it seemed to me that most of the ladies looked pale and nauseated; their general aspect gave me the idea that they were patiently enduring a horrible suffering.

This was nothing, however, compared to the suffering experienced by walkers who met with disaster. Edward Whymper, the mountaineer who led the first successful conquest of the Matterhorn, later wrote a guidebook to the Mont Blanc region which included an entire chapter on disasters to have befallen tourists. They include a French architect who leant against a balustrade and fell to his death into the Gorge du Trient, and another walker who slipped and fell seventeen hundred feet and whose body "presented a most ghastly spectacle of bloody raw flesh."

Although fresh air was a free and easily obtainable commodity all over the Alps, some places began selling themselves by stressing the medically beneficial quality of their high-altitude location. Throughout the nineteenth century the increasing popularity of Alpine spas went hand-in-hand with mountain tourism; some people spent months in them, cleansing their respiratory system with fresh, pure mountain air. Indeed in *La Nouvelle Héloïse* Saint-Preux says in a letter to Julie that he is "surprised that baths of salutary and beneficial mountain air are not one of the great remedies of medicine and morality... I doubt whether any violent agitation or any vapour sickness could withstand a prolonged stay in the mountains." His remarks were prophetic: although a couple of places, such as St. Moritz and Leukerbad, had been popular spas since early times, it was the mid-nineteenth century that really witnessed the surge in popularity of fresh-air cures. Alongside Switzerland, spas also grew up in Alpine (and also lowland) areas of Austria, France and Germany. As the medical evidence for the efficacy of spa treatment steadily grew, many people took to spending months at a time in their favoured spa; some, with recurrent complaints, came back year after year, or even decided to live in their chosen spa for their whole lives, establishing the first expatriate communities high in the mountains.

One of the best-known of all Alpine spas is Davos, situated at an altitude of 1,560 metres in the Alps of eastern Switzerland, its sanatoria and hotels strung out along an attractive and often sun-drenched valley. The development of Davos as a health resort is due to the influence of one man, a Swiss physician named Alexander Spengler, who came here in 1853 and discovered in this " roadless collection of crude wooden chalets" (as it was then) a very surprising phenomenon: none of the village's inhabitants suffered from tuberculosis. Spengler was fascinated by his finding, as in those days TB was a serious condition, responsible (for instance) for one in six deaths in Britain. Spengler decided that the absence of TB in Davos was ascribable to the climate of the area, with its heady mix of warm, dry weather with fresh air and bright sunshine; he published his findings in a German medical journal in 1862.

Not surprisingly, given the prevalence of TB in Europe, wealthy sufferers (those who could afford the expense of travel) soon began making their way to Davos in their droves. By the mid-1860s there were Dutch, German, English and English patients aplenty, with baths and sanatoria to cater for them. (Treatments in the sanatoria were rarely successful. They included a procedure known as artificial pneumothorax, which involved the injection of wax, gas or oil into the pleural sac, so collapsing the lung and resting it; or the phrenic crush, whereby the diaphragm was paralyzed by smashing certain nerves in the neck.)

One of the pioneering visitors willing to subject themselves to such treatment was an Oxford don named John Addington Symonds, who came here in 1877 after attempted cures of his TB in Corsica and the French Riviera failed. His time in Davos was successful and he was later able to write: "The one thing relied upon is air… to inhale the maximum quantity of the keen mountain sunlight is the *sine qua non*. Everything else—milk drinking, douches, baths, friction, counter-irritant applications, and so forth, is subsidiary." He settled in Davos and his home, known as Am Hof, became the focus of a burgeoning English community in the town: Robert Louis Stevenson, who wrote part of *Treasure Island* here while having his own consumption cured in 1882, even dubbed Davos "the neighbourhood of J A Symonds." Numbers swelled still further after the railway from Chur arrived in 1890, and ten years later there were 700,000 overnight visitors per year. (Many found staying in the town in winter tedious, and started tobogganing and later skiing during the cold season—which formed the origins of the Davos's renown as a centre for winter sports.)

The cosmopolitan clientele inspired the writer Thomas Mann, who came to Davos in 1912 and 1921 and set his long, dense novel *The Magic Mountain* (1924) in the resort during the era immediately before the First World War. The book deals with a group of recuperating patients (including an Italian liberal, a Jesuit who is a convert from Judaism, and a seductive temptress from Russia) whose lives and preoccupations are presented as an allegory for the problems besetting Germany at the time. In the novel, the train journey up from Landquart (just north of Chur) to Davos is described as being "a magnificent succession of vistas… a solemn, phantasmagorical world of towering peaks… that appeared and disappeared with each new winding of the path." Once in Davos the sanatorium is portrayed as "a long building, with cupola and so many balconies that from a distance it looked porous, like a sponge." For today's visitors, the journey up from Landquart is still just as exhilarating, and in the town itself there are plenty of elegant old spa buildings exactly like the ones Mann described, nowadays vying for space on the crowded valley sides with more anonymous ski-oriented shops and chairlift stations. As well as being a world-renowned spa and a fashionable centre for skiing and snow boarding, Davos has lately developed a new role, as a meeting place for the World Economic Forum: the meetings in 2000 and 2001 brought hordes of anti-capitalist protestors and violent scenes to this normally sedate and comparatively remote mountain resort.

Subaqueaous Penance

"Taking the waters" is, of course, as much a part of spa treatment as breathing fresh air: high-altitude spas such as Davos also have curative springs, and dozens of lowland, exclusively water-based spas are scattered across the valleys and fringes of the Alps, from Aix-les-Bains and Évian in the west to Bad Ischl and Badgastein in the east. All of these offer health treatment through immersion in, and drinking of, reputedly naturally curative spring waters. The treatment patients voluntarily endure in Évian or Bad Ischl has not changed much in a hundred years; in 1873 Baedeker was able to describe sanatorium inmates being "clothed in long flannel dresses, [and sitting] up to their necks in water in a common bath, where they remain for several hours together. Each bather has a small floating table before him, from which his book, newspaper or coffee is enjoyed." Naturally, "the utmost order and decorum is preserved." These days most spa towns are still places of subdued refinement, with peaceful lakeside walks to enjoy by day, and sophisticated cultural offerings in the evenings.

Typical of Austrian spas is Badgastein, which has been around since medieval times, its reputation resting on radon-rich hot springs that are meant to help rheumatism and arthritis. Kaiser Wilhelm I of Germany and Bismarck were both frequent visitors in the nineteenth century. Nearby, the Heilstollen, a set of underground galleries reached by a train, naturally exude radon from their walls, and are visited by both patients and the curious; they were discovered in the 1940s when prospectors looking for gold and silver noticed that the atmosphere in the tunnels they were digging had a beneficial effect on bodily aches and pains. Another Austrian spa, Bad Ischl, was a favourite of the emperor Franz-Joseph I, who came here to take the waters every year from early childhood to old age; this was where he was engaged, to a fifteen-year-old girl called Elizabeth of Wittelsbach, and where he oversaw the landscaping of an English-style garden, the Kaiserpark, which later incorporated villas for both Elizabeth and the Emperor's mistress, a Viennese actress named Katharina Schratt.

The origins of the curative treatment in Bad Ischl date back to the 1820s when Josef Gotz, a local doctor, discovered that the saltwater baths taken by local salt miners relieved their rheumatism. In fact, Franz-Joseph's mother was so convinced of the curative effects of the water that she nicknamed her son the *Salzprinze*, the Salt Prince. Over the border in Germany, more salt-water treatment is on offer at Bad Reichenhall, where patients can walk through an open-air colonnade in which spray is inhaled; or there is Bad Tölz, situated where the Alps begin to rise south of Munich. Here, in the Middle Ages, goods brought across the mountains by mule were offloaded onto rafts and sent off to the Bavarian capital along the grey-green Isar river. Then a local farmer discovered some iodine-rich mud springs and the town reinvented itself as a spa. Now thousands come each year to bathe in mud pools, and then maybe take in a concert by the town's most famous cultural export, the Tölzer Knabenchor, or Tölz Boys' Choir. The choir tours world-wide in addition to performing every month in the spa and providing boy soloists for opera houses in Munich and Salzburg. Posters with photographs of the choir can be seen all over Bad Tölz: ranks of thick-set blond boys wearing smart jackets and lederhosen, with coloured stockings and cotton shirts completing a distinctively Bavarian outfit. (Bad Tölz has always been *very* Bavarian: in the 1930s the Nazis established an elite military training college for SS cadets here.)

Further west in Switzerland, and much higher than any of the Austrian or German spas, Leukerbad is situated at an altitude of 1,411 metres, its lime- and sulphur-rich waters reputed to alleviate rheumatism, gout and paralysis. Perhaps surprisingly, Murray's 1838 *Handbook to Switzerland* had little good to say about the place: "From the dreariness of the situation, the coldness of the climate, and the defects of the lodging, few English would desire to prolong their stay here." The guide also observed that the bath houses had been swept away by avalanches on at least three separate occasions. Of the actual treatment, it states that "Four hours of Subaqueaous penance are, by the doctor's decree, succeeded by one hour in bed; and many a fair nymph in extreme negligee with stockingless feet and uncoifed hair may be encountered crossing the open space between the bath and the hotels. From their condition one might suppose they had been driven out of doors by an alarm of fire, or some such threatening calamity."

Mark Twain was much kinder about the place.

The patients remain in the great tanks hours at a time. A dozen gentlemen and ladies occupy a tank together, and amuse themselves with rompings and various games. They have floating desks and tables, and they read or lunch or play chess in water that is breast deep. There are several of these bathing houses, and you can always tell when you are near one of them by the romping noises and shouts of laughter that proceed from it.

The two most famous spas in the French Alps are both situated on the shores of lakes: Aix-les-Bains beside the Lac du Bourget, and Évian beside Lake Geneva. The former, lying at the foot of Mont Revard (1,537m), treats rheumatism and respiratory ailments. It has been a spa for two thousand years—the Romans knew it as *Aquae Gratianus*, "the waters of the Emperor Gratianus", and there is a handsome arch, the Arc de Campanus, built to honour the Pompeia family, outside the Thermes Nationaux, in whose basement are the remains of a Roman *caldarium*. In the second half of the nineteenth century Aix was fashionable enough to attract many crowned heads of Europe, including Queen Victoria, who visited on three separate occasions (though one imagines that there would have been little in the way of romping noises coming from any of the baths that *she* frequented). The Emperor of Brazil and the Empress Elizabeth of Austria also took the waters here, but nowadays the grand hotels above the town where they stayed, such as the Splendide and the Royal, with their spectacular views of the lake and their private walled gardens, have been turned into luxury apartment blocks, and Aix now seems more confident of its role as a yachting centre than as a spa. Rather as a testament to its decline, the old English church of St. Swithun's, built in 1870 for the town's large expatriate community, these days lies neglected along an unremarkable back street.

Évian, on the other hand, seems to be doing rather well for itself: its water is cold, filtered through glacial sands, and is used in the treatment of kidney and digestive problems, in addition to being sent around the world in plastic bottles. The fact that the town has become an international brand-name cannot fail to have helped its fortunes in an era when spa treatment is not as fashionable as it was; today its hotels are full and the elegant *Jardin anglais* beside the lake busy with strollers. But still, Évian is not to everyone's taste: in *Switzerland* (1950), John Russell remarked that "The water itself has a flavour so flavourless as to assume the proportions of a philosophical problem," and described the obsequiousness of the service in the hotels where "white-coat acolytes pad silently to anticipate one's whims… they will address [the visitor], as if by divination, in an elegant version of his own vernacular; English visitors may count upon an almost Wildean grace of diction."

Mountain Writing

Not surprisingly, the relaxing spas, sublime scenery and quiet lakeside resorts have made the Alps a favourite haunt of writers ever since the Romantic poets nearly two centuries ago. Those who came to write in the second half of the nineteenth century include Charles Dickens, Johann Wolfgang von Goethe, Henry James, William Thackeray, Thomas Mann and Sir Arthur Conan Doyle, many of whom included memorable descriptions of the mountains in their work.

Charles Dickens is best known, of course, for his novels set amidst the grime and grind of Victorian England. But the author travelled extensively in France, Switzerland and Italy (and also the United States), and published his reflections on these places in a number of essays. He was always very fond of the Alps. In 1844 Dickens left England and took his wife and five children to live in Genoa, on the Italian Riviera. He sent descriptive pieces week by week to John Forster, his future biographer, which were later published in a collection entitled *Pictures From Italy*.

Here is his evocative description from that book of crossing into Switzerland via the Simplon Pass at dead of night: "It was late in November… the air was piercing cold. But the serenity of the night, and the grandeur of the road, with its impenetrable shadows, and deep glooms, and its sudden turns into the shining of the moon and its incessant roar of falling water, rendered the journey more and more sublime at every step."

A little further along the road towards the pass, the Gorge of Gondo was "savage and grand beyond description, with smooth-fronted precipices, rising up on either hand, and almost meeting overhead. Thus we went, climbing on our rugged way, higher and higher all night, without a moment's weariness: lost in the contemplation of the black rocks, the tremendous heights and depths, the fields of smooth snow lying in the clefts and hollows, and the fierce torrents thundering headlong down the deep abyss." At daybreak the family reached the top of the pass and watched the rising sun strike "upon the waste of snow, and turning it a deep red," after which they began

> rapidly to descend, passing under everlasting glaciers, by means of arched galleries, hung with clusters of dripping icicles; under and over foaming waterfalls... down, over lofty bridges, and through horrible ravines: a little shifting speck in the vast desolation of ice and snow, and monstrous granite rocks... gradually down, by zig-zag roads, lying between an upward and a downward precipice, into warmer weather, calmer air, and softer scenery, until there lay before us, glittering like gold or silver in the thaw and sunshine, the metal-covered, red, green, yellow, domes and church-spires of a Swiss town.

In June the next year Dickens had cause to return to England, this time via another pass, the St. Gotthard, which was "not as fine as the Simplon... the loneliness and wildness of the Simplon are not equalled there." He was accompanied by Charley Dickens, his eight-year-old son, who later recalled "an extremely rocky and icy walk... I can see the pair of us now, he stalking away in the distance, I struggling in vain to keep up, very tired but extremely proud of being with him."

Although Dickens often mentioned the Alps in his travel writing, the mountains only appear once in his fiction—in the opening to Part Two of *Little Dorrit*, where parallels are drawn between the stark monastery at the top of the Great St. Bernard Pass and the Marshalsea prison in London, in which Little Dorrit's father had recently been incarcerated. The novel describes the monastery at night as "another ark... [floating] on the shadowy waves", although the next day "the bright morning sun dazzled the eyes, the snow had ceased, the mists had vanished, the mountain air was so clear and light that the new sensation of breathing it was like having entered on a new existence."

Although his descriptions of the pass and its monastery, in *Little Dorrit* and elsewhere, present the place as a dark, dismal refuge in the mountains, Dickens was charmed by most parts of the Alps, and towards the end of his life he had a mock-up Swiss chalet built in the garden of his house at Gads Hill Place just outside Rochester in Kent. The chalet, which came in kit form (ninety-four separate pieces in fifty-eight boxes), was a Christmas present from the French actor Charles Fechter, who had worked with Dickens on a number of dramatic productions in London. Dickens was so excited by his gift that he persuaded his guests to help him start putting it together, during their stay with him over the Christmas holiday period in 1864. When it was finally complete, the view from the window was very un-Swiss, encompassing fields of corn sweeping down towards the Thames, with its yachts and steam boats; but Dickens spent much time in the chalet, hanging mirrors throughout to give it a feeling of light and space. He wrote in it when the weather was warm enough, and was in fact working in the chalet on his last (and unfinished) novel *The Mystery of Edwin Drood* the day before he died, in June 1870.

Dickens could hardly be accused of cashing in on the Victorian mania for all things Alpine, but the same could not be said for another Victorian novelist, who used the drama of the Alps to good effect in one of his most famous works. In 1891 Sir Arthur Conan Doyle chose to kill off his hero, Sherlock Holmes, by having him plunge to his death in the Reichenbach Falls above the small town of Meiringen in central Switzerland. The fictional detective's death came as the result of a struggle with his arch-enemy, the diabolical Professor Moriarty, whom Holmes and Watson had been pursuing across Europe. *The Final Problem* recounts how, while staying at Meiringen, Holmes and Watson decide to take a break from detective work and indulge in some sightseeing. Reaching the falls, the pair find

a fearful place. The torrent, swollen by the melting snow, plunges into a tremendous abyss, from which the spray rolls up like the smoke from a burning house. The cleft into which the river hurls itself is an immense chasm, lined by glistening coal-black rock, and narrowing into a creaming, boiling pit of incalculable depth, which brims over and shoots the stream onward over its jagged lip. The long sweep of green water roaring forever down, and the thick flickering curtain of spray hissing for ever upwards, turn a man giddy with their constant whirl and clamour.

While the two friends are visiting the falls, Dr. Watson receives a hastily written note asking him to return to Meiringen to attend to an English woman who has suddenly been taken ill; but the letter is a fake, sent by Moriarty, and when Watson realizes the trick and returns to the falls, Holmes has gone—over the edge, Watson assumes, his body "deep down in that dreadful cauldron of swirling water and seething foam". The text in the original book is accompanied by a famous illustration by Francis Mosley, of Holmes in his deerstalker hat engaged in a struggle with Moriarty high above a swift-moving river which churns remorselessly at the bottom of a gorge.

The Reichenbach Falls are in fact just as Conan Doyle described them, crashing down the side of a wooded slope in a series of chasms and whirlpools in a charming spot overlooking the pretty town of Meiringen (which, incidentally, gives its name to a world-famous dessert: meringue). A bumpy funicular leads up to the lowest point of the falls, from where paths and steps lead around and over the cascading streams of water. One narrow track expires on a thin ledge with sheer rock faces above and below, and it is not difficult to see how a scuffle here could end in tragedy; a plaque on the cliff wall indicates that this is indeed the spot where Holmes supposedly met his end. (In 1903 Conan Doyle gave in to the pressure of popular opinion and resurrected his hero for some more adventures, coming up with the unlikely claim that the detective had never slipped to his death at all but had managed to grab hold of a tuft of grass in his fall.)

Down in the valley, Meiringen itself was very popular with the Victorians (according to the story, Holmes and Watson stayed in the Englischer Hof hotel), and appropriately the town is located on the curving, climbing, immensely picturesque railway line linking the two favoured resorts of the English, Lucerne and Interlaken. Nowadays the town has a Sherlock Holmes museum, situated in the basement of the former English church (which, as we have seen, was the first to be established in the Alps). Here is a lovingly-detailed mock-up of 221b Baker Street, crammed with books and Holmes paraphernalia, such as a folded copy of *The Times*, and the detective's violin. Other bits and pieces in the museum include school memorabilia from Stonyhurst College, the boarding school on the bleak Lancashire moors that Conan Doyle entered at the age of ten (it is interesting to see his name on a school roll that lists other boys named Sherlock and Moriarty). The museum opened in 1991 with the author's daughter Jean Conan Doyle present. The church sits on Conan Doyle Square, and needless to say, the town abounds in hotels and cafés whose names echo the Sherlock Holmes and London themes. The Holmes connection comes into its own every 4 May, when fans from around the world gather in Meiringen to commemorate the detective's demise, often dressed up in deerstalker hats and caps; the gathering is an eccentric homage both to Conan Doyle's creation, and also to the enduring English love affair with the Alps.

Besides English authors, the Alps played host to myriad other writers from Europe and America during the nineteenth and early twentieth centuries. The German poet Rainer Maria Rilke (1875-1926) spent his last six years in Sierre, in the Rhône Valley, where he wrote *Sonnets to Orpheus* and died after pricking his finger on a rose-thorn. The Philosopher Friedrich Nietzsche (1844-1900) had a summer home for eight years at Sils, near St. Moritz, where he wrote *Also Sprach Zarathustra*. At Montagnola near Lugano is the Collina d'Oro, home for forty-three years to the German writer Hermann Hesse (1877-1962), who came here came here in 1919 following a traumatic separation from his family. He wrote the classics *Steppenwolf, The Glass Bead Game* and *Siddharta* in two villas in the village, the Casa Camuzzi and the Casa Bodmer. He was awarded the Nobel Prize for Literature in 1946 and died in Montagnola in 1962; the Casa Camuzzi is now a museum dedicated to his life and work.

Grenoble, the greatest city of Alpine France, was the home town of Henri Marie Beyle (1783-1842), who wrote under the pen-name of Stendhal; his eccentric biography *The Life of Henry Brulard* contains much about his early life but says virtually nothing about the mountains. And other writers, even if they did not make their homes in the Alps, passed through the region and wrote of its beauty: Ernest Hemingway set a scene of *A Farewell to Arms* in the Grand Hôtel des Iles Borromées in Stresa, on Lake Maggiore; Henry James travelled in the region too, and wrote "One can't describe the beauty of the Italian lakes... Nor would one try if one could." (In former times, the lakes had inspired Pliny the Younger, who had a villa at Bellagio on Lake Como, and Goethe, who was imprisoned as a suspected spy after making a sketch of a castle on the shores of Lake Garda.) All these writers further enhanced the popularity of the Alps among Europe's middle classes, and ensured the tide of nineteenth-century tourists remained unabated.

Musicians and Artists: "that serene and glorious Switzerland"

Scores of artists and composers came to the Alps, too, from the mid-nineteenth century onwards. One of them was Gustav Mahler (1860-1911), who lived in a succession of remote retreats in Austria. The first was at Steinbach on the Attersee, where he stayed a number of times at what is now the Gasthof Föttinger, writing his second and third symphonies. The composer was notoriously sensitive to extraneous noise: organ-grinders were paid to stay away from the street outside and cows had their bells muffled, while children were resolutely kept at bay. Later Mahler sought solitude on another lake, the Wörthersee, close to Klagenfurt in the very east of the mountains. He purchased a grand house on the lake shore, and in a small clearing in the woods above it he built a simple wooden summer house in which he composed his middle symphonies; this delightful place, little more than four walls, a floor and a ceiling, and only reachable by walking up through the trees from the busy holiday beaches along the Wörthersee, is now kept as a virtual shrine to Mahler's memory. But in 1907 the composer's eldest daughter Maria died in Klagenfurt of scarlet fever, just before her fifth birthday, and Mahler never again came back to the area, spending his later summers in a remote spa in the Tyrolean Alps at Dobbiaco.

Another composer fond of finding lakeside retreats in which to work was Richard Wagner (1813-83), who lived in a villa at Tribschen, a district of Lucerne, from 1866 until 1872. Wagner was no stranger to Lucerne when he bought the property; he had written *Tristan* during a prolonged stay at the Schweizerhof Hotel in 1859, while the *Siegfried Idyll* was composed in another Lucerne residence, the Hôtel du Lac, in 1852. Wagner spotted the beautiful, secluded lakeside property at Tribschen when he was travelling in Switzerland with his partner Cosima, the daughter of Franz Liszt. "Nobody will get me out of here again," he later said of his new home. "The works I conceived in that serene and glorious Switzerland, with my eyes on the beautiful gold-crowned mountains, are masterpieces, and nowhere else could I have conceived them."

Wagner's peaceful villa, rising behind trees on its own promontory, overlooks water on three sides, and has fine views across the lake. In 1870 the composer married Cosima and his time in Lucerne became one of his most creatively fertile periods. In 1938 Arturo Toscanini conducted a concert in the house, inaugurating the first Lucerne Festival, which has grown to become one of the most prestigious music festivals in the world; not surprisingly, the house itself is now a museum dedicated to Wagner's life and work.

Many painters have also found that the mountains offered a secluded and inspirational environment in which to develop their craft. Gustav Klimt (1862-1918) frequently stayed in a house on the Attersee in the early years of the twentieth century, drawn by the same craggily beautiful scenery that had drawn Mahler a few years previously. His mistress Emilie Flöge owned a house in Unterach on the same lake, which often make appearances in his paintings. Murnau, an ancient medieval town in the Bavarian Alps, is a cradle of the modern art movement in Germany, thanks to the painter Gabriele Münter (1877-1962), who bought a country house on the shores of the Staffelsee in 1909. He spent many summers here, and it soon became the focus for a group that became known as Der Blaue Reiter, including such luminaries as Wassily Kandinsky and Franz Marc.

Another lakeside resort, Ascona on Lake Maggiore, has been attracting a diverse assembly of philosophers, spiritualists, and artists for well over a hundred years, starting with Mikhail Bakunin, the Russian anarchist, who came here in the 1870s. By the turn of the century Henri Oedenkoven and Uda Hofmann had established a vegetarian artists' colony on a hillside overlooking the resort, and in the inter-war era Ascona became the haunt of Isadora Duncan and many others. Lenin, Jung, Hesse, Kandinsky and Paul Klee all passed through the town at one time or another, lending the place a distinctively bohemian edge at odds with the somewhat staid character of Locarno, of which Ascona is a part.

Tobogganing and Skating: "A new excitement to the life of man upon his planet"

Until the later decades of the nineteenth century, tourism in the Alps was exclusively a summer affair. No-one wanted to come to the mountains during the dark, cold days of winter, when the passes were snow-bound and the days were short, dark and frequently freezing. When the first snow flurries of late autumn began to dust the valleys and the resorts, the last tourists packed their bags and headed home; for the next six months the Alps would once again be the preserve of farmers and hunters, and the only foreigners who remained were spa patients, shivering away high in their mountain sanatoria.

Yet by the 1860s the realization was gradually dawning that people might be missing out on something by so resolutely ignoring the Alps during the winter. John Ruskin travelled to the Alps in all seasons and wrote that "the finest things one can see in summer are nothing compared to the winter scenery among the Alps." His fellow Alpine enthusiast, Leslie Stephen, maintained that in winter "the whole region becomes part of dreamland... the very daylight has an unreal glow... the peaks are in a state of suspended animation... they are spell-bound, dreaming of dim abysses of past time or of the summer that is more real to them than life." But it would take more than wise words from eminent literary authorities such as these to kick-start winter tourism: an entrepreneur was needed, a businessman who was willing to take a risk, and that innovator came in the form of a St. Moritz hotelier named Johannes Badrutt.

Badrutt's big chance came on the day in 1864 when four Englishmen, enjoying the final hours of their summer holiday in St. Moritz, invited him to join them for a farewell drink in the Engadiner Kulm hotel, of which Badrutt was the owner. Trying to persuade his guests to return to the hotel in mid-winter, Badrutt made a bet with them that if they came back during December the weather would be as sunny as it was in summer. The suggestion was met with gasps of disbelief from the Englishmen, so Badrutt said that he would pay their expenses if the weather was not as fine as he'd promised. Intrigued, his guests returned to St. Moritz shortly before Christmas, and found themselves basking in the winter weather for which the town is famous—an apparently endless series of dry, cold, and brilliantly sunny winter days. The Englishmen stayed until March, indulging in the then novel pursuits of skating on the frozen lake, sledding down the snowy slopes and relaxing by sunning themselves on the hotel terrace; Johannes Badrutt had won his bet and the concept of an Alpine winter sports holiday had begun. (In 1954 modernization work at the hotel revealed hidden documents confirming that this bet had indeed been placed, and was set down on paper in the form of a written agreement; also unearthed was an entry in the visitors' book by one of the Englishmen concerned, Lord Shrewsbury, who described the weather during their winter holiday: "far from finding it cold, the heat of the sun is so intense at times that sun shades were indispensable," he wrote. "The brilliance of the sun, the blueness of the sky and the clearness of the atmosphere quite surprised us.")

In the same decade as Johannes Badrutt won his wager in St. Moritz, the first recreational skiers started to populate Switzerland's snowy slopes. Skiing had been around in the Alps for hundreds of years, but not as a form of outdoor sport. In medieval times hunters, traders and farmers regularly donned skis, simply to get around in the snowy valleys during the harsh Alpine winters. Even earlier, the Vikings had also used skis, and skiing as a form of sport appropriately originated in Scandinavia, its exact beginning marked by the journey on skis that a Norwegian named Sondre Norheim made from Telemark to Christiania (now Oslo) in 1868. Soon after, one of Norheim's fellow countrymen, Odd Kjelsberg, brought the first skis to Glarus in eastern Switzerland and yet another Norwegian, a man named Bjornstad, opened a ski shop in Bern (Norwegians are also credited with introducing skiing to Australia, California and New Zealand).

The sport took time to catch on: Christoph Iselin, one of the pioneers of Swiss skiing, had to practice in the dark at Glarus as he thought people would laugh at him. Then one winter in the 1880s, an Englishman named Colonel Napier rented Robert Louis Stevenson's old chalet at Davos, and discovered that his Norwegian manservant had brought a pair of skis with him; Napier was intrigued and strapped the wooden planks onto his feet. Thanks to the colonel, skiing quickly became popular in the spa, largely as an activity to kill time during the snow-bound days of winter.

Another early pioneer of skiing at Davos was Conan Doyle. Staying at the Hôtel Belvedere, supporting his wife who was suffering from TB, Conan Doyle found that his "life was bounded by the snow and fir," so took up "with some energy the winter sports for which the place was famous." In March 1894 he crossed the Maienfelder Furka from Davos to Arosa with two Swiss guides—and so might well have been the first English person ever to tackle a mountain tour on skis. Later, he presciently wrote in *Strand* magazine that "the time will come when hundreds of Englishmen will come to Switzerland for the skiing season between March and April."

Skiing was not the only form of winter recreation in the Alps: tobogganing was introduced at around the same time, and for a time was much more popular. Robert Louis Stevenson was an enthusiast of tobogganing; like Conan Doyle he took up the sport to give him something to do during the cold winter days at Davos: "the whole glittering valley and all the lights of the great hotels lie for a moment at your feet," was how he described hurtling down the slopes, feet-first and hanging on for dear life. "Tobogganing teaches the pulse an unaccustomed tune, and adds a new excitement to the life of man upon his planet."

In 1883 another English resident of Davos, John Addington Symonds, formed a Tobogganing Club; the Alpinist Arnold Lunn later declared that "the evolution of tobogganing at Davos, from a mere mode of transport among the Swiss into an organized sport among the British, is a characteristic episode in Anglo-Swiss relations." Once he had founded his club, Symonds encouraged the residents of the hotels at Davos to compete for prizes on a toboggan run established along the road from Davos to Klosters, and many races were staged between visitors and locals, the latter using the traditional *schlitti* (wooden sledges) deployed in the Alps to transport loads across the mountains for centuries. The English community at St. Moritz got to hear about the competition and, not to be outdone by their near-neighbours, established an even more exciting competition route, designed by an English major (W. H. Bulpett) and running past the tiny hamlet of Cresta. The first race along the Cresta Run was held in February 1884, when the over-confident local team from St. Moritz was beaten by a visiting team from Davos. (Nowadays the death-defying 1,200-metre track is the fastest and most famous bobsleigh run in the world.)

Ice-skating was also a popular sport in the years before skiing took hold: the International Skating Union was founded in Davos in 1892, and ever since the Hôtel Belvedere had opened there in 1875, English skaters could be seen every winter, gliding across the ice dressed in frock-coats, sponge-bag trousers, white ties, and top hats.

While Davos and St. Moritz were busy with skaters and tobogganists, skiing was having a harder time winning favours among English visitors. One early British skier was Gerald Fox, who learned to ski in Norway in 1889 and two years later took his skis to Grindelwald, where he used to put them on in his room in the Bear Hotel and clump down the corridors with them strapped to his feet before heading out onto the slopes. Such behaviour marked him down as an eccentric rather than a sportsman, a brush with which many early skiers were tarred (skiers in St. Moritz were at that time referred to as "plank-hoppers".) But in 1903 the Davos English Ski Club was founded, and skiing was on the way to claiming its place as the premier Alpine winter sport.

Henry Lunn and the Development of Skiing

The person who did most to further the popularity of skiing in the Alps was a Lincolnshire-born Englishman named Henry Lunn, who transformed the winter tourism scene in the region just as Thomas Cook had revolutionized summer tourism a generation before. Lunn was an ordained Methodist minister and in his early adult life was a key figure in the ecumenical movement. In 1892 he decided that a meeting of all the different Protestant churches was needed, in order that the various denominations could be given a chance to discuss some of their differences. Grindelwald, a mountain resort lying at the foot of the Eiger and easily accessible by train from Interlaken, was chosen as the venue, partly because it had been the former retreat of a saint, Bernard of Clairvaux, and partly because of its popularity among the English. Lunn started to make the travel arrangements for his delegates and found that he had a flair for administration and organization. He also found that he had a fondness for winter sports.

In 1898, six years after he had successfully organized the Grindelwald conference, Lunn was back in the Alps, this time in Chamonix, and accompanied by his ten-year-old son Arnold. Some Swiss guides were engaged to teach the pair how to ski. Arnold, who grew up to play just as important a part in the development of skiing as his father, and was knighted for his services to Anglo-Swiss relations, later recalled that at that time, around four or five Englishmen living there were keen skiers, but no locals indulged in what they must have thought was an odd, Anglo-Saxon habit. But the sport was catching on fast: the Lunns were there only three years before a local doctor, Michel Payot, started organizing instructional courses (which led to the first crossing of the Col du Géant on skis). During his visit to Chamonix Henry Lunn saw that skiing was about to undergo an explosion in popularity, and seized his business opportunity: the Public Schools Alpine Sports Club was born.

In 1903 the club organized the first winter sports package tours in the Alps; the resorts selected by Henry Lunn were St. Moritz, Davos and Arosa. The club was essentially a travel agency, but its name was deliberately chosen for its snob value. Arnold Lunn later wrote that the club appealed to those "who liked to preserve their social environment [and] dine with congenial Englishmen." With its membership limited to ex-public school boys, and those who had been to one of the older universities or had held a commission in the services, it was not surprising that a certain code of behaviour and dress was expected: "It would have been unthinkable for an Englishman not to dress for dinner at any one of the leading sports centres during the first decade of the century," Arnold Lunn wrote. "I remember one miserable outcast whose registered luggage did not arrive for a week... and then the cloud lifted. His luggage arrived. I shall never forget the expression on his face, when he appeared for the first time in evening dress. He looked like a man who had just been cleared by court martial of a disgraceful charge."

Soon Adelboden, Mürren, Wengen and Montana were full of parties of British winter holiday enthusiasts; a guidebook of the time, *Switzerland in Winter,* written by Will and Carine Cadby, remarked that "Mürren's winter visiting population was composed of skiing duchesses, skating lords and curling bishops." In January 1903 the first Public Schools Alpine Sports Club Challenge Cup was staged in Adelboden, bringing competitive skiing to the mountains for the first time. Less than twenty years later, in 1921, the first British downhill championships were staged at Wengen (which in the following year played host to a Varsity race between Oxford and Cambridge, while Arnold Lunn staged the first slalom competition down the valley at Mürren). In 1924 a group of Englishmen meeting in the Palace Hotel at Mürren founded a downhill racing club, which they named after the Roberts of Kandahar, the oldest skiing race in the world; thus the name of a remote town in the northwest frontier province of India (now in Afghanistan) became associated with the most prestigious skiing race in the Alps. (By 1930 St. Anton had a Kandahar race, too, and in 1930 over one hundred skiers competed in the Arlberg-Kandahar competition.)

Meanwhile, Henry Lunn was making a lot of money out of his organizational flair and his ability to spot gaps in a growing market; he later wrote of his love of being in the Alps in winter, under "the eternal sun... [where] the sparkling atmosphere is more of a tonic than the finest champagne." And although he abandoned his ecumenical role within the churches to become a full-time travel agent, Lunn still managed to find the time to found an English church in the Alps, St. Luke's, in the grounds of the Palace Hotel at Montana, thus continuing a tradition that had begun thirty years previously with churches in Meiringen, Davos and Zermatt.

During the first decades of the twentieth century, and spurred on by Lunn's pioneering efforts, mountain resorts such as Davos, St. Moritz and Chamonix gradually reinvented themselves as skiing centres. (St Moritz was the first to introduce drag lifts, when a local engineer, Gerhard Müller, strung some rope along a chain of makeshift pylons and attached one of the ends to an old motorbike engine.) Other resorts followed: in the 1930s Mussolini developed Italy's first ski resort, Breuil-Cervina, as part of his drive towards creating a healthy nation; the ski lifts here reached a previously unheard-of altitude of 3,500 metres, while the grand hotels ensured the patronage of a wealthy and influential clientele. Another well-known Italian resort, Sestrière, was targeted at a very different sort of visitor: it was developed (with *Il Duce*'s blessing) by the Fiat magnate Giovanni Agnelli as a means of alleviating poverty in the mountains, and it mainly attracted factory-workers from the northern industrial cities (Agnelli asked for the height of the sinks in hotel rooms to be raised so that people were not tempted to urinate in them.)

Appealing to a better class of visitor, Kitzbühel in Austria had been a mining town in the Middle Ages and then a spa, its peat baths reputedly offering curative respite; then Franz Reisch imported skis from Norway in the 1890s and within a few years the place had become the premier resort of the Eastern Alps. France was slightly slower to get going with its resorts; one of the first, Méribel, was created by a British aristocrat, Lord Lindsay, after the *Anschluss* rendered Austrian ski resorts off-limits in the 1930s. Val d'Isère was another resort that was quite a late starter: in 1923 Findlay Muirhead wrote in his guide to the French Alps that "the villagers practically hibernate in winter, as the cult of winter sports has not yet reached their solitude"; but in the years after the Second World War it grew into one of the world's most famous ski resorts.

Skiing was soon an immensely popular sport with a worldwide following, and in recognition of this the International Olympic Committee decided to stage a winter games in the season preceding the summer ones; Chamonix was selected to stage the first ever competition, in 1924. No longer was the little town beneath Mont Blanc an obscure climbing centre; now it was in the big league of the international sporting calendar. St. Moritz followed in 1928, and in 1935 the neighbouring resorts of Garmisch and Partenkirchen in Bavaria were officially amalgamated so that the 1936 games could be staged in Garmisch-Partenkirchen. Since the Second World War the games have been staged at many more resorts in the Alps, including Innsbruck in 1964 and 1976, while places such as Chamonix (1968) and St Moritz (1948) have welcomed the games back for a second time. Ski-jumps grew from the valley sides of these resorts like curly concrete appendages: the Planica jumps at Kranjska Gora in Slovenia were built in the 1930s and are still the longest in the world. By that time, Alpine recreational skiing had come a long way from its origins in places like Davos where only thirty years previously it had been little more than an eccentric hobby.

Skiing was also found to have military uses. Just before the turn of the century, a young army officer garrisoned in Briançon was so convinced of the usefulness of skis for travelling through the snow-covered Alps that he personally funded the kitting-out of seven of the men under his command. In 1901 these *chasseurs alpines* (Alpine troops) skied down the slopes of Mongenèvre in front of a panel of military experts. The army top brass were won over: in 1903 a military school was founded in the town (which is now a major ski resort) and from them on Alpine troops were properly equipped and trained.

At exactly the same time, in Austria, Colonel Bilgeri began to equip and train his men in skiing, and later wrote a 150-page instruction manual on Alpine warfare (which was captured and used by the Italians). Then during the First World War the Italian army set up climbing courses in the Dolomites consisting of cables, ladders and ropes; known as *via ferrata*, these courses were kept secret until the 1950s, and in the 1980s the first *via ferrata* course constructed specifically for recreational climbers was opened near Briançon. Nowadays *via ferrata* is a popular activity all over the Alps, with many a sheer rock face peppered with climbers fitted with harnesses and helmets and shinning up ladders attached to the cliff wall.

Because skiing took place in the winter, when it became dark early, and early resorts were still in effect small villages with no discernable cultural life to offer visitors, an *après-ski* scene had to be established from scratch by those who wanted it. The Scotch Tea Rooms in St. Moritz served crumpets, scones and tea-cakes during the winter evenings, while in Davos there was a literary society with guest lecturers: M. J. Michael spoke on "Some facts about the insides and outsides of insects", and another lecture, by John Addington Symonds, was on "Lyrics from the Elizabethan Song Book". Fashionable hotels such as the Palace at St Moritz, which boasted a Rafael original hanging in the bridge room, livened up the dark, cold evenings with fancy-dress parties.

Such activities were all very tame by today's standards, but were the forerunners of the clubs and bars that are now crammed with the *après-ski* crowd every evening during the season in Verbier or St. Anton. And it is these activities, more than any other, which have meant that Alpine resorts have had a long-standing appeal among the rich and famous: in the 1930s St Anton became a magnet for European film stars, and then the favoured watering hole for Luftwaffe flying aces in the 1940s; Alfred Hitchcock once remarked that he had been going to St. Moritz on and off for thirty-five years without ever once indulging in any winter sports. Nowadays, some of *the* places to hang out with the glitterati include Gstaad, whose guest list has included King Baudouin of the Belgians, Prince Rainier of Monaco, and Zaire's former military dictator, Mobuto; and St. Moritz, which has long been a prime winter resort of the international jet-set and European royalty (although Prince Charles has for a long time favoured its near-neighbour, Klosters).

The Monarch of Mont Blanc

With so many hundreds of books and articles written on the subject, it seems sensible to tell the story of Alpine mountaineering by focusing on the successful execution of just three climbs: Mont Blanc, because it is the highest mountain in the range; the Matterhorn, because its conquest in 1865 resulted in the first "great" mountaineering disaster; and the north face of the Eiger, because its ascent provides one of the greatest challenges in the entire field of mountaineering. Classic texts such as Edward Whymper's *Scrambles Among the Alps* (1865), or *White Spider*, Heinrich Harrer's 1959 account of the first successful conquest of the north face of the Eiger, are there for those who want to delve deeper into this vital chapter in the history of the mountains.

From Chamonix, Mont Blanc does not look as forbidding as it is supposed to be; rounded and smooth rather than steep and jagged, the mountain takes the form of a hump-shaped expanse of pure whiteness

that to the uninitiated makes its prospective ascent look encouragingly easy. But the tragic history of the climbing attempts on this mountain proves the optimist wrong, every time. The story of its conquest starts in the middle of the eighteenth century with the academic and mountain enthusiast, Horace-Bénédict de Saussure. He was the Professor of Natural History at the Geneva Academy, and grew up in that city, first visiting Chamonix at the age of twenty-two. "From childhood I have had an absolute passion for the mountains," he later wrote; "I still remember the sensation I experienced when, for the first time, my hands touched the rocks of the Salève and my eyes enjoyed its vistas."

In 1760 de Saussure's fascination with Mont Blanc led him to offer a reward to the first person to reach its summit (he also promised to meet the expenses of those who tried and failed to make the ascent). The first person to answer the professor's call was an egocentric, womanizing would-be writer and painter named Marc Théodore Bourrit, who duly failed on two attempts in the early 1780s. His attempts were followed by that of another local, Lombard Meunier, who was of the mind that no provisions were needed on the climb, save a scent bottle and an umbrella (not surprisingly, he was also unsuccessful). Clearly, ascending the mountain was not as straightforward as it looked.

Then in 1786 a young doctor from Chamonix named Michel-Gabriel Paccard joined forces with a local farmer and crystal-hunter, Jacques Balmat, in a bid to win de Saussure's extraordinary prize. Balmat was known to be boastful, vain and devious; Paccard, on the other hand, was more measured and intelligent. Starting from their bivouac point high on the mountainside at 4am on 7 August 1786, they managed to dodge collapsing snow bridges, brave the bitter cold, cope with altitude sickness and survive winds powerful enough to blow them off the mountainside, to reach the summit at 6.23pm on the same day. "The monarch lay at the proud foot of a conqueror," Balmat wrote modestly of his accomplishment. "Everything around belonged to me! I was the monarch of Mont Blanc! I was the statue on this unique pedestal!" As for the view, which stretched from Lake Neuchâtel in the Swiss lowlands all the way to the Mediterranean port city of Genoa, he could see "mountains all fleecy with snow, rising from meadows of the richest green." Below them, most of Chamonix was watching the mountain through spy-glasses, and saw clearly the signal that Balmat and Paccard gave signifying that they had reached the top—a handkerchief waved wildly from the end of a baton. (Balmat recorded that, from the summit, he in turn could see the crowds of people gathered on the town's market square, watching them.) The pair spent little more than half an hour on the summit, heading back down at 6.57pm and reaching their bivouac spot a little before midnight. By that time they were suffering dangerously from frostbite and snow blindness. Balmat later recalled that, on looking in a mirror, his "eyes were red, my face black and my lips blue... every time I laughed or yawned the blood spouted out from my lips and cheeks, and in addition I was half blind."

This first successful attempt on Mont Blanc was followed by a notoriously vicious literary spat. Balmat quickly claimed de Saussure's reward, which was augmented by money given by the King of Sardinia, the ruler of Savoy at that time. Marc Bourrit, already the author of a book on his own (failed) attempt at conquering the peak, wrote and published a book on the Balmat/Paccard attempt, in which he declared that Balmat was the hero and Paccard was nothing but a liability. Bourrit's animosity towards Paccard apparently stemmed from an earlier attempt the two men had made on the peak, which to Bourrit's shame ended when he became unsettled by the high mountain environment, forcing them both to come back down. Bourrit's *Letter on the First Journey to the Summit of Mont Blanc* became popular over Europe and his version of the story went largely unchallenged; Chamonix itself was soon divided into those who supported Bourrit's claims, and those who supported Paccard (on one occasion the two men actually came to blows outside an inn in the town). De Saussure was a supporter of Paccard and later wrote "this modest and sympathetic character has been very unjustly relegated to the second rank behind the somewhat theatrical figure

of Balmat". The argument rumbled on for the rest of both men's lives: Paccard was later elected mayor of his village and married Balmat's sister Marie, while Balmat continued as a mountain guide, meeting his death in 1834 at the age of 72 while prospecting for gold amidst the high peaks.

Next it was de Saussure himself who climbed the mountain. He was accompanied by eighteen guides and took along a copy of Homer to read, no doubt hoping to be inspired by tales of the Greek heroes. Like many climbers he was affected by palpitations, nausea and sleeplessness—but he succeeded, reaching the summit at 10am on 3 August 1787, and recording his exploits in *Voyages dans les Alpes*. The following year de Saussure climbed the mountain again, this time in the cause of science; while camped out on the Col du Géant, a thousand metres below the summit, he experienced the severest thunderstorms imaginable, during which the wind gusted in "blasts of an indescribable violence… we felt even the mountain shake under our mattresses; the wind penetrated through the cracks in the wall of the hut, it once lifted my sheets and rugs and froze me from head to foot."

More climbs were made during the course of the nineteenth century; indeed, ascending the mountain became so popular that huts were built for climbers at various places on the route up to the summit, and in 1821 the Compagnie de Guides was formed in Chamonix, allowing the authorities greater control over access to the mountain. (Initially, it seems that the quality of mountain guides was poor, since more or less any Chamonix man could put himself forward; but the situation gradually improved, and by 1995 there were over one hundred guides in this much-respected organization, taking around ten thousand clients a year up the mountain.)

In 1808 Marie Paradis became the first woman to make the ascent, and her feat was followed in 1838 when the Comtesse Henriette d'Angeville, a minor French aristocrat whose father had been executed in the revolution, went up dressed in trousers made from stout Scottish wool. The countess' attire rather scandalized polite opinion of the day; but she wanted to prove herself the equal of any male climber, and carved the words *vouloir, c'est pouvoir*—"to will it is to be able to do it"— into the ice at the top. (On the way up she made her guides promise that if she died during the attempt they would carry her body to the summit.)

Amidst the triumphs of successful climbs, the nineteenth century also brought tragedy to the slopes of Mont Blanc. One of the most poignant accounts of a disaster came in 1870 when a group of guides set off from Chamonix to try to discover what had happened to a party of missing American climbers. As they expected, the guides found some bodies in the snow, with one walker "sitting down, with his head leaning on one hand and the elbow on a knapsack still containing some meat and bread and cheese." The unfortunate man had written a final letter to his wife in his notebook: "We have been on Mont Blanc two days in a terrible snowstorm," it read. "We have lost our way and are in a hole scooped out of the snow at a height of fifteen thousand feet. I have no hope of descending. Perhaps this book will be found and forwarded. We have no food; my feet are already frozen, and I am exhausted; I have only strength to write a few words. I die in the faith of Jesus Christ, with affectionate thoughts of my family; my remembrance to all."

Mountain Mania in London

By the middle of the nineteenth century Mont Blanc was quite possibly the most famous mountain in the world. It had captured the public imagination not so much because of what had been written about it by the likes of Bourit and de Saussure, but rather because of the exploits of an English theatrical impresario named Albert Smith. This flamboyant character was the son of a doctor in Chertsey, and was hooked on mountains by the age of nine after reading a children's book entitled *The Peasants of Chamonix*. With an instinct for showmanship already apparent, the young Albert took to building miniature moving panoramas of the mountain, and used to frighten his little sister by telling her gory stories of disasters that had befallen climbers on its treacherous slopes. Later Smith studied medicine in Paris and in 1838 visited Chamonix on the cheap, entering the town on the back of a hay cart.

The visit changed Smith's life: he abandoned his medical studies, wrote humorous articles for *Punch* magazine and then became a theatrical producer, staging various pantomimes in London. In 1848 he wrote and published a monthly shilling serial entitled *Christopher Tadpole*, which concerned an ineffectual hero who climbs Mont Blanc (at one point the hapless man falls down a hole in the ice and emerges in Lake Geneva). The following year, Smith travelled to Egypt and created a stage show about the experience called *The Overland Trail*, which played to great acclaim in London. The success of this show gave him the money and confidence to return to Chamonix and to actually climb Mont Blanc, which he did in 1852, taking with him a bevy of porters who carried his provisions—sixty bottles of *vin ordinaire*, four bottles of cognac, six bottles of Bordeaux, four parcels of prunes, some raspberry syrup, ten small cheeses, four candles, six packets of sugar, and forty-six live fowls. Smith was elated when he finally reached the summit: "The ardent wish of years was gratified, but I was so completely exhausted that without looking around me I fell down in the snow and was asleep in an instant."

On his return to London, Smith set about staging his second travel spectacular: this was *The Ascent of Mont Blanc*, which was to run for seven sell-out years in the Egyptian Hall in Piccadilly. Each performance involved the participation of a brace of chamois, a live St. Bernard dog, pretty girls in Alpine costume, a diorama of the Alps at the back of the stage and a wooden Swiss chalet—and Smith exaggerating his exploits remorselessly. He was the ultimate showman: at the close of each season he personally presented a bouquet of flowers to every woman in the audience. Meanwhile, the merchandising opportunities were terrific: the show spawned board games and popular songs, such as the *Chamonix Polka*, while an ice rink (a glacarium) was opened on Baker Street, its walls adorned with snowy Alpine scenes. Smith gave royal command performances of his show at Windsor Castle and at Osborne House, Queen Victoria's home on the Isle of Wight. When one of his St. Bernard animal stars had puppies, Smith gave one of them to Queen Victoria, and another to Charles Dickens, who had seen his show and wrote of it that "the most timid ladies may ascend Mont Blanc twice a day... without the slightest danger of fatigue."

Not surprisingly, this explosion of Alpine bad taste had its critics. "There has been a cockney ascent of Mont Blanc... of which you will doubtless soon hear," mused John Ruskin in one of his letters. The *Times* of 1855 remarked that Britain was gripped with "Mont Blanc mania" but that "Mont Blanc has become a positive nuisance... really, the world cares very little about the matter." Nor did Smith care: he had recognized that the Victorians had a fascination with mountains and milked his opportunity for all it was worth; at the end of the sell-out run of his show, he was thirty thousand pounds richer, and interest in the Alps was at an all-time high.

"Better knowledge of the mountains through literature, science and art"

In the same decade that Albert Smith was presenting his crowd-pleasing spectaculars in London, some rather more scholarly Alpine enthusiasts were preparing to celebrate their enthusiasm for the mountains in a very different manner. The Alpine Club was founded at Ashley's Hotel in London's Covent Garden on 22 December 1857, its stated aim being "the promotion of good fellowship amongst mountaineers... and better knowledge of the mountains through literature, science and art". The membership was of a distinct social and intellectual type: most had been to public school and Oxford or Cambridge, and lawyers, dons and clergyman were the most strongly-represented professions. Founding members included the poet Matthew Arnold, the art critic John Ruskin and the publishers John Murray and William Longman; the first president was an under-secretary for the colonies and a keen Alpinist named John Ball. The club's most valuable activity was the publication of mountaineers' experiences in the Alps. These first appeared in 1859 in a volume entitled *Peaks, Passes and Glaciers*, and then from 1864 in the *Alpine Journal*, whose pages were crammed full of individual accounts of climbs, in addition to letters requesting guidance on climbing equipment, travel arrangements and so on. The journal forms a valuable account of the heyday of Alpine mountaineering and the contributions that British climbers made to it.

One prominent member of the Alpine Club (and for a time its president) was Leslie Stephen, one of the great men of letters of Victorian England. He was the editor of *Cornhill Magazine*, the founder of the *Dictionary of National Biography* and also a fellow of Trinity Hall, Cambridge. But he was no effete academic: he had been a distinguished rower and sprinter in his youth, and had also climbed the Bietschorn and the Monte della Disgrazia; once he walked all the way from Cambridge to London in twelve hours to attend an Alpine Club dinner. His daughter, the novelist Virginia Woolf, later wrote that her father was given to walking the streets of London wearing the same tweed coat he used in the mountains, its waistline stained yellow from the ropes that had been fastened round it. But Stephen, like so many Alpine Club members, was much inclined to snobbery: he wrote of encountering "the genuine British cockney in all his terrors" in St. Moritz and thought that the Grindelwald glacier was like the back end of a "wretched whale, stranded on a beach... hacked by remorseless fishermen" as American and Cook's tourists walked all over it.

Leslie Stephen was not the only culprit. Accusations of snobbery were to dog many of the club's members in the early days. It has been suggested that in the 1870s one climber, Albert Mummery, the owner of a Dover tannery, who had ascended the Matterhorn by a new and dangerous route along the Zmutt ridge, was blackballed for being in trade. Predictably, members of the Alpine Club looked with horror on the crowds of tourists and climbers who were now descending on the Alps each summer: Chamonix and Mont Blanc were written off as being too popular, and Zermatt was adopted as the favoured Alpine resort. The club also had an exclusively male membership: women were not considered to have the physical or moral stamina required for climbing mountains. In 1871 Meta Brevoort, an American woman in her forties, had to publish her account of climbing the Bietschorn under the name of her nephew, William Coolidge, because of club rules that forbade women from contributing to the pages of the *Alpine Journal*. (A Ladies' Alpine Club was founded in 1908.) The club also considered itself aloof from such trivial matters as winter sports, so when skiing and tobogganing gained in popularity a separate Alpine Ski Club was founded—by an Oxford undergraduate, Owen O'Malley, who held the first meeting in his rooms at Magdalen College. This organization was later to produce the very first skiing guides to the Alps.

The Matterhorn and the Eiger

The summit of the Matterhorn (4,478m) is nearly four hundred metres lower than Mont Blanc, but this mountain is infinitely more spectacular and dangerous: those who climb it have to contend with steep slopes, unstable snowfields, black ice, and the constant rumble of boulders bouncing down the slopes. Vaughan Hawkins, a nineteenth-century Alpine enthusiast, wrote that "the mountain has a sort of prestige of invincibility... which leads one to expect to encounter some new and unheard of source of peril upon it."

Edward Whymper was an engraver by profession, whose interest in mountaineering stems from the time he was asked by the publisher William Longman to make some engravings for a book on the Alps. He was immediately gripped by the challenge posed by the Matterhorn: "there seemed to be a cordon drawn around it, up to which one might go, but no further," he wrote. On 13 July 1865 he attempted to break through that cordon by leading an expedition from Zermatt to conquer its summit. Whymper's party included Michel Croz, an experienced guide from Chamonix, as well as two local guides, father and son with the surname Taugwalder; in addition, there was a Cambridge undergraduate named Douglas Hadow, a vicar, the Revd. Charles Hudson, and an English aristocrat, Lord Francis Douglas. They knew that another group had already set out for the summit from the Italian side and were racing up the mountain to beat them; but in the end this other party gave up and returned home, and Whymper's party reached the summit unchallenged, at 1.40pm the day after they had set out from Zermatt. Whymper later wrote that the view from the top was stunning, stretching all the way to Mont Blanc: "not one of the principal peaks of the Alps were hidden. I see them clearly now... snowy mountains, somber and solemn or glittering and white, with walls, turrets, pinnacles, pyramids, domes, cones and spires! There was every combination that the world can give, and every contrast that the heart could desire."

But after the triumph of reaching the summit, disaster struck on the descent. Hudson, Hadow, Lord Francis Douglas and Croz all perished in what became one of the most notorious mountaineering disasters of all time. A slip and fall from Hadow was all that it took, followed by a break in the rope held by Whymper and the older Taugwalder guide. Whymper later described his horror as "for a few seconds we saw our unfortunate companions sliding downwards on their backs, and spreading out their hands, endeavouring to save themselves. They... disappeared one by one, and fell from precipice to precipice on the Matterhorngletcher below... from the moment the rope broke it was impossible to help them." Three corpses were later found, stripped of clothing and mutilated by the precipitous fall; Croz had half his skull missing, and a rosary cross was jammed into his jawbone which had to be cut out with a penknife to aid in the body's identification. Nothing of

Lord Douglas was found except a shoe, a coat sleeve and a pair of gloves; all of these can be seen in the Alpine museum in Zermatt, along with Whymper's ice axe, the broken rope and the first report about the disaster, written in Whymper's own hand.

The golden era of mountaineering ended with the dreadful events on the Matterhorn. "Is it common sense? Is it allowable? Is it not wrong?" thundered The *Times*, condemning the cult of mountain climbing as "folly"; Charles Dickens agreed, and wrote that the climbing of the Matterhorn "contributed about as much to the advancement of science as would a club of young gentlemen who should undertake to bestride all the weathercocks of all the cathedral spires of the United Kingdom." The *Edinburgh Review* commented: "Has a man the right to expose his life, and the lives of others, for an object of no earthly value, either to himself or his fellow creatures? If life is lost in the adventure, how little does the moral guilt differ from that of suicide or murder?" Leslie Stephen wrote sadly that mountaineers were now considered little more than "overgrown schoolboys who, like other schoolboys, enjoy being in dirt, and danger, and mischief." The public, on the other hand, was fascinated by the story: for a while Whymper became the most talked-about person in Europe, and lectured on the Matterhorn disaster to packed halls in London; but he never returned to the mountain: his later career took him climbing in the Andes, dog-sledding across Greenland, and also to the Mont Blanc range, on which he wrote a famous climbing guide. Another of his books, *Scrambles Among the Alps* (1871), has become one of the classic mountaineering texts; Arnold Lunn wrote of it that "There is no book which has sent more climbers to the Alps... the closing scenes in the great drama of the Matterhorn move to their appointed climax with the dignity of some of the most majestic passages in the Old Testament."

The Eiger was first climbed in 1858 by an Englishman named Charles Barrington and two local guides. They did not, however, make their ascent via the infamous North Face, a vertical wall of ice and rock that rears up behind the prettily-situated hotels of Kleine Scheidegg (from where trains to the Jungfraujoch depart). In 1937 Colonel Edward Strutt, who was the editor of the *Alpine Journal* at the time, declared the climbing of the *Nordwand* (or *Eigerwand*) to be "an obsession for the mentally deranged... he who first succeeds may rest assured that he has

accomplished the most imbecile variant since mountaineering first began." Of the eight men who, by that time, had attempted to scale the North Face, six had died, and none had reached the top; parts of the face had been named the Death Bivouac (a narrow rocky ledge where climbers could just about pitch camp), the Traverse of the Gods and the "spider", on whose "limbs" climbers were trapped as stones and ice fell and bounced all around them.

The most notorious disaster to befall climbers on the North Face came in 1936, when the Austrian Toni Kurz perished from exhaustion and frostbite while dangling on the end of his climbing rope; when rescuers finally appeared (gaining access to the North Face through the *Eigerwand* station of the Jungfrau railway) he was only able to mutter "Ich kann nicht mehr"—"I can't go on"—before expiring. In his book *A Century of Mountaineering* Arnold Lunn wrote of his death that "his valiant heart had resisted the terrors of storm and solitude and misery such as mountaineers have seldom been called on to endure… he did not surrender. He died. In the annals of mountaineering there is no record of a more heroic endurance." After Kurz's death the German press renamed the *Nordwand* the *Mördwand*—the killer wall.

The first successful ascent of the North Face was made by an expedition party led by Anderl Heckmair in July 1938. With him was a fellow Austrian named Heinrich Harrer (who was married to the daughter of the "father" of plate tectonic theory, Alfred Wegener). Harrer, who died in January 2006, later wrote a classic book about the North Face entitled *The White Spider* (his other famous work was *Seven Years in Tibet*, in which he described his adventures in the Indian and Tibetan Himalayas). Harrer's book includes a memorable description of his traverse of the infamous "spider", where "ice particles and snow… get canalized in the cracks and gullies, shoot out onto the Spider under pressure, and there join up in a flood of annihilating fury [before finally flinging] themselves outwards and downwards, obliterating and taking with them everything which isn't part of the living rock." The second part of his book recounts other attempts made on the North Face, such as that in August 1953 which ended when "the gallery-minder of the Jungfrau Railway saw two shadows hurtle past the windows of the Eigerwand station [which are set into the wall of rock], enveloped in a cloud of snow, at noon. It was only a momentary glimpse, but long

enough for him to recognize the shape of bodies..."

"Those mysterious impulses which cause men to peer into the unknown"

The two men the Jungfrau station attendant had seen fall to their deaths on the Eigerwand were Uly Wyss and Karl Heinz Gonda, two exceptionally experienced climbers. What was the cause of their striving? Where did the need to climb mountains come from, that caused them and so many others to risk their lives in the Alps?

Some of the earliest climbers went up mountains to conduct scientific research. Conrad Gesner, who marked his 1555 ascent of Pilatus with a blast on his alpenhorn, was a prominent naturalist who wanted to investigate how plants coped with harsh conditions at high altitudes. In 1765, two brothers from Geneva, Jean-André and Guillaume-Antoine de Luc, climbed Le Buet to conduct some physics experiments: at the top they measured the air pressure and investigated the effects of altitude on the length of time it took water to boil. A few years later, the Abbé Murith, a priest at the Great St. Bernard monastery, climbed the Vélan and took various measurements with his barometer and thermometer at the summit, as well as investigating the plant species he found.

But later climbers had little interest in science; they just wanted to go *up*. Why was this? In some ways the need to excel, and succeed, is innate to the human condition. (In fact the word *excel* is derived from the Latin *excelsus*, meaning "high".) Successful mountain climbers literally find themselves on top of the world (and those with religious inclinations find themselves closer to heaven too). But there is more to it that this: for many climbers, the mountain is a foe, there to be conquered; it is a challenge, and some people find that they need to rise to such a challenge to prove themselves. In *The White Spider* Heinrich Harrer wrote that the North Face of the Eiger presents "an advanced school and supreme testing-place of a man's worth as a human being." And once climbers have reached the summit, they are masters of all they survey; they are empowered, yet also belittled, threatened into oblivion and reminded of their smallness in the world by the grand vistas and the awesomeness of nature they encounter. Many mountaineers have found this blend of powerlessness and triumph strangely intoxicating.

A number of climbers have described their own, personal reasons for risking their lives on the slopes—although sometimes these reasons defy meaningful articulation. In *Scrambles among the Alps* Whymper simply wrote of "those mysterious impulses which cause men to peer into the unknown". "We return from their precipices wiser as well as stronger men," wrote his fellow Alpine enthusiast Leslie Stephen, not actually making things any clearer. Michel Paccard, one of the first climbers of Mont Blanc, said that he climbed for France, for science, and for his own satisfaction—in that order. In 1843, after climbing the Weisshorn, the geologist James Forbes indicated that an Alpine ascent was similar to a military campaign: "It was mainly the quality of not knowing when to yield," he wrote, "of fighting for duty even after [ceasing] to be animated by hope". In the Leni Riefenstahl/Arnold Fanck film *The Holy Mountain*, the dancer asks a climber what he is searching for as he climbs: "one's self", comes the enigmatic reply. In another film set in the Alps, Clint Eastwood's *The Eiger Sanction*, a conversation in the restaurant at Kleine Scheidegg involves one character enquiring of another, "Tell me... do these men [ascending the North Face of the Eiger] climb to prove their manhood, or is it more a matter of compensating for inferiority feelings?"

It is no coincidence that the greatest era of mountaineering occurred during Victorian times, and that many of those who set out to conquer the peaks were British. This was, after all, the age of exploration, and the highest peaks of the Alps were as inaccessible and as challenging as the Antarctic or the Sahara; to attempt to conquer the Matterhorn was akin to searching for the north-west passage or finding the source of the Nile. And yet, unlike any of these places, the Alps could be reached in little more than a day's travelling from London! In addition, mountain climbing, like other forms of exploration, involved the championing of Victorian ideals of manliness and pluck, resourcefulness and courage; it was on the peaks of the Alps that the ex-public school types of the Alpine Club could demonstrate the grit, determination, prowess and moral fibre that had been beaten into them at school; and, in an era when so much of the world was coloured pink on the map, mountain climbing became both a symptom and a justification of imperial ambition. Gavin de Beer confirmed this when he wrote, in *Alps and Men* (1932), of "the almost proselyte fervour with which they [the members of the Alpine Club] acclaimed the virtues of their new pastime, which sprang from national pride that the last outposts of Europe were falling to the British." The comments of one Victorian climber, the Revd. J. F. Hardy, who sang the National Anthem at the summit of the Lyskamm, say it all: "the noble old anthem fills out English hearts with happy thoughts of home and fatherland, and of the bright eyes that will sparkle... at our success."

Mark Twain's account of his attempt at climbing the Riffelberg in *A Tramp Abroad* is one of the greatest accounts of Victorian-era mountaineering; but it is in fact a complete sham, a delicious satire on the endless stream of climbing accounts so popular at the time. Twain's expedition party apparently included four surgeons, a geologist, twelve waiters, a vet, a barber, and four pastry chefs; their provisions included two thousand cigars, sixteen cases of ham, one hundred and fifty-four umbrellas, and twenty-two ladders; the resulting procession leaving Zermatt was 3,122 feet long. "In point of numbers and spectacular effect, it was the most imposing expedition that had ever marched from Zermatt... out of respect for the great numbers of tourists of both sexes who would be assembled in front of the hotels to see us pass, and also out of respect for the many tourists whom we expected to encounter on our expedition, we decided to make the ascent in evening dress."

Riddled with failures and absurdities, the trip is truly a comedy of errors: at one point the guides, who had never ascended the Riffelberg before, "had a strong instinct that they were lost, but they had no proof—except that they did not know where they were." Later, one of the mules explodes after accidentally eating one of the cans of nitroglycerine. "The explosion was heard as far away as Zermatt; an hour and a half afterwards, many citizens of that town were knocked down and quite seriously injured by descending portions of mule meat, frozen solid." But it is all fanciful nonsense: in reality, the Riffelberg is not a mountain, but an inn located above Zermatt, easily reachable by road. It takes three hours to walk there from Zermatt (Twain's mock-epic trip took seven days); the road is unmistakable (Twain's party loses the way almost immediately on setting off); and guides are unnecessary (Twain has seventeen).

Later in the same book, Mont Blanc is the subject of a similarly satirical ascent: firstly, there is an account of reaching the summit "by telescope" from Chamonix: "choose a calm clear day; and do not pay the telescope man in advance. There are dark stories of his getting advance-payers on the summit and then leaving them there to rot." Then there is an account of the view from the summit, encompassing a succession of fictional peaks including the Wobblehorn, the Yodelhorn, the Fuddlehorn, the Dinnerhorn, the Bottlehorn, the Shovelhorn, the Saddlehorn and the Powderhorn, and beyond them the Ghauts of Jubblepore, the Aiguilles des Alleghenies, plus the "smoking peak of Popocatapetl [actually a volcano in Mexico] and the stately range of the Himalayas, dreaming in a purple gloom." This blend of superlatives and purple prose perfectly satirizes the accounts of dozens of genuine mountaineers who have written of the views from the summits that they conquered.

A Return to Lake Geneva

There are many lakes in the Alps. But there is something special about the crescent-shaped, azure-blue Lake Geneva that sets it apart from all the others. The lake, known as *Léman* in French, straddles both France and Switzerland. On its northern side it is fringed by a string of elegant, sophisticated Swiss resorts, such as Montreux and Vevey, whose villas occupy the hillsides above the neat gardens that edge the lake shore itself. The main focus of the opposite shore is the equally elegant watering-hole of Évian, one of the most famous French spas. Eastwards from Lausanne and Évian the lake enjoys a truly Alpine setting, with snow-capped mountains glinting in the sun above the still water, and mountain railways pushing up from Montreux through terraced vineyards towards the ski resorts of the Bernese Oberland.

Geneva itself has a reputation as a rather sterile (not to mention hugely expensive) city: in a letter to his sister the Russian novelist Dostoevsky called it "a dull, gloomy, Protestant, stupid town with a frightful climate, but very well suited for work." Home to the European headquarters of the United Nations and dozens of international organizations, Geneva's hinterland is the world, not the mountains, and for this reason it has received little mention in this book. But its lake is divine. For over two hundred years writers and artists have come here: a trend established by Byron and Shelley in the early nineteenth century has led to a myriad of names being associated with the lake, including the actors Charlie Chaplin, Richard Burton and Aubrey Hepburn, the writers Edward Gibbon, T. S. Eliot, Henry James and Victor Hugo, and, more recently, the pop singer Freddie Mercury. Many come here to retire, and eventually to die; they are attracted by the sunshine in summer, by the balmy breezes in winter, by the views, by the easy opulence and luxury, and by the arts festivals and the literary heritage and the exclusivity of the resorts. In his 1950 book on Switzerland, John Russell wrote that "it is here, if anywhere, that those artful and splendid survivors, the Emperor-Moths of western civilization, can still enjoy the eternal July of their leisured existence." Over half a century on, it only takes a casual glance at the elderly, elegantly-attired, softly-spoken residents of the lakeside towns to realize that he is still right.

There is a strangely melancholic air about the lake, too. It is hard to pin down its exact nature: perhaps it is the huge, gloomy hotels that line the shore, clinging with quiet pride to a previous age of refinement and deference that has now virtually disappeared; or perhaps it is the sense of transience which cloaks the place: people come here, after all, to die, or to convalesce in a place bathed in cool air and soft light.

Nowhere can this atmosphere of leaden stillness be sensed more than in the resort of Vevey, the setting for Anita Brookner's acutely observed 1984 novella *Hotel du Lac*. Although Vevey and Lake Geneva are never mentioned by name, the description of the Dent d'Ouche, the bulky, rocky mountain facing the resort from across the water, and the "gaunt remains of a thirteenth century castle", which can only be the Château de Chillon, means that the setting cannot be anywhere else.

The heroine of the novel is an overly cautious, lonely middle-aged woman named Edith Hope, "a writer of romantic fiction under a more thrusting name". At the opening of the book Edith comes to stay in a hotel besides the lake shore. It is the off-season, and the lake seems perpetually bathed in a mottled grey light, while the Dent d'Ouche is obscured by a soft mist, rendering it a "dark grey shape" rising from the still water. "It was late September, out of season," begins the description of the resort.

> The tourists had gone, the rates were reduced, and there were few inducements for visitors in this small town at the water's edge, whose inhabitants, uncommunicative to begin with, were frequently rendered taciturn by the dense cloud that descended for days at a time and then vanished without warning to reveal a new landscape, full of colour and incident: boats skimming on the lake, passengers at the landing stage, an open air market... for this was a land of prudently harvested plenty, a land which had conquered human accidents, leaving only the weather distressingly beyond control... [Vevey was] settling down for its long interrupted hibernation. No one came here in the winter. The weather was too bleak, the snow too distant, the amenities too sparse to tempt visitors.

All the guests in the Hotel du Lac are of a certain age, and possess a certain refinement and style; they are there for rest and recuperation. "It was assumed that [the guests] would live up to the hotel's standards, just as the hotel would live up to theirs... while the young of all nations hurtled off to the sun and beaches, the Hotel du Lac took a quiet pride, and sometimes it was a very quiet pride, in its isolation from the herd." Doctors and solicitors know about it, but travel agents do not. The Hotel du Lac is "a stolid and dignified building, a house of repute, a traditional establishment, used to welcoming the prudent, the well-to-do, the retired, the self-effacing, the respected patrons of an earlier era of tourism. It had made little effort to smarten itself up for the passing trade which it had always despised. Its furnishings, although austere, were of excellent quality, its linen spotless, its service impeccable." The hotel is proud of its traditional bearing: "the very sparseness of the terrace, the muted hush of the lobby, the absence of piped music, public telephones, advertisement for scenic guided tours, or noticeboards directing one to the amenities of the town. There was no sauna, no hairdresser, and certainly no glass case displaying items of jewellery; the bar was small and dark, and its austerity did not encourage people to linger." Here it is, in this refined, quiet hotel that Edith Hope begins to come to terms with the indiscretion that has caused her to seek a self-imposed exile in the first place (albeit encouraged by a friend in England); it is also the place where Edith opens her cautious courtship with the refined and wealthy Mr. Neville.

Hotel du Lac bears inescapable comparisons with another novel written over a hundred years earlier and also set in Vevey. In *Daisy Miller*, by Henry James, the eponymous heroine, a charming but wayward young American, is visiting the resort while on an extended European tour; like Edith Hope, she is beguiled by the charms of a suitor, whom she eventually decides to reject. James wrote his novel in 1878 when Vevey, to his mind, had the "characteristics of an American watering-place. There are sights and sounds which evoke a vision, an echo, of Newport and Saratoga." The novel is set during the time when the grand hotels along the lakeside were patronized by well-healed foreign visitors who had a sense of class and propriety about them—the sort of guests that one feels the proprietors of the Hotel du Lac rather missed.

Henry James was born in New York but was partly educated in Paris and Geneva, so was well acquainted with the behaviour of Americans in Europe. In *Daisy Miller* his heroine enjoys flouting the rigid social conventions of the "old world" but in doing so comes across as something of a brash but naïve innocent. Daisy is intrigued by Europe but is out of her depth when she tries to immerse herself in its culture and history: she is bored by a visit to the Château de Chillon, and her companion notes wryly that she "cared very little for feudal antiquities, and the dusky traditions of Chillon made but a slight impression upon her... the history of Bonivard [the prisoner whose story was recounted by Byron] had evidently, as they say, gone into one ear and out of the other."

Although the second half of *Daisy Miller* is set in Rome, it is difficult not to assume that Brookner was alluding to its preoccupation with manners and propriety by setting her own novel in exactly the same lakeside resort. Not surprisingly, given the scenic attraction of the location, both novels have been filmed: *Daisy Miller* in 1974, by the American director Peter Bogdanovich, and *Hotel du Lac* in 1987 by the BBC, with Anna Massey and Denholm Elliot in the lead roles.

Since then, another film has also used the lake's melancholic beauty as the setting for a love affair between two people who happen to be taking a holiday on its shores. *Le Parfum d'Yvonne* (1994) opens with the passage of a steamer across the lake, gloriously shot in widescreen, the harsh sunlight glinting on the water and the Swiss flag fluttering wildly behind the boat as it glides towards the distant, hazy shoreline. The film is set in the 1950s, and the two protagonists, one a young would-be writer hiding out in Switzerland from military conscription, the other an aspiring actress of appropriate glacial beauty with whom he begins a torrid affair, live a life of giddy socializing and erotic liaisons during their summer by the lake. Like *Hotel du Lac* and *Daisy Miller* the story is partly set in the sombre world of gloomy but expensive lakeside hotels, the austerity of the surroundings standing in stark contrast to the intensity of the relationship between the two young lovers. The film is the work of the noted French director Patrice Leconte; its rich visual atmosphere of sumptuous lakeside gardens and hazy days on the glistening water nicely sets the scene for a poignant but brief love affair whose intensity and passion can never be repeated.

The Lake Geneva Smart Set

The origins of Lake Geneva's literary, artistic and intellectual heritage can be found in a grand eighteenth-century chateau in the village of Coppet, on the north bank of the lake's westernmost part. The builder of this elegant lakeside retreat was Jacques Necker, minister of finance to Louis XVI of France up to the time of the French Revolution. Necker saw at first hand (and in fact carefully documented) the corruption of the regime in Paris and, realizing the revolution was probably coming, bought the chateau as a refuge from anti-monarchists. Later on his daughter Germaine married the Swedish Baron de Staël Holstein, and from the 1790s Madame de Staël turned the chateau into a bohemian haven for intellectuals and authors, who came here to talk, listen to lectures, to be treated to performances of plays in the library, and indulge in lavish soirées. "The first general meal was taken at eleven in the morning, and thenceforward Madame de Staël drew without mercy upon the talent and experience of her guests until midnight when, in the words of one regular guest, 'one either went to bed, or had to go on talking'," wrote John Russell in *Switzerland.*

One visitor, the Duke of Wellington, remarked that Madame de Staël was "a most agreeable woman… if you kept her away from politics." Byron was intrigued by her fame but also complained about

her long speeches, and warned his physician that, on meeting her, he should "speak as little as possible, and only when she addresses you. She has met everybody, and after Goethe, Schiller and Napoleon we are all inferior." Madame de Staël herself was a celebrated writer, and in particular was a fierce critic of Napoleon; she died in 1817 at the age of fifty-one. Nowadays, her old home is owned by her descendent, the Count of Haussonville, who lives here occasionally but also opens the place up to curious visitors. Those who make the trek here pass through wrought-iron gates still adorned with the letters NC, which refer to Jacques Necker and his wife Suzanne Curchod; through the courtyard there are rooms boasting superb examples of eighteenth-century furniture and hung with exquisite Chinese wallpaper.

The north shore of the lake between Coppet and Geneva is lined with peaceful and attractive villages. One of them, Cologny, gained a literary name for itself during the heyday of Madame de Staël's "Parliament of European Opinion", which was in almost permanent session further along the coast. The poet John Milton had come here in

1639, and nearly two hundred years later Byron and Shelley were to set up temporary homes in villas in Cologny as they wrote, talked and bobbed around on the lake; this was where Byron wrote parts of *Childe Harold's Pilgrimage* and where Mary Shelley conceived *Frankenstein*. The place is today known as the "Beverley Hills of Geneva" and is home to a number of internationally-known film stars. (In the town's Bilbioteca Bodmeriana a 160,000-volume library contains one of the few copies of the Gutenberg Bible, and the oldest extant copy of the Gospel of St. John.)

Heading from Cologny eastwards along the lake shore (although the crescent shape of the lake makes the direction more like northwards here) takes travellers on the lakeside railway line past Coppet to Céligny, where the links with the silver screen continue. The actor Richard Burton lived the last few years of his life here, in a villa that he named "Pays de Galles" after his homeland, Wales; it is a modest residence, and Burton is buried in a similarly humble grave in the village's Vieux Cimitière. Further on, as the lake widens, the Pavillon Audrey Hepburn at Tolochenaz is a loving museum to the great film actress, who lived here from 1963 until her death in 1993; on show are both her Oscars, a personal letter from Samuel Goldwyn, and the black dress she wore in *Breakfast at Tiffany's*. (In 2002 the museum was closed by members of Hepburn's immediate family who claimed that the place was becoming over-commercialized.)

Ten kilometres beyond Tolochenaz the slopes rising from the lake shore become steeper, and the mountains that enclose the eastern part of the lake rise fully into view. Lausanne, one of the most beautifully situated cities in Switzerland, dominates the lake's northern shore and has a truly Alpine setting. It is an ancient city, with Roman remains by the lake itself, but over the centuries the focus of the city has shifted up hill, and nowadays the cathedral and railway station and old town are built over a series of terraces rising, step-like, from the gardens and promenades along the water's edge. (As a result, it must be the only city in the world with a metro system operated by means of rack-and-pinion underneath the carriages.)

Victor Hugo provides an apt description of the view over the town from the terrace of the cathedral, which has remained unchanged since he came here: "I saw the lake above the roofs, the mountains above the lake, the clouds above the mountains, and the stars above the clouds. It was like a staircase where my thoughts climbed up step by step and broadened at each new height." Nowadays, Lausanne combines the conservatism of a resort and cultural centre with a distinctly avant-garde edge, which comes from being home to a university (the biggest in Switzerland) and from eccentric events such as the annual International Rollerblading Contest when a hundred thousand participants descend on the city. Lausanne has always been a very popular city with the English, and by 1900 there were forty retired British colonels living here. The town was also home to four English churches, a number of English schools, a cricket pitch, and an English library where afternoon tea was served. It is not surprising, then, that in the mid- nineteenth century Charles Dickens chose to stay here with his family for a number of weeks, during an extended tour of continental Europe.

Dickens wrote about Lausanne and the surrounding countryside in his memoir *Travelling Abroad* (by "The Uncommercial Traveller"). He recalled that he arrived in the town "on an exquisitely clear day [in 1846]... I stood looking at the bright blue water, the flushed white mountains opposite, and the boats at my feet with their furled Mediterranean sails, showing like enormous magnifications of this goose-quill pen that is now in my hand." It was his habit to walk ten miles each day, allowing the details of the books he was currently working on to develop in his mind before committing them to paper. Dickens discovered that the countryside around Lausanne was "leafy, green and shady... full of deep glens, and branchy places, and bright with all sorts of flowers in profusion." In the city itself he was pleased to see so many booksellers crammed "in the steep up-and-down streets". The novelist began writing *Dombey and Son* during his visit, reading parts of it out to friends on occasions, including Thackeray, who remembered being given biscuits and Liebfraumilch by his fellow novelist; the book's setting, amidst the grim mill towns of the north of England, must be as far removed from the environment of Lausanne as is possible.

Dickens is not the only writer to be associated with the city. In the 1780s the English historian Edward Gibbon had lived in a house in the St. François district, where he wrote *Decline and Fall of the Roman Empire*. The town seemed to leave a rather different impression on him than it did on a later generation of writers. Gibbon wrote that "affectation is the original sin [of Lausanne]... affectation of wealth, nobility and intelligence—the first two being very common, the second very rare." Byron wrote much of *The Prisoner of Chillon* in Ouchy, part of Lausanne's lakefront, in 1816, and during his visit he sought out the summerhouse where Gibbon had written his monumental work, but was disappointed to find it a ruin; nevertheless he gathered some rose leaves and acacia from the overgrown garden and sent them to his publisher John Murray in London. Another visitor at around the same time as Byron was Robert Southey, the prolific essayist and biographer who became poet laureate in 1813; he declared that, were he to settle on the continent, Lausanne would be the place he would most like to live in. A hundred years later, T. S. Eliot wrote parts of *The Wasteland* here, in 1921 and 1922, when he was convalescing after a nervous breakdown; "By the waters of Leman I sat down and wept," is one of the poem's characteristic lines of alienation and despair.

Twenty kilometres beyond Lausanne are the neighbouring towns of Vevey and Montreux, perhaps the most famous resorts on the Swiss side of the lake. Opposite them the Savoy Alps rise abruptly from the French shore as a series of unfolding peaks, the most dominant being La Dente d'Ouche (2,222m). Meanwhile, little trains push themselves up a steep rack railway from Montreux, past opulent villas with carefully tended back gardens and fantastic views, into vineyards and then forest, heading for the mountain settlements of Gruyères and Gstaad.

Both Vevey and Montreux have had links with litterati for over two centuries. When figures such as Byron and Turner came here in the nineteenth century, only a thin sliver of settlement clung to the terrace immediately adjacent to the lake; as Turner's 1802 painting of the Château de Chillon shows, the slopes above the road and castle were left bare for cultivation of vines or use as mountain pasture. They would hardly recognize the scene today: the south-facing slopes above both resorts are now smothered with whitewashed villas glinting and glimmering in the sunlight with as much sparkle as the lake immediately below them.

Over time, Vevey has acquired a sedate reputation, setting it apart from the brashness of Montreux and the big-city, internationally-oriented flavour of Lausanne and Geneva. (It is also famous as the headquarters of Nestlé, one of the world's biggest multinationals, which occupies a surprisingly drab modern office block next to the main road and railway line in the western part of the town.) It has long been associated with writers: Thackeray wrote part of *The Newcomers* here in 1853, and later on Dostoevsky wrote *The Gambler* and Gogol wrote *Dead Souls*. Nowadays, there is even a Poet's Ramble, a walk through Vevey where individual benches on the lake front are dedicated to a particular writer connected with the town; participants can press a button to hear extracts of each writer's work, while enjoying the same views that inspired them. One modern writer associated with Vevey is Graham Greene, who lived in the nearby village of Corseaux with his companion Yvonne Cloetta until his death in April 1991, and is buried in the cemetery. It is perhaps ironic that Greene is buried in Switzerland, as some of the most famously damning words ever written about the country have come from his pen: in his screenplay to the classic 1949 film *The Third Man*, Greene has the character played by Orson Welles, Harry Lime, remark that "In Italy for thirty years under the Borgias they had warfare, terror, murder, bloodshed, but they produced Michelangelo, Leonardo da Vinci and the Renaissance. In Switzerland they had brotherly love, and they had five hundred years of democracy and peace. And what did that produce? The cuckoo clock." (The British satirist Alan Coren once retorted that the Swiss *had* to invent the cuckoo clock as their other primary products, snow and chocolate, were both prone to melting; and anyway, Harry Lime was wrong—the cuckoo clock is a German invention, originating in Bavaria.)

Vevey's sophisticated lifestyle has also attracted film stars, and the small cemetery in the quiet village of Coursier, just above the town, contains the graves of two Hollywood legends who came to spend their final years here, James Mason and Charlie Chaplin. James Mason was in films for fifty years and his career as a leading man saw him play such roles as Brutus in *Julius Caesar* (1953), Captain Nemo in *20,000 Leagues Under the Sea* (1954) and Humbert Humbert in *Lolita* (1963); perhaps appropriately, his last film was *Dr. Fischer of Geneva* (1984), based on a novel by Graham Greene. Mason's near-neighbour in Vevey was Chaplin, who arrived in 1952 after being hounded from the United States as a result of the McCarthy trials, and lived in a villa in the hills overlooking the lake until his death in 1977. He is buried alongside his wife Oona, in a grave that has no adornments or photos, just a sea of yellow and purple flowers in front of large headstone bearing their names. Vevey now hosts an international festival of comedy films in Chaplin's honour, and by the shore there is a statue of him in characteristic pose, baggy trousers, cane and top hat, unveiled in 1989 on the 100th anniversary of his birth.

"Montreux, by contrast [to Vevey], is a stupid, temporary town… it has nothing interesting to say for itself," wrote John Russell. Although several writers are associated with it, including Shelley and Byron, Montreux has never rid itself of a certain air of brash vulgarity. Not that the town lacks association with artistic luminaries, who easily rival those of Vevey. Hans Christian Andersen wrote *The Ice Maiden* here, in nearby Clarens Tchaikovsky began *Eugene Onegin* in 1877, and Stravinsky composed *The Rite of Spring* between 1911 and 1914. "Clarens, sweet Clarens, birthplace of deep love," wrote Byron in *Childe Harold*; "Thine air is the young breath of passionate thought." Clarens, of course, was where Rousseau had set *La Nouvelle Héloïse*—although a nineteenth-century Murray guidebook is quite rude about the place, saying that it is "far less attractive than many of its neighbours, and it probably owes its celebrity to a well-sounding name, which fitted it for the pages of a romance. The spot on which the beautiful 'bosquet de Julie' is sought for is now a potato field."

Later, Vladimir Nabokov lived the last sixteen years of his life in apartments in the Montreux Palace Hotel and is buried in Clarens, while Noel Coward lived in Les Avents, in the mountains above the resort. When he bought his villa, the view over Montreux and the lake was partly obscured by trees, which brought the jocular comment from Ian Fleming that "Only Noel Coward could buy a house in Switzerland without a view"; Coward met this with the rejoinder, "On the contrary, it overlooks a wonderful tax advantage." The trees blocking the view were soon felled, and the house was later dubbed "chalet Coward" (or even "Silly chalet"). Like many writers and actors who came to live by Lake Geneva, Coward wanted a house surrounded by mountains as a defence against the modern world; he craved, and found, in Les Avents remoteness, seclusion and physical isolation. (Unlike most luminaries who lived by Lake Geneva, he is not buried here; he died and was buried thousands of miles away, on the Caribbean island of Jamaica.)

The most recent personality associated with Montreux is the actor, writer and wit Peter Ustinov, who lived in the resort until his death in March 2004. Ustinov won Oscars for his performances in the films *Spartacus* (1961) and *Topkapi* (1965), but in the latter part of his life moved away from acting to work as an ambassador for Unicef, and to write a number of novels; one of his last, *Monsieur René*, is a satire set amidst Geneva's plushest international hotels. He is buried in Bursins Cemetery in Nyon, further west along the lakeshore.

■

Montreux's modern-day brashness stems from its association with a very different set of celebrities—those from the world of rock music and showbiz, who are attracted on an annual basis by its world-renowned jazz and rock music festivals. The town has long been on the touring circuit of rock bands. In 1971, during a concert in the Montreux Casino by Frank Zappa, a member of the crowd set off a rocket flare which set the ceiling on fire; the flames were seen rising above the town and the lake by Ian Gillan, lead singer of the group Deep Purple, who was staying in a hotel nearby and subsequently wrote the song *Smoke on the Water* inspired by what he had seen. More recently, Freddie Mercury, lead singer with the rock group Queen, had a house for many years in the Montreux district of Territet, on one occasion commenting that "if you want your soul to find peace, go to Montreux." He spent the last few months of his life in Montreux before he died of AIDS in 1991. Four years later, the remaining members of Queen released a final album, *Made in Heaven*, which mainly comprised previously unreleased material recorded when Mercury was still alive. The distinctive cover of the album shows the singer outside his chalet beside the lake at sunset, his whole form silhouetted against the clear water and distant mountains.

Now, with his old villa in private hands and firmly off-limits, Mercury's fans flock to Montreux's Place du Marché, beside the lake, where a bronze statue of the singer portrays him in characteristic pose; he is holding a wireless microphone and has his right hand raised in triumph, as if standing before a crowd of tens of thousands of fans in a stadium during one of Queen's famously extravagant concerts. The plaque beside the statue simply reads "Freddie Mercury, lover of life, singer of songs."

■

Montreux occupies one of the most distinctive settings anywhere in the Alps. Its railway station is set on a ledge above the lake, and from here narrow-gauge trains grind up the steep hillside towards Gstaad and the Bernese Oberland, the lake appearing more and more jewel-like as the trains rise through the sloping vineyards. By the lakeshore there are landing stages for boats crossing over to St. Gingolph and Evian in France. Beyond these ports on the southern shore the mountains of the Mont Blanc massif begin to rise, a mighty chain of steadily rising peaks that includes the Dent d'Ouche (2,222m), Mont Buet (3,094m) and finally Mont Blanc itself.

These days the summit of Mont Blanc is thick with climbers. On clear mornings in summer there is sometimes standing room only on its snowy peak. The problems of cold (even in July), altitude sickness and exhaustion are the same ones that confronted the early climbers on this mountain back in the eighteenth century. But the feeling of triumph of having reached the top is nowadays dulled through the knowledge that the experience has been shared by so many others. When Balmat and Paccard first conquered the mountain in 1786, and when Percy Shelley gazed at its summit in awe from Chamonix in 1816 and honoured it with his famous poem, Mont Blanc was still known by some as "the accursed"; now there is a road tunnel underneath it, a cable car three quarters of the way to the top of it, and a succession of mountain huts and refuges on its slopes to support the hundreds of people who make their way to its white summit every year. Benign and serene (but still claiming a number of lives each year), the mountain bears witness to the whole spectrum of Alpine history and geology: it rose through the squashing together of mighty tectonic plates; its sides have been worn down by the glaciers whose source lie in its massive snowfields; it has been perceived at various times as an abode of fantastic monsters and horrendous devils, and as a challenge to mountaineers and engineers;

and for two centuries it has been eulogised by writers, fawned over by tourists, and skied down by winter sports enthusiasts.

Yet despite all this, its formidable wildness remains intact. In his *Ode to Mont Blanc* Shelley writes of the "giant brood of pines" around the mountain's flanks, swinging in the winds with an "old and solemn harmony", and goes on to describe how, "in a trance sublime and strange", he watches the rainbows stretch across the ethereal waterfalls, and hears the sounds made by the gushing Arve and the cries of circling eagles. Two hundred years on, much of what Shelley observed is still there for today's visitor to experience, if they look carefully enough: to re-read his poem is a reminder of how much of the Alps remain "remote, serene and inaccessible"—a place where silence, solitude and wild thoughts are still distinctly possible.

Bibliography and Further Reading

Travel guides

A number of books in the *Rough Guides* series provide excellent practical coverage of the Alps for today's travellers, and also contain background articles relating to the politics, culture, history and society of this region. The *Rough Guide to Switzerland* and *The Rough Guide to Austria* are particularly invaluable; the relevant sections of *The Rough Guide to Slovenia* and *The Rough Guide to Italy* also provide excellent coverage of the Alpine regions of those countries. Michelin's *French Alps* in the *Green Guide* series, and the book on Bavaria in the *Lonely Planet* series, provide thorough accounts of the Alpine regions of France and Germany.

Part One: Landscapes

Richard Fortey's *The Earth: an Intimate History* provides an excellent account of the geology of the Alps and how the nature of their formation came to be discovered. Some may find the book rather specialized in places, but Fortey writes stylishly and manages to spin the otherwise rather dry history of the development of earth sciences into a good yarn. The book is partly a travelogue and Fortey tells his story of the earth through visits to places as far apart as Iceland, Hawaii and New Zealand. The book is published in paperback by HarperPerennial.

Part Two: History

The quotations from Schiller's play *William Tell* are taken from the edition of Schiller's Historical Dramas published in 2001 by the University Press of the Pacific in Honolulu.

Martin Gilbert's *First World War* (1994) provides coverage of the various battles fought in the Alps during that time.

Part Three: Imagination

Elma Dangerfield's *Byron and the Romantics in Switzerland* (Ascent Books, 1978) is a short but lively account of the time that Byron and Shelley spent in the Alps in the early nineteenth century. There are numerous editions of Mary Shelley's *Frankenstein* available (including one in the Penguin Popular Classics series that also includes separate introductions to the work by both Mary and Percy Shelley). The poetry of Byron, Wordsworth and Shelley is also published in numerous editions.

The quotations from Rousseau's *La Nouvelle Héloïse* are taken from the edition translated by Judith H McDowell and published in 1968 by the Pennsylvania State University Press. There are dozens of English-language editions of *Heidi* available; the Kekec books, however, are not available in English translation. Kessinger reissued John Ruskin's classic work *Modern Painters* in five separate volumes in 2005.

Ian Kershaw's magnificently detailed biography of Hitler (*Part One: Hubris* and *Part Two: Nemesis*) includes a fair amount of information on the Eagle's Nest and Berchtesgaden; it is published by Penguin. Audrey Salkeld's 2004 biography of Leni Riefenstahl is published by Pimlico.

Mountains of the Mind by mountaineer and historian Robert Macfarlane (Granta Books, 2003) provides an outstanding history of how mountains in all parts of the world have been perceived during different eras, from medieval times to the present. The book focuses mainly on the Alps although there are also chapters on climbs in the Andes and the Himalayas. Simon Schama's wide-ranging *Landscape and Memory* includes a good account of the shifting perspective on mountain landscapes that came with eighteenth-century Romanticism. It was republished by Fontana in 1996.

Part Four: Visitors

Many extracts from nineteenth-century guidebook series such as Baedeker and Murray are quoted and discussed in *Leading the Blind: a Century of Guide Book Travel, 1815-1914* by Alan Sillitoe (Macmillan, 1995), which examines how guidebooks helped and encouraged travel in Europe and the Middle East during the early days of mass tourism. R. L. J. Irving's *The Alps* (1947) and John Russell's *Switzerland* (1950) are half-way between travelogues and practical travel guides and provide an insight into travel and tourism in the Alps in the middle of the twentieth century. Both are, however, now out of print.

There are many modern editions available of Mark Twain's *A Tramp Abroad* and *The Innocents Abroad. Pictures from Italy* by Charles Dickens was republished in 2004 by Kessinger, and the anthology *Dickens in Europe*, containing the author's accounts of his travels in France, Switzerland and Italy, was published by the Folio Society in 1977.

Anita Brookner's 1984 novel *Hotel du Lac* is published in its most recent edition by Penguin. A *Complete Sherlock Holmes* was published in October 2005 by the Collector's Library, but many other editions are also available. Penguin Popular Classics publish modern editions of *Daisy Miller* by Henry James and *Little Dorrit* by Charles Dickens.

Savage Snows: the story of Mont Blanc by Walt Unsworth (Hodder and Stoughton, 1986) provides a thorough history of the various attempts that were made to climb Mont Blanc, leading up to the bitter arguments surrounding the first successful attempt in 1785. Heinrich Harrer's classic 1959 book *White Spider*, an exhilarating account of the various ascents of the North Face of the Eiger, was republished in 1995 by HarperCollins. *How the English Made the Alps* by Jim Ring (John Murray, 2000) provides a thorough and entertaining account of the influence of British pioneers of tourism, winter sports, mountaineering and transport engineering in the Alps during the nineteenth century. *Killing Dragons* by Fergus Fleming (Granta Books, 2000) is an absorbing and well-researched account of the development of Alpine mountaineering during the same era, telling the story of how the "dragons" that were thought to live among the peaks were gradually slain, one by one, as each new summit was conquered. Edward Whymper's classic mountaineering book *Scrambles among the Alps* was republished by National Geographic Books in 2002.

Index of Literary, Mythical, Scientific & Historical Names

Index of Places & Landmarks